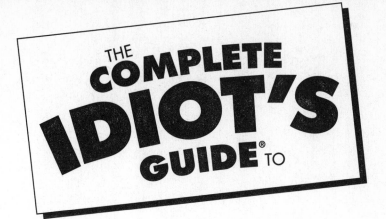

THE COMPLETE IDIOT'S GUIDE® TO

Success as a Property Manager

D1511201

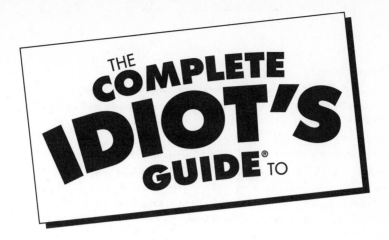

THE COMPLETE IDIOT'S GUIDE® TO

Success as a Property Manager

by Melissa Prandi, MPM, and Lisa Iannucci

ALPHA

A member of Penguin Group (USA) Inc.

ALPHA BOOKS

Published by the Penguin Group

Penguin Group (USA) Inc., 375 Hudson Street, New York, New York 10014, USA

Penguin Group (Canada), 90 Eglinton Avenue East, Suite 700, Toronto, Ontario M4P 2Y3, Canada (a division of Pearson Penguin Canada Inc.)

Penguin Books Ltd., 80 Strand, London WC2R 0RL, England

Penguin Ireland, 25 St. Stephen's Green, Dublin 2, Ireland (a division of Penguin Books Ltd.)

Penguin Group (Australia), 250 Camberwell Road, Camberwell, Victoria 3124, Australia (a division of Pearson Australia Group Pty. Ltd.)

Penguin Books India Pvt. Ltd., 11 Community Centre, Panchsheel Park, New Delhi—110 017, India

Penguin Group (NZ), 67 Apollo Drive, Rosedale, North Shore, Auckland 1311, New Zealand (a division of Pearson New Zealand Ltd.)

Penguin Books (South Africa) (Pty.) Ltd., 24 Sturdee Avenue, Rosebank, Johannesburg 2196, South Africa

Penguin Books Ltd., Registered Offices: 80 Strand, London WC2R 0RL, England

Copyright© 2009 by Lisa Iannucci

International Standard Book Number: 978-1-59257-920-4
Library of Congress Catalog Card Number: 2009924908

11   10   09   8   7   6   5   4   3   2   1

Interpretation of the printing code: The rightmost number of the first series of numbers is the year of the book's printing; the rightmost number of the second series of numbers is the number of the book's printing. For example, a printing code of 09-1 shows that the first printing occurred in 2009.

Printed in the United States of America

Note: This publication contains the opinions and ideas of its authors. It is intended to provide helpful and informative material on the subject matter covered. It is sold with the understanding that the authors and publisher are not engaged in rendering professional services in the book. If the reader requires personal assistance or advice, a competent professional should be consulted.

The authors and publisher specifically disclaim any responsibility for any liability, loss, or risk, personal or otherwise, which is incurred as a consequence, directly or indirectly, of the use and application of any of the contents of this book.

Most Alpha books are available at special quantity discounts for bulk purchases for sales promotions, premiums, fund-raising, or educational use. Special books, or book excerpts, can also be created to fit specific needs.

For details, write: Special Markets, Alpha Books, 375 Hudson Street, New York, NY 10014.

Publisher: *Marie Butler-Knight*
Editorial Director: *Mike Sanders*
Senior Managing Editor: *Billy Fields*
Senior Acquisitions Editor: *Paul Dinas*
Development Editor: *Nancy D. Lewis*
Production Editor: *Kayla Dugger*
Copy Editor: *Christine Hackerd*

Cartoonist: *Steve Barr*
Cover Designer: *Bill Thomas*
Book Designer: *Trina Wurst*
Indexer: *Brad Herriman*
Layout: *Chad Dressler, Rebecca Harmon*
Proofreader: *Laura Caddell*

Contents at a Glance

Appendixes

Contents

Introduction

The real estate industry has faced a significant downturn for the last few years, but that hasn't affected the property management industry at all. As a matter of fact, it has only underscored the need for good property managers and management companies that can keep buildings running properly, tenants satisfied, and bottom lines financially sound.

Think about it: investors purchase a building with the hope that it will be profitable. Some investors oversee day-to-day operations, but it's not a common scenario. Instead, they know that to maximize the building's potential, it's best to bring in a qualified, educated professional who knows the building and its systems and who can manage all of the particulars.

That's where you come in. Being a property manager is a thrilling career. No two days are alike and the career is extremely rewarding. A property manager incorporates multiple business aspects—problem-solving, financial, legal, communications, and more. Your career also includes contact with tenants and the community.

Whether you enter the career the traditional way, through a college education and an entry-level job, or the roundabout way, as a superintendent or concierge who is moving up the ranks, property management has myriad opportunities to find a position that works for you.

The property management industry has been steadily growing over a number of years. Why? Others are recognizing the need for these professionals, and individuals are recognizing the rewards of this fabulous career. So, cheers! Here's to the beginning of a wonderful career that is constantly evolving and growing!

What You'll Find in This Book

The Complete Idiot's Guide to Success as a Property Manager is written in four parts. Each one addresses a different aspect of being a property manager.

Part 1, "Getting Started," teaches you everything you need to know about starting a property management career. First, you'll examine what skills are necessary to be a successful property manager and determine whether this is a career for you. Read the job description of a property manager and learn the differences between commercial and residential management.

Next, you'll learn what kind of education is required—from college to continuing education classes. Part 1 also explores the different property management designations you can earn in both residential and commercial property management. You'll learn how to land that first job and what your starting salary will be, and how you can choose to fly solo and start your own business. Finally, the last two chapters in this part will provide an in-depth analysis of each type of commercial and residential property management position.

Part 2, "Nuts and Bolts," is all about what you need to do and how you need to do it. You'll get a tutorial on setting financial goals, organizing paperwork for income taxes, collecting rents and fees, and keeping records. With the financial basics in hand, you'll learn how to negotiate contracts and leases that make tenants and management happy.

This part also delves into the literal nuts and bolts of the building systems—from the roof to the basement, and everything in between. You'll also get the basics on being an environmentally friendly property manager, getting residents involved in recycling, choosing healthier building materials, and reducing energy use and costs.

Finally, this part gives you what you need to know about commercial and residential leases and provides tips and suggestions on negotiating those leases. You'll learn the legalities of your job in a simple language that doesn't take a law degree to understand.

Part 3, "People Management," examines the relationship between property manager and tenant. First we focus on hiring the right personnel to do the job. From there, you'll learn the ins and outs of improving your relationships with tenants and those tenant-to-tenant relationships.

This part also provides an in-depth analysis of various real-life management issues, and tells you how to solve them. Are you an enforcer, a negotiator, or a pleaser? It gives you the ins and outs of handling a small staff and a large staff and where to turn to for help when things go wrong.

Part 4, "Handling It All," provides the insight you need to handle any scenario that comes your way. We examine the safety and security of your building and what you need to do to keep your tenants and building safe in case of an emergency. In today's world, nothing happens without the media present and this part provides a primer for how to work with reporters who want the scoop. Being able to handle it all means utilizing whatever technology can help you do your job better.

Property management can be a stressful job, and having techniques and solutions in place to handle those stressful moments is vital to your success. This part provides tips and suggestions for assessing and prioritizing your day, and recommends a variety of technologies that can reduce your workload. If the job does stress you out, this part examines job burnout and how to put out the burnout flame and return to your job as a successful property manager. Finally, it's time to build your business. With experience and knowledge in hand, learn how to add clients to your repertoire and promote yourself within the industry. You've achieved success as a property manager and it's time to let others know just how good you are. And finally, this part speaks to the entrepreneur in you. If you're ready to branch out on your own and start your own property management business, this part is vital to your success. It will tell you what you need to know to become a successful property manager who owns a successful property management firm.

Of course, this book wouldn't be complete without some additional information for you to reference. The glossary in Appendix A is a good reference tool for understanding the lingo of the property management industry. Appendix B is a thorough reference list of sources you can turn to for additional information on everything we discussed in this book. Appendix C provides sample pages of leases and other documents you need to know about. Turn to these appendixes often.

Extras

Throughout the book, you'll find tips, warnings, facts, and definitions to make your reading experience more enjoyable and informative. Look for these special highlights for more information:

def•i•ni•tion

Learn the lingo of the property management industry. Here we'll tell you the words or phrases you need to know and what they mean.

Things to Avoid

Be warned! These sidebars advise you on what to steer clear of and why. The more hazards you remove from your path, the better.

Productivity Tips

Learn how to more efficiently do your job. These sidebars include tips from the authors and property management experts in the field.

Notes from the Field

These sidebars are like having a property manager talking directly to you and telling you like it is. Learn tips of the trade and read anecdotes about the ins and outs of the business.

Acknowledgments

There are so many people that help make a good book great and I'd like to take time to thank them. First and foremost, I'd like to thank my editor, Paul Dinas, who had faith in my ability to write this book and who supported me through the entire process. Thank you to my technical expert Melissa Prandi, MPM, President, PRANDI Property Management, Inc., CRMC, for her professional input; my development editor Nancy Lewis; and everyone at Alpha Books.

I'd like to thank my amazing agent, Marilyn Allen of Allen O'Shea Literary Agency. I'd also like to thank Hannah Fons, my editor and friend at *The Cooperator*, a Yale Robbins publication in New York. Hannah is a wonderful editor, writer, and friend who also provided guidance and suggestions for this entire book. Every writer needs an editor like Hannah in their life.

This book couldn't be complete without input, anecdotes, and advice from real-life property managers, so I'd like to thank the following individuals: Kimberly Smith, AvenueWest Corporate Housing (Denver, CO); Roxana Hammock, Guardian Management LLC (Portland, OR); Kirk Steinbruecker, Ashton Condominiums/ Apartments (Arlington Heights, IL); Robbin H. Pearson, Colonial Properties Trust (Atlanta, GA); Mike Levy, Levy Consulting, LLC (Fort Collins, CO); Pam McKenna, Guardian Management LLC; Chip Hoever, Somerset Management Group (Somerset, NJ); Janet Bledsoe; Ian M. Gopin, G&G Management and Development (Needham, MA); JoAnn Duncan, MSL Real Estate Services (San Antonio, TX); Meghan Martin, Gateway to the Summit (Keystone, CO); Rebecca Marston, Marston Voss (Boston, MA); Jeffrey T. Lame, Readco Management, LLC (CT); Richard J. Fry, RCP Management Company, Inc. (Princeton, NJ); and Barbara Kansky, Mediate Management Company, Inc. (Boston, MA). Also, special thanks to the following: Megan Etling of Schroder PR (Atlanta, GA), and Joshua Dorkin, Founder and CEO of BiggerPockets, Inc. (Denver, CO).

And last—but really first in my life—is my family. They are always patient with the chaos of a writer's career and the deadlines, and provide more love and support than I can ever ask for. So, to my children, Nicole, Travis, and Samantha, and my mother, Patricia Quaglieri, thank you and I love you.

Trademarks

All terms mentioned in this book that are known to be or are suspected of being trademarks or service marks have been appropriately capitalized. Alpha Books and Penguin Group (USA) Inc. cannot attest to the accuracy of this information. Use of a term in this book should not be regarded as affecting the validity of any trademark or service mark.

Part 1

Getting Started

Congratulations! You're ready to embark on a career as a successful property manager. You're probably filled with questions about how to get started. In addition, you're probably wondering about the type of property manager you will be, the salary you can expect, and the opportunities for advancement in the industry.

The first part of this book answers all of those questions and then some. It provides information on the array of property management positions that are available. It helps you kick-start your education and explains the licensing requirements you need to obtain a job. With education complete, you'll learn about what the industry is really like and what kind of job market you can expect. You'll then read a commercial property manager's and a residential property manager's real-life stories. It's time to get started!

Chapter 1

An Overview

In This Chapter

- ◆ Understanding the role of a property manager
- ◆ Learning about the different types of property managers
- ◆ Utilizing personality traits and job skills

Owning a building is an investment for an owner or developer. Like all investments, it needs to be properly taken care of in order for it to grow in value and become a source of income and profit. Nobody wants to own, live, or work in a rundown building that has out-of-date systems, shoddy landscaping, and cracks and holes in the walls and roof. That simply isn't the type of building that will attract the interest of a potential homeowner, renter, or commercial tenant.

On the other hand, a building that is properly maintained—complete with a maintenance schedule—can hold its value and even appreciate in value. An added benefit is that existing tenants like the fact that their building is well-cared for and, as a result, they will renew their lease again and again. In almost every successful building, the property manager is the person in charge of caring for the building, property, staff, and tenants.

This chapter reviews the job description of a property manager, compares the job's current and past responsibilities, and provides an inside look at a commercial property manager and a residential property manager.

The Role of a Property Manager

A property manager is someone who is responsible for managing real estate "assets" on the owner's behalf. Assets include residential properties like condominiums, apartment buildings, or senior communities, as well as commercial properties such as office buildings, malls, medical facilities, business parks, warehouses, or *mixed-use* projects that can include any and all of the above.

def•i•ni•tion

A typical **mixed-use** building is a popular form of building development, where the street level of the building is devoted to commercial use and the upper floors is for residences. Thus came the expression "living above the store." Today, mixed-use properties include mom-and-pop stores as well as national franchises, such as Home Depot. Mixed-use can also mean commercial properties that combine medical, dental, and retail.

A property manager is responsible for the day-to-day operations of buildings. For example, they make sure that the tenant rent is collected on time and that all invoices—the mortgage, taxes, insurance premiums, landscaping, janitorial, and so on—are paid on time. The manager also negotiates all of the contracts for services performed on the building—for example, janitorial, security, snow removal, window washing, heating, venting, air conditioning, roof work, preventative maintenance, and landscaping contracts. Managers also are responsible for visiting properties and conducting property condition evaluations.

They are responsible for making repairs, administering warranties, and maintaining the structural integrity of the building. They must guarantee that the building meets the building codes and applicable laws for any local, state, or federal regulations.

And the most interesting part of the job is that you have to do all the aforementioned while maintaining, and hopefully improving, the bottom line.

Improving the Bottom Line

Who would invest in real estate if they didn't think it would generate a return? The ultimate fiscal goals of a property manager are to …

- Stay on top of the current rental market values so properties are priced for profit.

- Increase how much money a property is making (its net operating income) through rents, and so on.

- Protect the property by making certain its insurance is in place and the building stays maintained.

- Increase the property's value by keeping it maintained and upgraded.

- Provide the client with an accurate monthly accounting report showing cash flow.

Property managers also keep financial statements and work with an accountant regarding financial matters. They must make sure that income-generating properties are doing just that, and money-saving budget cuts are made when needed. Managers must also administer legal documents to the benefit of ownership, while creating an environment that no one wants to leave.

> **Notes from the Field**
>
> According to the U.S. Bureau of Labor Statistics Office of Occupational Statistics and Employment Projections, there were 329,000 property managers employed in the United States in 2006. That number is expected to rise by 50,000 between 2006 and 2016.

Handling People

The property manager is a people person in charge of communicating with doormen, porters, supers, vendors, vagrants, city officials, politicians, employees, and visitors. He must also be available to tenants to answer any complaints or concerns. If there are problems with a building, the manager is responsible for seeing that things are taken care of, either through the superintendent, the building engineer, or an outside repair company or vendor. And don't let reasonable expectations—such as those related to the hour of the day or the actual level of "emergency"—cloud your judgment. Perception is reality, and if Mrs. Ferguson's ice dispenser isn't working at 2 P.M. on a Saturday, the fact that it can wait to be fixed during regular business hours on Monday for less money isn't really relevant.

The property manager's job is to walk the tight rope between meeting the owner's economic needs, while maintaining the building and keeping the occupants happy.

Types of Property Managers

A property manager can be employed as an individual by the building's owner or through a condominium association's board of directors. A property manager is the middleman between the tenants and the owner/developer. A property manager can work as an employee of a property management firm or a real estate company. He can be responsible for one or more properties, and he can manage residential, commercial, or mixed-use properties. He may work onsite (appropriately called an "onsite manager"), or work offsite as a middleman between the onsite manager and the property management company or developer.

It's important to note that property management isn't an all-day desk job, and most managers aren't working a typical 9-to-5 day. You may work 8- to 12-hour days, and continue to be on call after hours to address any problems or emergencies as they arise. You will also spend a great deal of time away from your desk visiting properties, checking repairs, talking to tenants, attending meetings, and showing homes and office space to potential tenants.

Residential Property Managers

A residential property manager can be responsible for apartment buildings, condominium developments, single-family home associations, townhouses, duplexes, mobile homes, and more. You can work in a traditional apartment building, a luxury high-rise, or student or military housing. You can also be a community association manager who takes care of one or more apartment complexes, such as a *cooperative* or condominium complex.

def•i•ni•tion

A **cooperative,** or "co-op," is a group of apartments—often a high-rise apartment building—where the units are owned by the corporation and the residents are the stockholders of the units.

Subsidized housing is housing that the government supports. It is meant for those who have low to moderate incomes.

Residential property managers also manage public or *subsidized housing* facilities—sometimes known as social housing or low-income housing—which are apartments for those who pay less than the going monthly rate. The building owners or developers receive financial assistance in a variety of forms from the various government agencies. This assistance pays for the building and any operation costs, including utility or maintenance costs and services.

You can also manage an age-restricted community (often limiting tenants to individuals 55 years of age and older) of single-family homes, condominiums, apartments, or co-ops. As more baby boomers continue to age, senior housing is one of the fastest-growing areas of property management.

In both cases, it's best to have special skills for dealing with these demographics.

Notes from the Field

A report released by the Building Owners and Managers Association—a national network of professionals involved in building ownership, management, development, and leasing—states that aging baby boomers are increasing the need for retirement communities and assisted living facilities. These specialized housing facilities can require property managers that have specialized health facility experience.

Commercial Property Managers

A commercial property manager oversees retail, *flex*, and/or industrial space, as well as office buildings, business parks, or medical campuses. The key is that the commercial property produces income. A commercial property can be an industrial building that is home to a manufacturing plant or an industrial park that houses multiple manufacturing facilities. It also includes warehouses for personal use, as well as high-end commercial storage. Office properties can include a building with only one type of business or one building with multiple business types. Retail properties can be a traditional shopping center, a strip mall, or even a stand-alone building like a restaurant. Nursing homes, college housing, and hotels/motels also fall under the commercial property management heading.

def•i•ni•tion

Flex space refers to light industrial warehouses that are converted to office space.

Some of the responsibilities of a commercial property manager are similar to that of a residential manager. For example, both are responsible for leasing and renting properties, collecting rent, negotiating contracts for building services, and maintaining the inner workings of a building. The leases for commercial properties and tenants, however, are vastly different than those for a residential tenant. These differences will be discussed in greater detail in Chapter 8.

In addition, commercial property managers work closely with local governments and the community, especially when an existing building needs to be expanded or renovated, or when it is being considered for an alternate use.

Mixed-Use Managers

Mixed-use properties, also known as multi-unit, are those that typically combine commercial and residential units. For example, a row of stores might be located on the bottom floor of a building at street level, while residents live above. A mixed-use building can also be where commercial and industrial businesses share space. Property managers who want to manage mixed-use properties should understand that they need experience or knowledge in both commercial and residential property management to handle these responsibilities.

Past, Present, and Future Property Managers

Do you remember that famed television character Schneider from the sitcom *One Day at a Time*? Schneider was a fast-talking, suave superintendent who took care of the building and the tenants. He collected rents and tended to leaky faucets. He showed potential tenants the vacant units and helped new tenants move in.

But Schneider wasn't the property manager. He was the superintendent, or "super." At one time, the manager's job was done by a super, who collected rents, tended to tenant complaints, and fixed leaky faucets. You can think of him as the property manager of the past. Like many professions, however, property management has evolved over the years. New federal and state laws, rapidly changing building systems, security issues, complicated legal paperwork challenges, and advanced computer technologies are just some of the issues that have substantially altered the way property managers complete their jobs. Although they are responsible for making certain all repairs are made, they rarely do the hands-on work themselves.

Notes from the Field

Although there isn't a definite recording of property management's beginnings, the industry seemed to explode after the development of co-ops and condos following World War II. Someone was needed to help take care of these buildings, which were investments for corporations. Without any onsite help, many of these buildings were beginning to fail financially and fall apart. A property manager was brought in to handle the day-to-day tasks.

Managing in Today's Market

Throughout the last few decades, the property manager's role has been redefined. As larger properties were built, managers took on more responsibilities, working hard to keep buildings financially sound, especially during hard economic times. Over the last few years, property managers have been put to the test in this area. The housing market has slumped, the economy has slowed, and utility costs have risen. Property managers have had to think outside the box to fill vacancies and cut costs while still providing quality service to its tenants.

In addition, managers of yesteryear typically managed only one building at a time. Today, property managers can handle multiple buildings, each worth millions of dollars. Managers are also more involved with the decision-making process. They forecast the building's potential income and anticipate real estate market trends in today's economy.

In 2001, *The National Real Estate Investor* magazine looked into the growth of the property management role. The article recognized that property managers now disseminate market research and conduct cost/benefit analysis to make recommendations on the property's future. There is tremendous pressure to boost revenue through additional forecasting and analysis. But the bottom line is that, regardless of the additional responsibilities, customer service is still the manager's top priority.

A Future Look

There are still Schneiders in today's buildings, but in most cases they now report to property managers. Looking down the road, the property management role will continue to evolve even further as the industry faces other new challenges that crop up. For example, the challenges of incorporating more environmentally friendly changes into the building.

In addition, the housing crisis of the last few years has underscored the need for a property manager that can ride out the housing industry rollercoaster, while keeping the property maintained and costs level. A well-prepared property manager is a must for any successful building. But what makes a successful property manager?

Personality Traits and Job Skills

To be a successful property manager, you need more than a real estate license, a college degree, or a certificate hanging on your office wall. You even need more than basic work experience. You need a specific personality. Let's face it. Someone who wants a slower-paced desk job or who isn't good at confronting people or making decisions is not going to succeed in this industry. Consider whether you see yourself when you read the following personality traits:

- **Confidence:** When you are confident, you believe in yourself and the decisions you make.

- **Leadership:** A good leader can motivate others to achieve a task at hand.

- **Firm and fair:** Property managers develop friendships with tenants and vendors, but you must still be firm and fair in your decision-making. You must also solve problems between residents and the landlord.

- **Awareness:** You must be aware of problems that are brewing.

- **Proactive:** Don't wait for someone to tell you about a problem. You are the type of person who stays on top of things.

- **People person:** Property managers communicate with people all day. You have to be able to quickly establish rapport.

- **Sense of humor:** Property management jobs are stressful; having a sense of humor helps.

- **Professional:** Showing up to work on time, getting the job done, and having a positive work ethic is key to managing a property.

- **Hard working:** Be ingenious in your work habits. Work hard. Work smart, but remember that this is a "do-ers" occupation.

- **Salesmanship:** Managers sell the prospects on the location, the owner on the contract fee, the vendor on the lower price, and the community on the benefit of the project—every day.

To be a successful property manager, it's also important that you come into the job with certain skills:

- **Organizational:** With all of the paperwork and tenants for which you are responsible, it's important to be able to stay organized.

- **Communication:** You will be talking to vendors, real estate agents, tenants, community members, and more. Good communication skills—listening *and* talking—is vital. We'll delve into this more in Chapter 13.

◆ **Marketing and public relations:** You will be selling properties as a property manager, so basic marketing and advertising skills are helpful.

◆ **Computer:** Basic computer skills are necessary, although they can be learned on the job. Having advanced computer skills, however, will allow you to more quickly and more efficiently do your job.

◆ **Financial:** An accounting, finance, or taxation background may be helpful for you in this job because you will be dealing with numerous financial reports.

◆ **Legal:** Any familiarity with local, state, and federal laws and regulations will help.

◆ **Real estate:** You will need a real estate license (see Chapter 2), but any previous knowledge and experience in the industry is a plus.

◆ **Time management:** This isn't the same as being organized. It's about controlling what can be controlled within each 24-hour period to the best of your ability.

If you have most of these skills, you're off to a great start. And don't worry, if you don't have these skills, many of them can be learned along the way if you have the drive and ambition to succeed.

Successful Property Managers

You're obviously reading this book because you have either just started in your career as a property manager and want to learn more or you already are a property manager and you want to be successful at your job. But what does it mean to be a successful property manager? Well, of course, it depends on who you ask.

If you read what historical icons have said about success, you will see that they each measured success very differently. For example, Albert Schweitzer, a famed theologian, once said, "Success is not the key to happiness. Happiness is the key to success. If you love what you are doing, you will be successful." Winston Churchill once said, "Success consists of going from failure to failure without loss of enthusiasm."

Although Donald Trump's success could be measured in dollars and cents, he measures it in the amount of passion you have for your career. He once said, "Without passion, great success is hard to come by."

When we asked property managers to tell us what success means to them, one answered, "Having satisfied unit owners." Another said, "Keeping costs down." Still another said, "Making money for the investor"; another said, "Preventing as many surprises as possible."

So, is being a successful property manager something you feel or something you do? It's truly both. Being a successful property manager means working hard, staying organized, handling emergencies, keeping a cool head, and having the personality to take it all in stride.

Property management requires knowing the ins and outs of the building, and knowing how to quickly and easily get the job done within the budget. It's also essential to love what you do; to work through the challenges that this important career places in front of you; and to balance the building, its tenants, and the bottom line. Managers prevent as many problems as possible and solve those that come along.

Being a successful property manager is not an impossible task. Armed with the right information (this book), tools, and mindset, anyone can succeed as a property manager. Keep in mind that you up your chances of success if you have certain personality traits.

Real-World Example

Throughout the book, we'll offer tips and suggestions, stories from the trenches, and stories of success. Here we profile Harry Conley, CPM, president and general manager of Fifth Street Management.

Before launching Fifth Street Management, Harry held senior management positions with national real estate firms, including Trammell Crow, Prentiss Properties, and Hines. His commercial real estate career spans more than 20 years, and he has managed corporate portfolios in excess of 10 million square feet. In addition, Harry has directed many state and national facilities services accounts for corporate clients, and has opened more than six million square feet of Class A office assets across the United States. Harry has obtained the Certified Property Manager (CPM) designation from the Institute of Real Estate Management, National Board of Realtors.

What drew you to your career?

"I was living/working in Houston, Texas, in 1979 and the oil industry was booming. I was seriously considering entering that industry when a chance encounter with a former school buddy occurred. We were discussing work and careers and he was working at a company called Hines. I had never heard of them but he quickly gave me an introduction into their development and property management business. I liked what I heard about property management because I had worked in the construction of office buildings during my summers in between school sessions both in high school and college. I had worked as a welder's helper, plumber, and general laborer and had somewhat of an interest in buildings.

For one summer session I was employed at an upscale condominium development and worked as a maintenance person. I have always liked the broad range of operations that property management requires every day—from highly technical operating systems, to detailed financial requirements, to the interpersonal relationships required to effectively manage a real estate asset."

Why work in both commercial and residential properties?

"My earliest opportunities for involvement and training were in the commercial office sector. I have spent the majority of my career operating and managing large office properties. The move to include high-rise condominiums occurred as I perceived that the market was underserved for qualified high-rise expertise in that genre of real estate.

Both types of real estate require solid technical knowledge of building systems and the requirements for long-term preventive maintenance. You can't fake this. Over time the absence of an appropriate maintenance program will have painful consequences for the property and the occupants in the form of unnecessary expenses and disruption of services. In both environments I enjoy working with the owners."

What is your day like?

"The typical day in the life for me begins with a cup of coffee and a review of my calendar. At Fifth Street, I have six direct reports. Each person has an area of responsibility to oversee. I review financials for every property, and that activity is scheduled for the second and third weeks of the month, depending on the property. I usually visit each property we manage at least once per month, or more frequently if there is a special project underway. I have a PDA and stay in touch via e-mail and phone regardless of my location. I try to spend approximately 25 percent of my time on business development and planning.

My training at both of these firms has provided a foundation for successful property management throughout my career. The Hines organization was a model of systematic approaches to every aspect of building operations. Whether it was preparing a budget or sourcing a contract for a large construction project, preparation and research were the hallmarks of their culture. My time at Trammell Crow was similarly very valuable. In addition to their excellent planning and operations, I think it was there that I began to be more aware of the entrepreneurial aspects of the business."

Why did you start your own company?

"I always had a desire to head up my own company. Throughout my career, even prior to beginning in real estate, I had dabbled in entrepreneurial projects. Each project taught me new lessons that I draw on today in running Fifth Street. When I was introduced to Kim King Associates (KKA) in 2002, the timing was right for both of us to come together to create this company. We were fortunate to be able to assume the management assignment for several pre-existing properties that KKA was managing and also the timing was right for the opening of their newest development, Centergy. I never doubted that we could deliver first-class operations management, and we have simply focused on each asset as it comes. Growth has been a product of our successful execution at each property. We have never advertised or solicited business. My approach has been to perform well for our existing clients and through those relationships referrals have steadily come to us."

The Least You Need to Know

- ◆ Residential, commercial, and mixed-use buildings have many property management opportunities.

- ◆ The role of a property manager has changed significantly over the years.

- ◆ Successful managers are leaders who are confident, organized, and personable.

The Property Management Career

In This Chapter

- ◆ Educating yourself and learning as you go
- ◆ Earning designations to further your career
- ◆ Reviewing earnings expectations and the industry outlook

When a new home is being built, the foundation is the first thing laid. Without a strong foundation, a house can't be correctly built and will eventually crumble. The foundation is the basis for building the rest of the house. Similarly, your education is your strong foundation to a successful career in property management. This chapter reviews the different types of property management education to give you a strong starting point for a long, prosperous career. It will also review on-the-job training, provide tips on finding your first job, and identify the salary you can expect—everything you need to know to go from classroom to job, and then some!

Getting an Education

A successful property management career should start with a college education, but it's not mandatory. There are other paths you can take to becoming a property manager.

def•i•ni•tion

A **Realtor** is a real estate agent who is a member of the National Association of Realtors. In most states, you must be certified as a real estate agent or Realtor in order to become a property manager.

Notes from the Field

In a 2006 report by *Money* magazine, property manager was named one of the top 50 jobs in America. Coming in at #23, this career choice experienced a 15.3 percent increase in job growth with an average salary of $78,735.

For example, you can get hired in an entry-level job with a real estate or property management company, learn the ropes, and then work your way up from there. You can also start out as a *Realtor* and move on to managing rental properties. Or you can start off as a building superintendent or in another building staff position and climb the ladder. These are all good ways to start your career.

Attending college, however, gives you a step up in the field. You will already have some of the education that others are still learning on the job. And in a classroom, industry experts will teach you and you will have opportunities to ask them questions. You will also learn how to read and analyze real estate industry information (this is a plus when you need to determine rental pricing, values of properties, etc.). A college degree may also enable you to obtain a higher starting salary.

Going the College Route

When choosing a college, search for one that offers a degree in real estate and/or property management. There are four-year and two-year schools that offer this learning track. You can travel to a school in another state or, if you choose, you can stay close to home. You can attend a community college as well. To find colleges that offer this curriculum, search www.collegeboard.com. Simply put in your criteria—state, price, and so on—and the website will offer you a list of choices.

If your school of choice doesn't offer a real estate or property management degree, you could obtain your degree in one of these fields:

◆ Business administration

◆ Accounting

- Finance

- Real estate

- Public administration

These are specialized skills that you will use in your job. A degree in any of these specialties, combined with a real estate license and any on-the-job training, will help to further your career.

> **Notes from the Field**
>
> According to the U.S. Department of Labor, about 90 percent of the fastest growing jobs in the future will require some postsecondary education or training. Property management falls under that "fastest growing" category.

Taking the On-the-Job Training Track

Learn as you go—that's what on-the-job training is about. You might be hired as an assistant property manager, a concierge, a super, a supervisor, or some other staff position in the building. You report to the property manager and begin to learn more about the building's inner workings as you do your job. Every day, you learn more and more, and you may soon find yourself interested in—and eligible for—a long-term property management position.

What could you do when you're on the job to help your career? First, be sure to ask a lot of questions. Second, share any ideas you have to make the property run in a smoother or more efficient manner. This will show initiative. It's also important to help the current manager see you as an asset, so share what the tenants talk to you about. Third, let your superiors know your future goals. They can offer you guidance so you get there.

Licenses and Designations

In order to be a property manager, a real estate license is a must. There are also highly recognized property management educational programs that allow you to earn certain designations. These designations show your clients and tenants that you have worked hard to achieve a certain level of educational training. For example, there is one program where you can earn a Certified Property Manager (CPM) title.

> **Notes from the Field**
>
> Almost all states have age requirements for property managers. In many states, you must be either 18 or 21 years of age to be a property manager, but check with your state's real estate board for your requirements.

Earning a Real Estate License

If you are going to rent, lease, manage, or sell any residential or commercial property as a property manager, most states require that you obtain a real estate salesperson's or broker's license. A broker is a real estate agent who has had additional training and education and passed a real estate broker's exam. The amount of classroom training hours required for a real estate salesperson's or broker's license differs depending on the state in which you want to work. Whether or not you need a license also depends on what type of property manager you are. For example, an HOA or Community Association Manager is not required to have a license in all states.

In New York, for example, 75 hours of classroom training are required. Courses cover real estate law, regulations, and procedures and ethics. Virginia only requires 60 hours of classroom training, but California requires 135 hours of courses. Broker training usually requires additional classroom hours, as well as a minimum number of years as a realtor. To determine your state's licensing requirements, search the Internet for "(your state) real estate commission." In addition, your particular state may have age, citizenship, or other types of requirements.

You can take courses that will prepare you for your real estate license through community colleges or through continuing education programs. While some states allow for course completion over the Internet, some do not, so it's best to ask your state association of realtors for your state's information. These courses can run approximately six or eight weeks and can cost up to $500 for a basic real estate license course and additional fees for the test and for the license. If you are currently working for a property management firm, they may pay all or a portion of these fees for you.

Once you pass the real estate salesperson test, you'll need to work under the supervision of a broker if you are going to sell/buy properties as a property manager.

If you are already a licensed sales agent or associate broker who wants to be a property manager, a principal broker must supervise you. The only exception is if you are working on behalf of a property owner, but you do not transact any sales or purchases of property. It can get a little confusing, so the best thing to do is check with the real estate commission in your state.

Productivity Tips

If you're working your way through school, consider a part-time job with a real estate or property management company in the interim. It could turn into a full-time job when you've graduated!

Earning a Property Management License

While all states require a property manager to have a real estate license, only some states require that a property manager actually have a property management license. Other states are still debating the value of such a license.

Those who support mandatory licensing say that managers should earn additional educational credentials, answer to a governing authority, undergo a background check, and agree to a code of ethics and standards. These folks also believe that a license will reduce the possibility of unethical property managers.

On the other side of the debate are those who are against additional licensing beyond a real estate license. They say the educational requirements are fine just the way they are, and they say governing agencies are simply looking for additional income streams. The debate is still raging on in states that don't currently have property management licensing and even some that already do.

> ### Notes from the Field
>
> Although most states require property managers to have a license, you can find out your state's requirements by searching the Internet. In your search field, put "(your state) property management license requirements."

Continuing Education

Today's property manager has many responsibilities, including supervising all aspects of the building and managing contracts, budgets, tenant relations, and more. A good manager stays up to date on the building's inner workings and is familiar with the changing building codes and laws. Federal, state, and local laws change all the time, so the schooling is never really over.

Some states (and certification programs) require that a property manager take additional courses every few years to stay licensed, certified, and current. Maintaining your real estate or broker's license requires continuing education courses as well. Some continuing education courses focus on specific programs—for example, building systems or financial analysis. Some states require that you take specific courses, such as Plumbing 1 or Lead Issues. Check with your state to find out exactly what courses you will need to take and when you must take them to meet the requirements for keeping your real estate and/or your property manager's license.

Productivity Tips _____

Remember the old saying "It's not what you know, it's who you know"? In the property management industry, it's both. When you're taking a course, chat it up a bit before class starts! Sitting in a classroom gives you the opportunity to network with other students and real estate professionals, giving you an advantage in the competitive job market. Ask for business cards—these contacts can help you later in your career.

Continuing education courses are offered in a variety of venues and include day, evening, and weekend classes. If these opportunities are difficult to attend, some organizations and schools offer correspondence courses through which you can conveniently complete home-study courses or online classes at your own pace. Trade organizations also hold various seminars and workshops to refresh your skills.

Once school is out, you'll receive your certificate or your passing letter grade by the sponsoring school or association. You're not required to be a member of a trade organization to enroll in their courses, but being a member may score you some discounts on enrollment. Again, if you're employed by a property management company, ask your boss if he'll foot the bill. It can't hurt. Otherwise you may have to pay for it out of your own pocket—but your potential for advancement could easily make these classes pay for themselves.

Things to Avoid _____

Don't sign up for any online real estate license or property management certification courses before making sure they are legit. Check out the organization or company, its instructors, and the courses they are offering before signing up. Make sure that the courses and the organization are recognized as real estate continuing education providers by the state in which you work. You don't want to invest time and money only to find out that your courses aren't acceptable for recertification. If you are unsure, ask one of the trade organizations to recommend legitimate online courses.

Earning Designations

You can also continue your education by taking specialized courses or by participating in workshops provided by various trade organizations. Once you complete them, you earn designations and continuing education credits that show you've successfully completed the program. Here are just a handful of designations and the requirements you need to fulfill to get them:

◆ **Real Property Administrator (RPA)**—RPA is a certification available through the Building Owners and Managers Institute (BOMI), an organization of property management firms, owners, and trade associations. It requires completion of six mandatory courses, one elective course, and an ethics course.

◆ **Facilities Management Administrator (FMA)**—This certification is provided by BOMI. It requires completion of seven mandatory courses, one elective course, and an ethics course.

◆ **Systems Maintenance Technician (SMT) and Systems Maintenance Administrator (SMA)**—These certifications are provided by BOMI. Each requires completion of eight mandatory courses, one elective course, and an ethics course. Both SMT and SMA courses detail specific operating systems, but the SMA program includes additional courses covering environmental issues, administration, and building design and maintenance.

◆ **Certified Property Manager (CPM)**—This designation means the individual has met the requirements of the Institute of Real Estate Management (IREM), an international organization that serves the multifamily and commercial real estate sector. This designation is also recognized by the National Association of Realtors, which represents 1.3 million commercial and residential real estate members. You must pass 10 required courses—including marketing, human resources, asset management, and ethics—and complete a management plan on a subject building. These courses are offered in the classroom, online, or via home study. References and a real estate license are required. The candidate must be working as a full-time real estate decision-maker for three years prior to obtaining CPM.

◆ **Certified Manager of Community Associations (CMCA)**—This designation is from The National Board of Certification for Community Association Managers (NBC-CAM) and signifies that a manager has passed NBC-CAM's national exam and met the requirements for managing condominium, cooperative, and homeowners' associations. The Community Associations Institute offers several other designations as well.

> **Notes from the Field**
>
> According to the IREM, the average CPM member has more than 18 years of real estate management experience. Together, they also manage over $879 billion in real estate assets comprised of approximately 10.2 million residential units and 8 billion net square feet of commercial space.

- **Accredited Residential Manager (ARM)**—This designation means the individual has met IREM's requirements for specialists who manage residential and apartment properties, rental mobile homes, rental condominiums, and single-family houses and condominiums.

- **Residential Management Professional (RMP)**—This designation means the individual has met the requirements of the National Association of Residential Property Managers (NARPM), a national association designed for real estate professionals. To become an RMP, you must have been a currently licensed real estate agent for at least two years. You must manage a minimum of 25 residential units during the candidacy period and at the time of achieving the designation. Applicants must complete 18 hours of NARPM-approved RMP coursework, plus their ethics course. They must also attend a NARPM convention, submit letters of recommendation, and more.

- **Master Property Manager (MPM)**—This designation means the individual has met the requirements to be a current member of NARPM and has been a currently licensed real estate agent for at least five years. They have achieved the RMP designation, and they must manage a minimum of 50 units during and at completion of candidacy. In addition, they must complete 24 hours of NARPM-approved MPM coursework, attend two or more NARPM National Conventions, submit letters of recommendation, and much more.

> **Productivity Tips**
>
> If your certification program does not require recertification, take the initiative to revisit the classroom within the next few years. It's always a good idea to stay on top of this ever-changing industry. It should be noted that every designation for management professionals requires taking an ethics course.

- **Certified Residential Property Management Company (CRPMC)**—This designation from the NARPM is awarded to professional property management firms that demonstrate a high standard in both procedures and customer service. A detailed examination of the company and recommendations from clients and peers are required for this designation.

Your First Job

Real estate license in hand, you're ready for your first job as a property manager! Congratulations! You're on your way. We don't want to burst your bubble, especially after everything we just said, but you're probably not going to be handed a building to take care of right off the bat. After all, it's a huge responsibility. Look at the online job listings for property managers. Most are looking for property managers with experience, and you need to work under someone else for a while to gain that experience.

In the interim, you might be hired as an assistant manager, as a leasing consultant, or in another supervisory position. After some experience, you'll be able to manage a building on your own.

Things to Avoid

If you haven't gotten your driver's license yet, do so before you apply for jobs. A property manager usually travels from the building to the property management office for meetings, and so on. You'll need a driver's license with a good record.

Salary

What are you going to be earning? According to the Bureau of Labor Statistics, the median annual earnings of salaried property, real estate, and community association managers were $43,070 in May 2006. The middle 50 percent earned between $28,700 and $64,200 per year. The lowest 10 percent earned less than $20,140, and the highest 10 percent earned more than $95,170 a year. Median annual earnings of salaried property, real estate, and community association managers in the largest industries that employed them in May 2006 were as follows:

- ◆ Land subdivision: $78,040

- ◆ Local government: $55,210

- ◆ Activities related to real estate: $40,590

- ◆ Offices of real estate agents and brokers: $40,500

- ◆ Lessors of real estate: $37,480

Although it's not required, many residential apartment managers and onsite association managers include the perk of an apartment as part of their compensation package. Managers can also be reimbursed for the use of their personal vehicles. In some cases, managers employed in land development receive a small percentage of ownership in the projects that they develop.

Job Outlook

You might think that, with the housing crisis over the last few years, you will have a hard time finding a job or that the jobs are fading away. Get that thought out of your head. The truth is property managers are needed now more than ever before. They are needed to keep the buildings running for the owners and the tenants, without breaking the bank. A building can't fail now.

The good news is that, as the current population ages, there is also going to be a greater need for assisted-living facilities, which opens up more property management opportunities. This is an industry that is expecting tremendous growth, and if you have training or experience in a specialized area such as health care, you'll have a better chance of getting a job. In the commercial real estate industry, the job outlook is also going to improve because there is more commercial growth than ever before. Employing property managers to care for property is a smart investment for both commercial and residential owners.

Real-World Example

Robbin Pearson has been a commercial real estate professional for more than 15 years. She earned her Bachelor's degree and holds a real estate salesperson license. She completed the required coursework for Georgia Appraisal licensure. Robbin earned a Certified Property Manager (CPM) designation and is a member of several trade organizations, including the Building Owners and Managers Association (BOMA) and IREM.

Why a career in property management?

"It was an accident. I always had some sort of real estate element in my jobs even going back to when I was an RA in college. My first job out of college was with a job placement firm, and part of what I handled was the management of our satellite offices, which included assisting in negotiating our leases.

My next job was with a software firm where I handled 13 offices, including the real estate transactions. It was from that job, and when I moved to Atlanta, that a job in property management seemed to be a good fit for my skill set. It was from that job that I really considered that my career was in property management."

Robbin worked her way up to her current position, working as a senior property manager. She manages a number of low- and high-rise office buildings and industrial and retail properties. She also works closely with senior management on business development and portfolio oversight. She is a portfolio manager and is responsible for nearly one million square feet of retail property located in the mid-Atlantic region.

Her career spans international facilities management and commercial real estate with positions overseeing retail, industrial, and office properties. Robbin has experience in corporate real estate, tenant and owner representation, third party management, and leasing.

Why commercial real estate?

"I never considered residential real estate. It's an entirely different industry that bears no resemblance to commercial real estate except that one of the goals is to achieve a high rate of occupancy. I love everything about my career. I think this is because it happened through me focusing on things that I'm good at and that I enjoy when looking for jobs in my young adult life.

As a property manager, there is rarely a daily routine. Responsibilities and tasks run the gamut and include dealing with tenants, vendors, and employees; problem solving and troubleshooting both urgent and long-term issues; accounting and financial reporting; and working with equity partners."

What experience have you taken away from your job?

"I think the take-away is that the more years of experience you have dealing with different property types, asset managers, budgets, reports, and so on, the more you've seen and learned and the more valuable you become. Things like budgeting become second nature so you're able to focus on more innovative ideas and thinking."

The Least You Need to Know

- There are many different routes you can take to a property management career.
- A real estate license is a must to get started, but look into additional educational opportunities to stay up to date and earn designations.
- The job outlook for the property management industry is solid.

Chapter 3

Residential Property Managers

In This Chapter

- ◆ Managing all types of homes
- ◆ Working in a retirement community
- ◆ Taking care of one, two, or more buildings
- ◆ Understanding mixed-use opportunities

Home sweet home! A tenant or homeowner wants to feel happy about where they live. They want to know their property is being taken care of, repairs and upgrades are being made, and the building—and their investment—is financially sound, safe, and secure. This is a residential property manager's job.

At the same time, that building's owner wants to make sure his tenants are being well taken care of; his investment is financially sound; and the property is being maintained, repaired, and upgraded. This is also your job as a residential property manager.

This chapter focuses on residential property management. We will review how you can be a residential property manager for many different types of residences, including apartments, student housing, and senior complexes.

Each comes with its own set of rules, situations, and problems. How you determine which type you work for depends on your likes and dislikes, as well as the current job market and job availability.

Apartment-Style Management

Typically, apartment buildings with more than 20 units are managed by an entire professional property management company. These companies appoint one or more property manager(s) to handle a particular building. Buildings with fewer than 20 units may be managed by either one property manager who lives onsite or by the building's owner.

There are two types of apartment-style properties: high-rise and garden-style.

High-Rise Apartments

A mid-rise building is 5 to 10 stories high, while a high-rise apartment building is higher than 10 stories, and might be called a *skyscraper*. There are also luxury high-rise apartments, which cater to higher-income tenants and feature special amenities, such as a view, top-of-the-line appliances, concierge services, and high-end security systems. Each unit's cost depends on its size and location. For example, a penthouse unit is going to cost more than a unit on the first floor with no spectacular view.

def•i•ni•tion

A **skyscraper** is a tall, continuously habitable building. There is no official rule that states how high a skyscraper has to be, but most are those that are higher than other buildings in the area and that stick out over the skyline.

The conversion of high-rise residential buildings has increased over the last few years. Why? Sitting unused in areas across the country are industrial buildings and other commercial buildings that were once used as factories, warehouses, and so on. Developers recognized the potential space and attraction of these buildings, and converted them to condominium apartments.

One prime example of such a converted building is the historic 1957 Downtown Dallas high-rise condo in Dallas, Texas. The building was converted from office space to high-end condominiums in 2003.

Being a property manager for a high-rise apartment building comes with its own set of challenges. Topping that list of these challenges is safety. Making certain all residents are able to get out of the building in case of a fire is a huge concern. (We'll tackle safety issues in Chapter 15.)

Garden-Style Apartments

Garden-style housing is considered a low-rise apartment with access to common lawn space or gardens. They are usually no more than two or three stories, and are most often found in the suburbs.

Student Housing Management

When you think of student housing, what's the first image that comes to mind? Is it a scene from the collegiate classic movie *Animal House*? Well, the good news is, although having students as tenants can get a little crazy from time to time, it's far from fraternity living. Student housing does however, carry its own challenges. For example:

♦ Students need reminders to pay their rent on time. Remember that these kids are young, and many of them are on their own for the first time in their lives. Some may be responsible, but be prepared for others who need guidance and reminders.

♦ Parties, cleanliness, and roommate issues are par for the course. Student housing comes with rules and regulations that the students must abide by, but often many of them will try to get away with whatever they can. When this happens, being a property manager may sometimes feel like being a parent.

Notes from the Field

According to the National Center for Education Statistics, college enrollment will grow by 11 percent between 2003 and 2013. Higher education is less affected by economic trends. Even during bad times, more people seek a college degree to improve job prospects. During good times, an education becomes more important. Today, students are taking longer to graduate, and need housing for longer stretches of time.

♦ Speaking of cleanliness, students have a tendency to not leave apartments the way they found them. Budgets for repairs and upkeep for student housing are usually higher.

♦ You're not just dealing with students. Oftentimes, parents will become involved in payments, and communicate with you about information regarding their child, repairs, and conflicts.

◆ Every year, the population changes. Students living in student housing this year may not be living there next year. This is a higher rate of turnover compared to other housing leases.

If you decide to specialize in student housing, you need a sense of commitment, tolerance, and patience.

Managing Cooperatives

The process of buying and owning a cooperative is much different than buying a single-family home or a condo. When someone buys a single-family home, they are responsible for taking care of the home—both inside and out. When someone purchases a condominium, they are responsible for what's inside the home, but they pay the management association dues that are used to maintain the property's common or shared elements.

Notes from the Field
According to The National Cooperative Business Association, there are more than one million units of cooperative housing scattered throughout the United States, with large numbers located in major urban areas like New York City, Chicago, and Washington, D.C.

However, in a cooperative, tenants must be approved by the building's board of directors before they can own their home. The corporation is the building's legal owner and the tenant is the stockholder. The owner pays a lender for the mortgage and is also required to pay a monthly fee to the corporation so they, in turn, can pay the cooperative corporation's underlying mortgage payment, property taxes, and property manager and maintenance charges. There is also a little matter of the bylaws and the proprietary lease.

Cooperative Bylaws

In a cooperative, there are rules to abide by called bylaws, which dictate the building's do's and don'ts. The condominium association's bylaws are self-governing and vary from building to building. For example, some buildings do not allow pets, while others limit guest visits to no more than a few days.

The bylaws explain meetings, voting, proxies, budget, *special assessments*, insurance coverage, and restrictions on the use of the units and the common areas. For example, condominium bylaws will state whether or not unit owners can own pets, but the cooperative owner's proprietary lease will state the rules of pet ownership.

def•i•ni•tion

A **special assessment** is a one-time fee levied on residents to raise money to cover an unexpected expense. Usually an assessment is only done in an emergency situation, when other methods of raising money have been unsuccessful or when a building's reserve funds are not adequate to cover a sudden expense.

As the property manager of a cooperative, your responsibilities in a cooperative are similar to that of other styles of residences. You will, however, be required to know and work with the board of directors to enforce these bylaws, especially if there is a complaint against another shareholder.

Cooperative Proprietary Leases

A proprietary lease is a lease used for co-ops that gives a shareowner the right to live in his particular unit. The lease gives him the right to live there and the bylaws tell him about what's expected of him when they do.

Managing Condominiums

When a homeowner buys a condominium, they are buying their own home. A condominium isn't a style of home—it's a type of home ownership. Condos can be in apartment buildings, townhouses, and even old warehouses or industrial spaces that have been converted into condos. Owning a condominium means owners own everything inside the walls and share the other areas of the association—tennis courts, pools, playgrounds, and clubhouses—with the other owners. Owners pay a maintenance charge to the association so that maintenance, repairs, and upgrades are made.

The good news about managing condominiums is homeowners usually take pride in their home ownership and will do what they can to maintain a high standard of living to protect their investment.

Condo Associations

The Community Associations Institute (www.caionline.org) says that homeowner and community associations deliver services that were once the exclusive province of local government, including trash pickup, street paving, lighting, and snow removal, to name but a few. The association members pay for these services, which were once paid for by local governments. Living in a community association allows residents to enjoy services such as snow removal, garbage pickup, and pool maintenance. They can also enjoy amenities such as playgrounds, swimming pools, tennis courts, health clubs, and clubhouses.

> **Notes from the Field**
>
> A study by the Community Association Institute shows that 73 percent of community association residents surveyed said that a manager provides value and support to the residents and the community. There are an estimated 60,000 community association managers in the United States.

These associations determine what homeowners can and cannot do, as related to such concerns as pets, parking, additions, and paint colors. Being a property manager in a community association is pretty much the same as being a property manager in other housing developments. For example, property managers prepare financial statements, negotiate contracts, and take care of tenant relations. The board of directors hires you to oversee the property, assist the board, and take care of financial records.

Condo Rules and Regulations

Condominiums come with their own set of rules and regulations. Unlike cooperatives, condominiums do not have proprietary leases. Instead, condominiums have more detailed bylaws. Covenants, conditions, and restrictions (CCRs) are rules written into the deeds or bylaws that define how property may be used. It prevents property owners from making changes to their individual properties that could adversely affect other owners.

Board of Directors

Condos not only come with their own rules and regulations, but they also come with a board of directors. This board, made up of volunteers from the association, decides what is and isn't going to be done to the property. If you manage a condo association, you will be reporting to a board on a regular basis. We'll discuss working with a board of directors in more detail in Chapter 13.

Managing Retirement Communities

In the United States, there are 36.3 million people age 65 and over as of July 1, 2004. This age group accounts for 12 percent of the total population. There are 4.9 million Americans age 85 and over in the United States. By the year 2050, it is anticipated that there will be 86.7 million Americans age 65 and over. They all need a place to live and a manager to manage them.

Independent Living

Seniors who can care for themselves want to live on their own. They may choose to live in independent living facilities, which are equipped with special features that make it easier for residents to get around. The facilities provide recreational activities— bingo groups, day trips, lectures, shopping, and more. They have a gym, pool, tennis courts, and more.

Congregate Care Communities

Congregate housing, or congregate living, offers seniors independent living in their own apartments, which they can own or rent. These homes may offer additional care services, such as nursing or Alzheimer care.

Active Adult Communities

Meant for the age 55 and up crowd (some can narrow it down to 55 to 65), active adult communities typically offer recreational amenities, security features, and social functions to its residents.

Section 202

Not all seniors can afford a place to live. As some get older, their income drops, and housing options become extremely limited. Section 202 Supportive Housing for the Elderly Program and the Low-Income Housing Tax Credit (LIHTC) helps provide housing. The Section 202 program helps increase the supply of affordable housing with supportive services for the elderly. It provides very low-income elderly individuals with options that allow them to live independently in an environment that provides support activities such as cleaning, cooking, transportation, and more. The program is similar to Supportive Housing for Persons with Disabilities (Section 811).

According to the American Association of Retired Persons' *AARP Public Policy Institute Data Digest*, the supply of both Section 202 and LIHTC housing is inadequate to meet the growing needs of low-income older renters, as evidenced by long waiting lists and low *vacancy rates*.

def•i•ni•tion

A **vacancy rate** is the percentage of all the units that are not occupied or rented at a given time, compared to the entire building.

NORCs

If you haven't heard of a NORC, the best way to describe it is with an example …

Andrea is 70 years old. Every day she gets up and does her yoga, something she's been doing for the last 40 years. She's great about seeing her doctor, her cholesterol is low, and her blood pressure is perfect. She lives alone in an apartment, but she has a lot of friends and she is active in the community. An assisted living center or a nursing home is not for her. She is happy in an apartment she loves so much, with neighbors her age all around.

Andrea is in what's called a NORC, a "naturally occurring retirement community." These are apartment buildings, housing complexes, or neighborhoods that started out as communities for tenants of all ages. They weren't originally designed or built as a senior community. But they turned into NORCs over time, as the tenants aged.

And, with over 76 million baby boomers scheduled to retire from the workforce and eyeing their golden years, the number of NORC communities is growing.

Single-Family Home Management

Property managers also manage single-family homes. Why would an owner need a property manager for just one home? Perhaps the owner hasn't been able to sell the property and has moved on to another home. Having someone take care of the home while he is gone keeps the value of the property intact. Some homes are also extremely large—think Oprah's Chicago-based multimillion-dollar mansion, for example—and can need more maintenance than a small homeowners' association.

Single Site vs. Portfolio Management

As a property manager, you will be handling either one property, such as a single-family home or single apartment building, or multiple properties. Manage one property, and it gets your full, undivided attention. Manage more than one property, and you need to be highly organized to make certain that records, leases, and reports are kept on track for each building. You must also be available to travel between buildings, even at a moment's notice.

When deciding whether you can handle multiple properties, consider your personality and skills. You don't want to fall behind on paperwork, fail to visit all of the properties, or give inadequate attention to any of the buildings. Later in Chapter 17, we'll discuss some time- and stress-management tips to help you handle multiple properties.

Deciding whether you want to be responsible for one building or more is a personal decision. Only you know how much you can handle. Also, if you start out your career handling one property, you can slowly add more responsibility and see what you're comfortable with.

Working with a Board of Directors

With certain types of property management, such as condominiums and cooperatives, you are responsible for reporting to a board of directors.

A board of directors is made up of volunteers who live in the building and it is, in a sense, your boss. You report to them and let them know about the happenings with the building. Most boards are comprised of anywhere from three to seven members, although larger buildings may have more. They hold posts such as president, vice president, secretary, and treasurer. They are elected to make decisions that are in the best interest of the co-op or condo they serve. Volunteering on a board is a time-consuming responsibility.

Board members are in charge of the association's money, and their first responsibility is to the budget. The treasurer receives your financial reports and invoices, and reviews financial matters and the budget with the accountant, the manager, and you. They review how the building is doing financially and make sure deposits are made properly and in the right accounts. They have the final say as to what repairs and upgrades get done and how money gets spent. Board members may also hear from tenants about the job you are doing and any problems with the building. The board will pass along any complaints and praise. The board can also fire you if you are failing to live up to your job responsibilities.

Mixed-Use Property Management

Mixed-use properties typically combine residential properties with commercial businesses. In most cases, the businesses are located on either the street level or lower floors while the residents live on the upper floors. There are also mixed-use properties that combine types of commercial properties—for example, retail and medical business.

Mixed-use buildings have several benefits:

◆ They preserve land. Many old commercial buildings sit vacant and unused. Developers and city planners have been converting these buildings to mixed-use facilities instead of building new. This option saves precious land.

◆ They raise revenue. Mixed-use properties can earn additional income for the building by renting out space to commercial businesses. It is possible to have multiple businesses renting space or one business renting multiple spaces.

Property managers for mixed-use properties have to be able to handle both commercial and residential residents, which requires that you know both sides of real estate. You must also keep up with both industries.

Notes from the Field

With mixed-use buildings comes the so-called 80/20 rule. Section 216 of the Internal Revenue Code requires that 80 percent of the co-op's total revenue come from stockholders' fees and assessments. No more than 20 percent can come from commercial space. If not in compliance, penalties can abound, including forfeiting valuable tax credits and more.

A Mixed-Use Case Story: Lucky Platt

One prime example of a mixed-use building that was converted is The Lucky Platt Building in Poughkeepsie, New York. Formerly a thriving department store business, the store closed in 1980. The building was abandoned until 2004, when it was purchased for $1, under the stipulation that the buyers would rebuild the historic department store site. It is now a landmark city location and was recently renovated to include 141 newly built studios and one- and two-bedroom unit apartments.

It includes 23,100 square feet of street level space and 22,000 square feet of lower-level retail/office space. These spaces can be used for shops or corporate offices, making it a mixed-use building.

Real-World Example

When you're a property manager, it's important to expect the unexpected as Kimberly Smith, a corporate housing property manager in Denver, Colorado, describes here:

"We were managing a newer condo in a San Francisco high-rise—the homeowners' association (HOA) decided to sue the developer over some construction defects. In order to prove the defect they needed to do some destructive testing. The owner of our unit wanted to volunteer to help the process. We made all the arrangements with the tenant—the testing team was to enter the unit while the tenant was at work.

They were to cut open a section of drywall, inspect the inner wall construction, document it, and repair the wall before the tenant returned home for the day. All went as planned until the tenant returned home and was unable to locate her cat. Turns out the cat was extra curious and had also inspected the construction! He was now trapped inside the wall! Don't worry; the cat was fine. The drywall was cut open again, the cat was released, and the wall was again repaired."

The Least You Need to Know

- There are many opportunities to work in residential property management—houses, apartments, condos, co-ops, retirement communities, and mixed-use.

- Working with specialized groups requires a slightly different skill set. Dealing with seniors will not be the same as managing student housing.

- Mixed-use buildings provide the opportunity to combine commercial and residential property management.

Chapter 4

Commercial Property Managers

In This Chapter

- ◆ Reviewing the commercial property industry
- ◆ Managing shopping centers and office buildings
- ◆ Discovering the unique aspects of managing medical buildings
- ◆ Working with industrial parks and "smart" buildings

In addition to residential property managers, there are commercial property managers. *Commercial property* refers to retail shopping centers, office buildings, hotels, warehouses and other industrial facilities, and shopping centers.

This chapter will review the types of commercial managers and their day-to-day responsibilities, which are similar to those of a residential property manager—working with the tenants, collecting rents, repairing and maintaining building systems and structures, negotiating leases and contracts, and so on. They also must help the property become more profitable and enhance its resale value. But certain aspects of commercial property management, such as the details of leases, negotiations, and how rents are structured, are different than in residential real estate.

Commercial Industry Overview

The last few years have been difficult for commercial real estate property, but there's good news and bad news about what's in the future and your prospects of becoming a commercial property manager. A successful commercial property manager is vital all the time, but it's especially important to know that a developer can depend on their property manager, especially when the going gets tough.

The Good News

The National Association of Industrial and Office Properties Research Foundation (NAIOP) issued a report that detailed the tremendous impact commercial real estate development has on the nation's economy. According to their report, in today's unstable economy—with frozen credit and capital markets and policymakers poised to act on key issues—understanding the commercial real estate development industry's significant economic contributions is more valuable than ever.

According to their release, in 2007 (the latest comprehensive data available), construction-related spending reached $549 billion and 839 million square feet of existing building space was added.

Notes from the Field
"The magnitude of commercial construction's economic impact is tremendous. This report reconfirms that a healthy real estate economy is vital to a prosperous U.S. economy," said Thomas J. Bisacquino, president of the NAIOP. "Commercial real estate development has an immense ripple effect in the economy, providing wages and jobs that quickly roll over into increased consumer spending."

According to the report, three phases of development contribute to commercial real estate's *sustainability:*

def•i•ni•tion

Sustainability means the ability to remain in a certain state for a long period of time.

1. Hard costs (actual construction costs): $283.7 billion

2. Soft costs (architecture, engineering, marketing, legal, management, site development, and tenant improvements): $265 billion

3. Building operations (maintenance, repair, custodial services, utilities, and management): $5.1 billion

The commercial real estate development industry is also one of the leading employers in the United States. In 2007, the industry supported 4.89 million full-time equivalent jobs and generated personal earnings of $170.1 billion.

Overall, commercial and residential construction spending totaled $1.16 trillion—approximately 8.5 percent of the nation's Gross Domestic Product (GDP), which was $13.8 trillion in 2007. Of the $1.16 trillion, nonresidential building construction (office, industrial, warehouse, and retail) accounted for $400.6 billion, or 34 percent of all construction spending. Sounds good, right?

> ### Notes from the Field
>
> According to Real Capital Analytics, medical office sales have grown from $857 million in 2002 to $2.1 billion in 2005. Medical office space now averages $211 per square foot, compared with $203 for all other office buildings. In 2002, medical office rents averaged $142 per square foot.

The Flip Side

According to Property Wire (www.propertywire.com), at least $107 billion of income-generating commercial property in the United States was already in distress in 2008 or was heading that way in 2009. This includes prestigious buildings, hotels, offices, apartment blocks, and warehouses across the United States in New York. Some buildings are carrying more than a billion dollars of debt! Real Capital Analytics' list includes a total of 268 properties in the New York area alone, with a value of $12 billion, as already or potentially in trouble.

So there are many opportunities in managing commercial properties, because more are being built every day. However, it's a particular challenge to be a commercial property manager in today's economic environment, so be prepared if you choose to enter this field. By working hard to make certain your property is successful, you'll reap the rewards and good feeling of a job well done. Let's review the various types of commercial property management careers you can choose from.

Shopping Centers/Retail

Retail buildings and shopping centers include big box stores like Wal-Mart; strip malls; markets; town square plazas; factory outlets; and neighborhood, community, and regional shopping centers. Retail property managers should have strong accounting skills to be able to handle multiple tenants of various sizes. You may manage a smaller strip center of just a few stores in a shopping mall with 100 stores. These malls can include local mom-and-pop stores, combined with national franchised stores and *anchor stores.*

def•i•ni•tion

An **anchor store** is also called the "key tenant" or "draw tenant." It's one of the larger stores in a mall, usually a department store, typically found at the end of the mall—thereby "anchoring" the mall. Lose the anchor store and usually the smaller stores follow.

The last few years have been very difficult for the retail industry. Thanks to the economic crisis, consumers have had to deal with rising energy costs and mortgage bills, home foreclosures, and job losses. As a result, consumers have significantly reduced or halted their spending, and many stores have closed.

According to National Real Estate Investor online, major retailers announced closures of more than 2,100 stores in the first quarter of 2008 alone, compared to 4,603 closings in all of 2007. For the retail property manager, this means that you need to be more conscious of cost-saving measures to prevent an increase in vacancy rates.

Office Buildings

Facilities managers manage large commercial properties such as offices or colleges. Office buildings are classified as either Class A, B, or C in order to maintain comparative market data in the industry.

- **Class A:** Think of Class A buildings as getting an A on a test—it's considered top-of-the-line, or the best score out of all the other buildings. They represent the highest or best quality of office buildings. They usually are new or recently built, well-constructed with high-quality infrastructure, and located in a prominent area. They have state-of-the-art fixtures, technologies, and amenities. Class A buildings also can command high rents from its tenants.

  Examples of Class A buildings are offices occupied by financial firms, high-priced law firms, and other large, high-profile buildings. This class has what's called "brass and glass," which are Class A medical buildings that include the highest technology capabilities.

◆ **Class B:** According to Building Owners and Managers Association (BOMA) International, Class B buildings compete for a wide range of users with rents in the average range for the area, and are not in competition with Class A. Building finishes are fair to good for the area. With sufficient restoration, a Class B building can be turned into a Class A building.

◆ **Class C:** This is the lowest class of office building. Class C buildings are usually older and in lower-income areas. They may be poorly managed or in bad physical shape and in need of renovation and repair. The systems and technologies may be outdated and, as a result, they do not command the higher rental rates that Classes A and B can command. They are also the hardest to lease. They may be eligible, however, for renovation grants and tax incentives.

◆ **Class D:** A building in this class is in very poor shape, has very low rental rates, and has low occupancy.

Your responsibilities as property manager may vary depending on the building's class. For example, a Class A building may feature additional state-of-the-art building systems that you'll need to maintain. As manager of a Class C building, however, you may be responding to more break-ins and security issues because these buildings are typically without a security system.

Medical Office Buildings

Medical office buildings (MOBs) are sites with either one medical company that takes up the entire building space or several different medical companies located in one building. For example, the tenants may include a medical laboratory who rents the entire building or a mixture of tenants, including a medical laboratory, mental health professionals, physicians, dentists, drug stores, eye doctors, and more. There are also buildings with on-site x-ray facilities and other testing equipment, and even same-day operating rooms.

Real estate developers have recognized the profit behind such medical buildings that rent to medical facilities. As a result, this has opened up additional opportunities for property managers. However, managing these buildings brings its own challenges. Although all property managers are taught to handle emergency situations, managing a medical office building increases the risk that there may be additional emergency situations. You must be prepared at all times to drop whatever task is at hand. There are several other unique aspects of managing medical buildings, which includes handling emergency building access for doctors and their patients, additional janitorial duties to keep the offices germ-free, and maintaining building systems so important medical equipment does not break down during procedures.

Emergency Building Access

Doctors and medical facilities traditionally offer their patients extended office hours from early morning to late evening. In some cases, tenants and doctors may also need access to the office after hours because of medical emergencies. For example, a dentist may have a patient who needs an emergency root canal and needs to be seen right away. Property managers need to allow emergency access and, for security reasons, need to keep an eye on who is coming in and out of the building after hours.

Additional Janitorial Duties

Medical buildings are high-traffic areas. Depending on the size of the building and the amount of tenants, there can be hundreds of sick and well patients and visitors coming in and out of the building all day long. To prevent any bacteria transmission and other hazards, medical buildings require daily cleaning and extra sanitary conditions in order to protect the patients and staff. To cover the expense, property managers often charge tenants a slightly higher rental fee to cover additional housekeeping responsibilities.

Maintaining Building Systems

Medical buildings may also contain testing supplies, emergency medical equipment, and ample supplies of medications that have special storage requirements, such as materials that must be stored at certain temperatures. Many medical buildings come equipped with individual heating, ventilating, and air conditioning (HVAC) control units in each office to meet their specialized needs. A building system that breaks down can lead to a loss of medications and emergency medical equipment. In some cases, rushing a patient from one floor to another in an emergency, only to encounter a broken elevator, can have tragic results. Properly working backup generators are vital as well.

Notes from the Field

When considering the heating and air conditioning temperatures in a medical building, remember the patients! Patients disrobe for various examinations and medical procedures. As a result, it's best to have the patient areas at a warmer temperature in the winter, unless the tenants explain it must be a certain temp for equipment or supplies. In the summer, don't have the air conditioning blasting. Instead, keep the rooms slightly warmer.

In the near future, MOBs will remain an active market that brokers and other real estate professionals should not overlook. As regional medical centers continue to grow, as the corporate structure of hospitals and managed care facilities change, and as the field of specialty medicine continues to grow, the medical office building market will continue to offer opportunities to investors and real estate professionals.

Industrial Properties

Industrial real estate includes all land and buildings used or suited for use by an industry. An industrial "site" is any location where industrial activity occurs. As an industrial property manager, you may be responsible for managing an entire *industrial park*.

Examples of industrial facilities include:

def•i•ni•tion

An **industrial park** is a combination of office and industrial space within one building. Some of these parks are now called business parks.

◆ **Heavy manufacturing plants.** Heavy manufacturing facilities make big-ticket items such as cars, appliances, and airplanes. The facilities are huge to accommodate the large number of workers, materials, inventory, noise, and so on.

◆ **Light manufacturing plants.** Light manufacturers make smaller items—for example, a pool-cut maker, an industrial laundry facility, or a knitting needle company. They are the opposite of the heavy manufacturing facilities—they don't need big trucks or a large number of employees, and they aren't terribly noisy.

◆ **Loft buildings.** Although loft space can often be converted to residential apartments—condos and co-ops in particular—many are converted to commercial office space.

Notes from the Field

According to Entrepreneur.com, many industrial incubator tenants are mom-and-pop businesses. Rents are handled very differently from other warehouse rents, too.

◆ **Incubator spaces.** A business incubator is a short-term office or warehouse space for a business. Leases for the businesses are generally short-term, even month-to-month. In large incubators, there may be a dozen or more tenants. Ideally, during the duration of the lease, the business—possibly a start-up—will get on its feet. If the business fails, it's easy to replace the tenant without breaking leases.

◆ **Distribution facilities.** A distribution facility is a warehouse that stores goods that are to be sold to customers or businesses. A distribution center (DC) can also be called a warehouse, a fulfillment center, a cross-dock facility, and a package handling center. These buildings are usually air conditioned.

◆ **Storage facilities.** Storage and self-storage facilities might seem easy to manage—put the items in the storage center, lock the door, and wait until the client (an individual or business) shows up again to check on their contents. There's much more to it than that. Property managers are needed to take care of every aspect of a storage facility, including collecting rent, maintaining the building, hiring and training personnel, and leasing and selling the property. Often, the property manager of a storage facility manages multiple sites.

◆ **Mixed-use.** There are mixed-use properties that are a combination of residential, commercial, and sometimes industrial properties, too.

As an industrial property manager, your responsibilities are similar to that of any other property: collecting rent from the business or businesses leasing out the facility, financial reporting, bill payment, staff supervision, maintenance, building systems maintenance, showing vacancies, lease negotiations, attracting new tenants and evicting others, being prepared for emergencies, and more.

High-Tech Properties

Property managers can now run what's called a "smart" building. One of the most common trends in commercial property management is to include top-of-the-line technology to entice tenants and stand out from other outdated buildings. While many buildings offer additional technologies, such as wireless access throughout the building, these smart buildings pretty much run on technology from top to bottom. It can also include such high-tech features as the following:

- Satellite dishes
- Security systems
- Communications with tenants

A smart building might seem like it's protected from the elements, but the biggest risk to a smart building is a power outage. What happens if your building suffers from power loss? Does it have an *uninterrupted power supply*? Can tenants still get in and out of the building? Can they get in and out of the elevators? Can building systems still work? What would happen if the systems failed? How would the tenants feel? Would your tenants lose their computerized inventory? What kind of financial impact would it have on both the tenants and the property management company? These are the issues a smart building property manager deals with every day.

def•i•ni•tion

If the power were to go out, an **uninterrupted power supply (UPS)** supplies emergency power to a building for approximately 5 to 15 minutes until power is restored. A backup generator is also vital to the smart building as well as medical facilities. Generators may protect your systems for up to another 30 minutes.

Although technology is supposed to make our lives easier, it's vital that you calculate the risks of each system, be prepared with a backup plan, and move quickly to restore the system before serious damage is done and data is lost. You will work closely with the utility companies to evaluate your power supply and make sure you're protected in case of failure. Preventive maintenance will be the key to preventing system failure.

The Least You Need to Know

- The last few years have been particularly difficult for the commercial real estate industry, but there is still much growth on the way.
- Medical buildings depend on properly run building systems with a backup generator in case something goes wrong.

- Storage facility management has become a bigger part of the industry, with an association and annual convention.

- Even smart buildings, which include top-of-the-line technology to run the building systems, still need a property manager, especially one who is computer savvy.

Part 2

Nuts and Bolts

Part 2 of this book supplies the nuts and bolts required to perform your job as a property manager. From the top of the roof to the bottom of the parking garage to outside on the property, you'll get all the ins and outs of how these systems run.

Then it will be time to tackle the paperwork: leases, financial reports, contracts, and more. Filling out forms and negotiating contracts and leases are a big part of a property manager's job. This part provides practical, valuable negotiating strategies and time-saving techniques. Finally, after reading this part, you'll be well versed in the federal, state, and local laws you need to know as a property manager.

Finance 101

In This Chapter

- ◆ Learning the basics of budgeting
- ◆ Different jobs, different reports
- ◆ Tightening the belt
- ◆ Keeping good records

Here it is—literally, the bottom line. Budgets and financial reports provide a crystal-clear picture of how the property you are managing is doing. From an investment perspective, it shows you, shareholders, tenants, the property's owner, the board of directors, etc., whether the property is (or properties are) profitable. If it is profitable, rest assured you're doing a job well done, making the right decisions and properly taking care of the building. You can continue on your successful path. If you're in the red, you can determine what needs to be done differently and how money needs to be managed to turn the profitability around.

It also gives an indication of how well you are doing your job as property manager. The tenants may love you, but if the building or property is struggling financially, it might be a sign that you need to make some changes. This chapter is all about budgeting basics. You'll learn how to prepare a budget and the differences between residential and commercial finances. You'll recognize a troublesome budget and how to trim the fat and raise cash if money gets tight.

Honestly, this chapter can be an entire book in itself, so we'll just cover the basics. We suggest that you consult with your accountant or board treasurer for additional suggestions and particular tax laws and financial situations that are specific to your state or that are geared to a specific type of property.

Financial Team

You're going to have questions and concerns about your property's financial condition. Therefore, you should have a team of experts that you can turn to for advice. These experts will advise you and guide you to the right decisions for the property. Your team should include experts such as a certified public accountant and an asset manager. If you are working with a board of directors, they often have these financial experts at their disposal. Feel free to ask their advice on any situations that arise.

Accountant

Most management teams utilize the services of a certified public accountant (CPA) or an accounting firm, preferably one with experience in your management area—such as commercial, residential, or mixed-use management. Accountants complete audits, reviews, budgets, and more on a monthly, quarterly, or annual basis.

Your accountant or accounting firm should be a member of the American Institute of Certified Public Accountants (www.aicpa.org), a national organization that requires members to be qualified and professional.

Asset Manager

An asset manager focuses on a property's finances for an investor. He looks at the big picture, considers properties, and advises whether the value is worth the risk. An asset manager can also be turned to for advice on other financial matters.

Maintaining Records: Financial Software

Team in place, check. Now you need an accounting system—some way of keeping track of the money that's coming in and going out. Remember, you can't accept any money without making some sort of notation. Traditionally, an accounts receivable ledger was the way to record money that came in, while an accounts payable ledger recorded money that went out for expenses. Believe it or not, some property managers who handle smaller properties still rely on this simplistic type of accounting system.

But today there's something better. Financial software programs keep track of your data and help to forecast for your next budget. It can do the math for you and even make financial and investment suggestions. These programs can also manage multiple properties, budget, complete work orders and purchase orders, conduct inventory, provide reminders, and keep track of management fees, owner payments, and special *assessments*. These programs can be installed on your computer, or there are financial software programs that you sign in to your own account on the Internet.

def•i•ni•tion

An **assessment** is an extra payment from each unit homeowner that covers the estimated repair cost.

TReXGlobal.com (also known as The Real Estate eXchange) is one example of a simple web application for real estate investors and property managers. According to TRexGlobal.com, there are 10 million real estate investors in the United States, and 9 million of them own fewer than 10 properties. Only a very small fraction of them uses software applications to organize rental finances.

TRexGlobal.com also says that research shows that while 90 percent of rental transactions are recurring—like rent collection and mortgage payments—investors spend hours tracking over and over the same items. Their program, SimplifyEm.com, is a web-based program that allows investors and property managers to easily manage rental transactions and generate tax forms with just one click. The program automates transactions you'll do every day.

Creating and Balancing Budgets

Now that you can track the income and expenses of the property you are managing, you'll have to create and balance budgets as a regular part of your job. You probably already know this, but a budget determines how much money is going to be made—through rentals, fees, etc.—and how you are going to spend that money. In property management, there are several types of budgets:

- ◆ **Developer budgets.** This type of budget is created for an association while the homes or buildings are being built. The developer budget makes sure the association has enough money once the developer has finished building the project. Once some time has passed, if the association feels that it needs to make any changes to the budget, they can do so at that time.

◆ **Operating budget.** An operating budget is an annual budget that includes such expenses as salaries, taxes, utilities, maintenance fees, and insurance.

◆ **Capital budget.** A capital budget is a budget that plans for long-term repairs and replacements or for equipment or systems. These budgets usually are for several years, but they should be looked at annually in case of changes, corrections, and so on. What is priority in a capital budget depends on a professional assessment, called a reserve study, of the buildings' needs. More detail on this later in the chapter.

Budgets are an integral part of a property management financial plan. They help you set goals for achieving an income and monitoring how much you're spending. No matter what size property you are managing, a budget is necessary to keep your eye on the profits.

Preparing a Budget

Preparing a budget for a cooperative or condo association is different than making a budget for a commercial property or for multiple properties. In condo or co-op associations, the final budgets need to be presented in front of the board of directors for their stamp of approval. The board of directors must vote on and approve the budget, depending on the association's bylaws.

Keeping accurate, complete budgets is important for any one property. But, if you're managing multiple properties, it's even more essential. The last thing you need is to get your monies confused. The main parts of any budget are income and expenses.

Income

Income is money you've gained that can come from several sources, depending on the type of property you're managing. It can come from rental monies, dues, assessments, interest on bank accounts, financial penalties, user fees, and *security deposits*.

def•i•ni•tion

> A **security deposit** is collected from a tenant when they sign a lease and before they move in. It is collected by the owner or manager and is held in trust. It is only returned after the tenants move out, minus any damages caused by the tenants that are above and beyond normal wear and tear or any unpaid charges.
>
> A **vacancy** is an unoccupied space. The vacancy rate is the percentage of all rental units that are unoccupied or not rented at a given time.

Income is calculated by looking at various factors, including lease terms, *vacancy*, and ownership expenses that are not reimbursable. Net Operating Income (NOI) is collectible income from a property, after all the fixed and variable operating expenses have been deducted.

Expenses

Expenses are what you pay. There are direct expenses, set expenses that are paid every month, that include items such as personnel costs and maintenance expenses. Variable expenses—which vary from month to month—include utilities and other maintenance charges.

In commercial and residential leases, tenants are responsible for their part of certain expenses. For example, in commercial leases, tenants are responsible for their share of capital expenses (such as building renovations and roof and parking lot replacements), as well as their portion of the taxes, insurance, utilities, maintenance, advertising, and management costs. In residential leases, tenants are responsible for paying common charges, which are fees to cover their share of maintenance of the common areas, etc.

The Bottom Line

In simple terms, your bottom line is the last line of your budget—it's the line that shows whether you have a profit or a loss. Finding this number can be done by taking the fixed and variable expenses and subtracting them from your total income (but not the mortgage). This should give you your net operating income. Once you have this number, subtract the mortgage payments and reserve deposits and you have your cash flow—or how much money is flowing in.

There may be other factors to think about, but this gives you a basic start. Consult with your accountant if you're not sure how to figure this out or if your situation is different. This is the number that will give you vital information on the strength or weakness of your property.

Establish Financial Goals

All successful property managers—and it doesn't matter what size residential or commercial properties you manage—are goal oriented, especially when it comes to finances. Like any good consumer looking to get out of debt or manage their investments and savings, it's important to understand your bottom line, recognize when things aren't going well, and learn how to make changes to get your goals back on track. To establish your financial goals for your property, you need to ask yourself two important questions.

Where Are We At?

Do you know how much money is in your personal checking account on a given day? Most likely you do (or you have a very close idea). The property's budgets and other financial statements should be treated the same way. They should be examined on a regular basis to keep track of how much money is coming in and what expenses have been and need to be paid. This evaluation should be done, at the very least, on a monthly basis.

So, how is the property doing? What about when you compare the numbers to last year's budget? Is there too much spending and not enough savings? Have there been unexpected repairs? Did heating and cooling costs increase and eat up the budget or decrease and save you an unexpected sum of money? You'll get all your answers to these questions when you review the documents.

Where Do We Want to Be?

Now you have an idea of how much income has come in and where it's going, so it's time to ask yourself if the property is where you want it to be. Is it in the black and showing a profit, or is it in the red and showing a loss? Is it far enough in the black, or will one emergency wipe out your profit? Are you happy with the numbers, or do you need to improve in a particular category? For example, do you need to do a better job of collecting fees or penalties for late payments? Without a good system in place, this money is down the drain.

For example, if you are losing income because you aren't doing a good job collecting fees, you might want to invest in an online financial software program that notifies you when tenants are late. If your budget can't afford this program, perhaps you can set one day aside to send out e-mail reminders and another day to follow up. Do you need to cut back on expenses? What expenses will you cut? If your building is not where it needs to be financially, it's time to make a plan so you can get back on track.

Covering the Emergencies

Emergencies are going to happen. For example, even though it has been properly maintained, the boiler suddenly breaks down (of course it's on a weekend in the middle of winter). To pay for the repair, you use your building's reserve fund, which is exactly what it sounds like—reserved money in case something goes wrong. Each month, part of the rent or dues collected from the tenants is designated to pump up the reserve fund to cover emergencies. How much money should be in the reserve is determined by a reserve study.

Reserve Studies

Reserve studies are done by a qualified engineer who calculates how much money is needed to cover replacements and repairs throughout the building or property. For example, let's say the engineer determines your roof has seven life years left before it needs to be replaced. The replacement cost is $100,000. To raise that much money, you'll need to save a minimum of $14,000 per year just to cover this replacement (it's assumed that you don't have anything put aside). The reserve study calculates all of the systems. Then you can see if you need to raise fees to cover the costs.

Things to Avoid

What repairs should you do first? That's easy—repair anything that puts your tenants' and staffs' lives at risk. Next, complete preventative repairs or replacements that will prevent emergency repairs down the road. Next, complete repairs or replacements that reduce operating costs and those that improve basic comfort and aesthetics of your tenants. Of course, follow local and state guidelines when making your list.

Special Assessments

An assessment is made when you need money for an immediate project. For example, if the furnace breaks, a new one costs $10,000. In your building, there are 100 owners, so each owner would be assessed $100 ($10,000 divided by the number of owners) to raise money for a new one (this depends, of course, on whether the assessment is based on the percentage of shares that each owner has in the association and not per unit). In cases of a budget shortfall, a special assessment should always be the last resort for providing funds necessary to meet the association's obligations.

Tighten the Budget

Costs should always be on the forefront of a successful property manager's mind, and there may come a time when you have to tighten the budget. Although many managers don't even consider cost-cutting techniques until the budget gets too tight, it's a smart idea to always think about how you could save some bucks. Circumstances such as rising energy costs, the nation's economic crises, and local economic situations may leave tenants struggling to pay rents, businesses closing, and college students opting to stay closer to home instead of paying for campus housing. It's important to know how and when it's time to trim the budget.

Reviewing the budget on a monthly basis gives you plenty of opportunities to find those hidden dollars.

For example, it's springtime and you have been chatting with a property manager of another building in town. You find out that your landscaping contract is a little pricey compared to others in the area. So you do a little research and find a great new vendor who is less expensive than the one you use now, but who provides the same quality service. You decide to either a) ask your current vendor to match the new offer or b) choose not to renew the contract of your current landscaper and hire the new company, saving thousands of dollars for the year. Look into other ways you can call for new proposals and scale back. But remember a successful property manager never sacrifices good quality service.

Postpone Projects

When money is tight, you may need to also reconsider any capital projects you have had on the schedule. When the economy is rough, it's harder for some properties to obtain a bank line of credit—one method of payment for making repairs and improvements. Unfortunately, it's harder to borrow today than it has been in the past, so consider what's most important to do and wait a bit to see if the banking climate improves or if you find another method of raising capital.

Struggling Tenants

This is a common scenario. You may either have a tenant who has hit a rough patch in her life or several tenants who have been affected by a struggling local or national economy. This may lead to late payments of fees and rental payments. Keep on top of the situation. You don't need to know the exact finances of your tenants to know how they are struggling. For example, if a commercial tenant's company begins to lay off employees or if they seem to be straining for customers, consider this a red flag. Read the local business newspapers to keep on top of what's happening in your business market. If a residential tenant has taken ill or lost a job, they may miss their payments, so stay on top of the situation.

You can work with them to solve the problem. Perhaps they just need a slight extension, which you might be able to grant. Keep in mind, however, that you are obligated to follow the rules of the bylaws and contracts, but it's important to work one-on-one with the tenant to come up with a solution.

Raise Extra Cash

Unfortunately, just cutting back expenses may not be enough. There may be a time that you need to raise extra cash to help the building's bottom line. The best way to raise extra cash is to think about out-of-the-box ways you can use your property. Here are a few ideas and hopefully this list will help you spark a few of your own:

- ◆ Making vacant parking spaces available for rent
- ◆ Renting out the property's community center to local businesses or individuals who need meeting or party space
- ◆ Renting out the building's roof space for meeting or party space
- ◆ Selling advertising space to local businesses in your community newsletter or on association websites

Productivity Tips

Instead of raising money by significantly increasing dues in one shot, include a small percentage increase every year in the lease. It's not so dramatic, and tenants can regularly budget it in.

◆ Renting out your super and other maintenance personnel to residents for any minor work that might need to be done which goes beyond the scope of their regular job responsibilities

◆ Increasing your laundry room rates (the laundry room is a moneymaker, so consider installing one or upping the rates charged to your residents in order to make some extra money)

Financial Reports

Each month, a financial report should be generated to give you an idea of where you are at. This report should compare where you are to where you thought you would be—in other words, it should compare projected budget to actual budget. In addition, it should also have a listing of all the bills that were paid and all the monies that were collected. In other words, anything financial that happened that month should be presented in a financial report.

Profit and Loss Statement

You've established your budget for the year and have been following it, but now you'd like an idea of how all of your hard work is doing. A profit and loss statement shows the financial results of a specific time period. You can do a monthly, quarterly, semi-annual, or annual profit and loss statement. Here is the general formula for figuring out profit and loss:

gross receipts – operating expenses – total mortgage payments + mortgage loan principal = net profit

Simple, right?

Once you have the profit and loss statement completed, compare those numbers to your current budget and financial goals. Look for any problems. For example, assume you are the property manager for a small office building. You estimated, based on last year's expenses, that the gas and utilities would cost $3,000 for the year. But, uh oh, this year the costs of your utilities have skyrocketed and you're on track to pay much more than that. What do you need to adjust to bring in more income and cover the costs of the utilities.

Perhaps when you reviewed your statement you noticed that you're short on income (revenue). Why? Did you have more vacancies than usual this year and aren't receiving as much rental income? In the book, *Property Management* (Dearborn Real Estate Education, 2004) by Robert Kyle, he uses an example to show how to overcome this. He writes:

> "For example, a residential building with four five-room apartments, each of which rents for $300 per month, billed $14,400 in rents during the past fiscal year (4 × $300 = 1,200 × 12 = $14,400), but actual rental collections only amounted to $13,680. Based on these figures the *occupancy rate* for the building can be calculated at 95% ($13,680 ÷ $14,400 = 0.95 percent)."

def•i•ni•tion

The **occupancy rate** is the percentage of all rental units in a property that are occupied or rented at a given time.

Kyle explains that the manager should, when preparing the budget for the upcoming term, deduct 5 percent from projected gross rent receipts to allow for vacancies or loss of rent.

Bad Debt

Oh, we're sorry to report that Mr. Jones has vacated his apartment. Unfortunately, he hasn't paid his rent in six months and, while you weren't on the property, he packed and left without paying. And, who can forget Ms. Annoying who drove the other tenants crazy? Ms. Annoying thankfully relocated to another state, but on moving day, she took her aggression out on the unit to the tune of $2,000 in damages. This is what's called "bad debt," and it can't be entirely eliminated.

According to just-released data from the National Apartment Association, in 2008, owners and property managers of market rate properties lost on average $70 per unit—or $2 billion industry wide—to bad debt.

The Financial Audit

Just the mere mention of the word "audit" makes everyone jittery and emotional. You can just picture Uncle Sam sneering at a taxpayer. But audit simply means to review the financial statements you've created all year. For co-ops and condos, it's pretty much required to do one for the shareholders.

This can be a complex report, so it's important to work with your accountant on this one. Once the audit has been completed, a certified financial statement is issued, which is an income statement, cash flow statement, or balance sheet that has been audited and signed off on by an accountant.

> **Things to Avoid** _____
>
> Keep accurate records and hold onto the paperwork. The Internal Revenue Service suggests that all businesses save financial records for a minimum of seven years. These records may be needed for tax reporting purposes or to settle landlord/tenant disputes. Commercial leases are more complex, and keeping records is extremely important when language changes.

Management Performance

Your job is to keep tabs on how the building is doing, but who is keeping tabs on how you are doing *your* job? Property management is a client service industry. No matter what, you should be given a periodic review of your performance by either the board of directors, your management company, developer, or other supervisor to assess how you're doing, what your strengths are, and what areas need improvement. The budgets—and the performance of any property managers you supervise—are just a few ways to measure your performance. If the bottom line of the financial statements isn't looking good, it could be a reflection on how well, or how poorly, you are doing your job.

How often you are evaluated depends on your employment contract, but the budget is a great place to start, whether it is done on a monthly, quarterly, or annual basis.

To help evaluate your performance, tenants can also provide regular feedback to your company. These evaluations should include key criteria such as your responsiveness, knowledge, and supervisory skills, as well as the property's physical and financial performance.

Red Flags

Of course, you want a perfect score on any evaluation, but it's unrealistic. There might be a problem with a tenant or a budget from time to time. You may also be concerned if your evaluations show that you're slow to respond to the tenants and that your performance isn't up to par. These problems can be corrected, and you can get your performance back on track. How?

♦ Make sure any complaints against you aren't personal. Maybe you clashed with Mr. Jones over a particular issue, but don't take it personally.

♦ Take additional courses. Are finances your weakness? Were your budgets or financial statements missing important information, or did you compute the wrong formulas? Perhaps you just need a refresher course. Go back to school and take courses on financial subjects that could help you improve. Recognizing and improving your weaknesses makes you a stronger manager.

♦ Find a mentor. Ask another property manager that you know to help you out. Ask questions and have him explain something with which you may not be familiar. His experience might help you solve a particular problem.

♦ Provide incentives. If you're in a supervisory position of other property managers who aren't doing their job well, provide an incentive for meeting their goals or even for meeting your own. A little self-push goes a long way.

And, finally, if one of your managers isn't doing his job or making ends meet, maybe it's best that he is removed or moved to another property. For example, maybe your manager, Eric, who handles several properties, would do better just handling one. Sometimes, it's hit and miss placing the right property manager with the right property. It's important to keep thinking of ideas that would make your buildings run more efficiently and successfully.

Financial statements and evaluations are done so the goals and objectives of the company can be met. Use these tools as a way to garner your progress, improve your performance, and most importantly, create new goals for yourself and the property.

The Least You Need to Know

♦ Finances are a very important aspect of property management, so be sure to ask for professional advice when you need it.

♦ Just as you would with your own personal checking account, be sure to check and double check your bottom line.

♦ Ask other property managers for a good recommendation for a property management software program.

♦ If something is going wrong, ask for advice or make some changes—don't hide the problem or neglect it.

Chapter 6

Building Systems and Services

In This Chapter

♦ Keeping systems in check

♦ Maintaining the building's exterior

♦ Detecting hidden dangers

♦ Knowing when and how to hire a pro

It's time to get into the nitty-gritty of keeping the building working right. When you think of building systems, you can compare it to your own body. You have a circulatory system, a nervous system, a digestive system, and a host of other systems that work together to keep you alive. Your building's systems—heating and cooling, electrical, and plumbing—are what keep your building running.

This chapter focuses on keeping these systems in check, so that the building runs smoothly. At the same time, this chapter is a lesson in evaluation. If something goes wrong with part or all of one of them, that part—or even the entire system itself—will need to be repaired or replaced. Depending on the problem, basic maintenance and repairs can be carried out by the super or a handyperson. If the problems are more complicated, call a professional.

Productivity Tips _____

This professional should always be licensed and insured and have the vendor paperwork filled out in advance prior to hiring. Many times the vendors/contractors you use will name the company as additional insured; you must verify that the person you hire carries proper insurance and licensing.

Do Your Homework

A successful property manager knows the building systems inside and out, even if you aren't the one to actually fix the problems. Property management and trade organizations offer basic courses on building systems, so ask if yours offers any. For example, in New York, the New York Association of Realty Managers (NYARM) offers a 30-hour Basic Building Systems program and a Facility Management for Residential Properties program.

The Basic Building Systems curriculum consists of 12 classes at 3.75 hours each, and covers various aspects of building systems and maintenance—including plumbing; heating, ventilating, and air conditioning (HVAC); fire protection; and building envelope—with related New York City building code requirements. They focus on system fundamentals; maintenance and repair; and environmental, safety, and security issues. The Facility Management course also offers a building maintenance session.

It's also vital to stay on top of new systems and technologies. If you have new equipment installed, check to see what the differences are with that equipment and what was used before. Doing your homework will prevent any problems later.

The ABCs of HVAC

An efficient HVAC system is vital to the success of a building. Your tenants want to be comfortable living or working in the building—and perhaps just as importantly, they don't want to pay more than they have to in order to keep that consistent level of comfort. And you want a system that doesn't cost too much to operate.

Traditional heating systems are forced hot water (also used in radiant, or floor, heating), steam heat, forced air, electric floor heating, heat pumps, and fireplaces and wood stoves. Some use gas, oil, propane, or electricity as fuel.

Boilers

Boilers are one of those pieces of equipment that nobody really thinks about until it stops working when you need it the most. A well-functioning boiler, however, is vital to every building and its occupants. A regular maintenance plan should be established to include a contract with a professional company to clean and repair the unit at least once a year. The cleaner the boiler, the more efficiently it runs—helping to save money in the long run. Boilers that are not maintained work harder and cost more money.

In between professional check-ups, your maintenance staff should make sure to keep filters clean and perform regular inspections to check for leaks or broken pipes. But leave the bigger repairs to the professionals.

You don't want to ignore a potential problem and have something go wrong in the middle of a storm or on a weekend—when a repairman's prices go through the roof. For those buildings located in areas that experience frosty weather, regular maintenance and cleaning is especially important before the temperatures plummet and the snow and ice begin to fall.

If a problem should arise, you and/or your maintenance person should first perform a cursory check of the unit to see what the problem might be. Look for the following:

◆ Inadequate oil or other fluids

◆ Cracking

◆ Leaking (rust is also an indicator that water has escaped)

◆ Dangerous odors

If you spot anything that might seem dangerous or beyond your scope of knowledge, immediately shut down the unit and contact a professional. Your state may mandate an inspection of the boiler every few years. Check with your department of buildings to learn your state's requirements.

Things to Avoid

In case of an emergency, every staff member should know how to shut down any building system. They should also be told when it needs to be done. For example, everybody should know how to shut the water off if a pipe breaks, to reduce damage until help arrives.

Air Conditioning Units

When the temps heat up, the tenants will flip on the air conditioning units to keep cool. Depending on the lease arrangement, those air conditioning units may or may not be your responsibility to maintain and repair.

Room air conditioners are typically installed in the tenant's windows and are sized according to their cooling capacities. Remember, the higher the BTU (it's listed on the unit), the more powerful the air conditioner. As a rule of thumb, an 8,000 BTU air conditioner can cool two small rooms (10 × 12 feet) or one large room (15 × 20 feet). Central air conditioning uses ductwork to send air throughout the building or home. The air conditioners should be kept in working order, especially the drain lines and pans of the central air system.

Heat Pumps

Some homes use a heat pump to stay warm. A pump extracts heat from the outside air and delivers it inside the home (it can also extract cooler air from the outside and deliver it inside), but it typically delivers cooler air than a standard furnace. Heat pumps are generally used in individual homes and units and don't typically heat an entire building. A property manager or super can, however, be called on to have the heat pump repaired.

Evaporative Coolers

Evaporative coolers, also known as swamp coolers, use a lot less electricity than standard air conditioners and are a great alternative to traditional air conditioning systems. They also do not use refrigerants, such as chlorofluorcarbons (CFCs) and hydro-chlorofluorocarbons (HCFCs), that can harm the ozone layer.

There are two types of coolers. Direct coolers force air through a water-soaked pad, which is then filtered and cooled. An indirect evaporative cooler prevents humidity from being added to the air. Only one system—traditional A/C or evaporative coolers—can be used at a time.

Fireplaces

Today, thanks to the known dangerous effects of fossil fuels, many homeowners are returning to wood-burning and pellet stoves. As a property manager, it's important to know that The National Fire Protection Association advises, "Chimneys, fireplaces, and vents should be inspected at least once a year for soundness, freedom from deposits and correct clearances. Cleaning, maintenance, and repairs should be done if necessary." Fire spreads quickly, so this is particularly important when you are managing such communities that share walls—condominiums and townhomes, for example.

Time to Replace the HVAC

Eventually, systems need to be replaced. Perhaps a system is getting too old and replacement parts are harder to find, or the system has already been repaired several times. Or it might be showing signs of wear and tear (such as rust), and there may have already been piping problems.

In Chapter 7, you'll learn how to choose products and building systems that are more energy efficient and that are better for the environment. Although an initial investment in a new HVAC system can be pricey, the return on investment begins immediately because the new system is much more efficient than the old one.

Remember, if you are a property manager of a co-op or condo, major purchases may need board approval. You can let them know that replacing older, less efficient HVAC equipment with newer, more efficient equipment can cut energy costs by about 20 percent, according to the Environmental Protection Agency (EPA). It can also improve the environment by decreasing contamination of mold, viruses, etc.

Electric

What the building's electrical costs are will depend on how much power your building systems use and how much power the tenants use. At different times of the year, that usage will go up. For example, in the summer, tenants run their air conditioning and home cooling devices more often, which may lead to an increase in costs and a strain on your electrical system. With all of today's electric gizmos and gadgets—such as computers, televisions, stereos, and washers and dryers—the costs of electricity are going higher and higher all the time, and systems are always being strained. Unfortunately, making the building's electrical system work for everyone when it doesn't have enough

Notes from the Field

According to the U.S. Fire Administration, home electrical problems cause 67,800 fires each year claiming 485 lives, causing 2,305 injuries, and resulting in $868 million in property damages. Most of these fires started because of faulty electrical outlets and old wiring.

juice or when it's in poor condition can lead to serious problems, including shock and fire.

When it comes to electrical problems, you don't need an electrician's license to do your job. You just need to be able to recognize an emergency and convey to your contractor what the problem might be. For example, can you tell your contractor that there seems to be a short in the ground? Or that a wire has been tripped? What should you look for?

Warning Signs and Safety Tips

What potential hazards are you looking for? Here are some signs of potential electrical problems on the property:

- ◆ Crackling or buzzing sounds when flipping a switch or plugging something in
- ◆ Frayed or broken wires
- ◆ Odors when the electricity is turned on
- ◆ Flickering, blinking, or dimming lights
- ◆ Plugs that are warm to the touch
- ◆ Circuit breakers that "trip" frequently

If these warning signs or problems are ignored, the results could be serious—even tragic. However, do not attempt any of the electrical repair jobs on your own. Most states require that these repairs be done by a licensed electrician, and you really wouldn't want it any other way. Install an electrical product the wrong way or repair something incorrectly and you can start a fire that might destroy the building and take lives. The best thing that you and your staff can do is stay alert and perform periodic checks on the fuses, generators, and fire alarms.

Depending on the system, it should be tested every two to five years, but circuit breakers, connections, and outlets should be tested every year. During the inspection, any loose connections or broken circuit breakers should be fixed and any wires that seem damaged or frayed should be replaced or removed.

Keeping a building safe also depends on keeping your tenants aware. Here are some electrical safety tips you can suggest to them:

- ◆ Keep space heaters away from anything that's combustible, including bedding, clothing, and rugs. Unplug them when they are not in use.

◆ Do not use extension cords. Plugging too many items into a system can overload it.

◆ Don't just check the plugs that keep getting tripped; check the appliance that keeps tripping it.

Upgrading Electrical

To determine whether your building needs an electrical upgrade, first have an assessor or electrical engineer inspect the system. He will check switches and perform tests to see what the system needs and whether or not the current one can support it. If not, there are special calculations he does to determine what the new electrical load should be. The size of the building and the units will help to determine that number.

This is one of those situations where the safety of your building and its occupants will outweigh any expense of a new system. By upgrading the system, the building's insurance premiums may even be reduced, and the building may be eligible for tax breaks or government incentives. When upgrading the system, remember to install energy-efficient upgrades, such as lighting (see Chapter 7) that can also help to reduce the building's overall electrical costs.

Plumbing

Plumbing is another system that is taken for granted. It's not given much thought until the pipes break and the bathrooms are flooded with water. What causes these plumbing problems? First, it's important to understand the system itself.

Many high-rise buildings use a gravity-style plumbing system. This is when the water comes into a tank in the building, is pushed to the top to rooftop tanks, and is then fed downward. Pressure-tank systems maintain a tank that uses pressure systems to distribute the water to each floor on the way up.

Some of the problems are caused by …

◆ Rusty pipes. Corrosion leads to broken pipes and they will eventually have to be replaced.

◆ Harsh water supply, which leads to corrosion. This depends on where you live, because some areas have harsher water than others.

◆ Misuse. Stuffing items down the toilet or the sink can cause pipes to break.

Productivity Tips _____

In a co-op or condo building, which party is responsible for repairing a building system depends on the governing documents. In most cases, a condominium owner is responsible for anything within their own four walls. In a co-op, management is responsible—but, again, it depends on the problem.

Here are some suggestions to keep in mind when dealing with plumbing repairs:

◆ Repair as you go. Don't wait until that little drip turns into a big puddle—and no, duct tape doesn't solve everything. Investigate why these leaks or cracks are happening and correct the problem as soon as possible. Small drips can lead to bigger problems (and bigger bills) later, including mold, decay, and rot.

◆ Leave it to the pros. Professional plumbers should repair bigger problems, especially anything behind walls or in floors. They have the tools, equipment, and experience needed to fix the problem, add new fixtures, and replace pipes.

◆ Think green when you replace or upgrade. No, not the water color (ew!). Every time you replace or upgrade something in the building, you should think about how you can be more energy efficient. For example, upgrade to low-flow valves and fixtures. These upgrades will reduce the amount of water used in the building and reduce your water bill over time.

As with any system, the key to good plumbing is maintenance. Take care of the system before something happens that costs a great deal of time and energy—especially when tenants are complaining.

Elevators

Like other building systems, elevators need safety measures and regular quarterly maintenance and inspection to prevent accidents. Depending on your building, hundreds—if not thousands—of people may ride the elevator each day, so safety is of the utmost importance. One part of the elevator that needs special attention is its cables. Elevators must have proper emergency controls, including smoke detectors and emergency switches that return the elevator to the ground floor in an emergency. There must also be a telephone emergency system inside the car, as well as a way for the disabled passengers to communicate.

If an elevator malfunctions, it's important to know ahead of time what steps you and your staff will take to fix the problem, get the elevator moving, and get any passengers stuck inside to safety.

Your number one responsibility during an emergency is to make contact with those inside, see if anyone is hurt, and assure them they are safe. Many people panic when stuck in an elevator, so it's important to make sure they do not overreact and try to leave on their own. Keep in contact with them until they are evacuated and let them know when rescuers have arrived.

If no one is in the elevator when it breaks down, the first step is to mark the elevator "out of service" and contact the service company. Similar to other building repairs, only qualified professionals should fix an elevator. If the problem occurs but is rectified before the serviceman arrives, have the elevator serviced anyway before it is used again.

Things to Avoid

Make sure that all staff knows that only emergency personnel should remove occupants from an elevator that is broken or stuck. This is especially important if the elevator is stuck between floors. Pulling out someone who is stuck in an elevator can lead to tragic results, especially if the elevator starts moving again.

Exterior

Have you heard the old saying, "put your best face forward"? That saying goes for buildings, too. If your building's façade is in bad shape, people are going to wonder how bad the inside is. Whether a building is old or new, built of stone, brick, glass, or some other material, any trouble with or damage to its façade is a serious emergency. The last thing you want as a property manager is for a piece of your building's crumbling mortar to fall to the ground below, with tragic results.

Signs of Trouble

When you are searching for signs of trouble on the outside of the building, you should look for rust spots; algae formation; and cracks in the mortar, caulking, and sealants—of course, this all depends on what material the building exterior is made of.

Water seepage is the biggest cause of exterior problems. During construction, the building's envelope—which consists of the walls, foundation, and roof—needs to be waterproofed to prevent unwanted moisture from entering and getting trapped inside the walls. Some moisture is almost always present within a building, but the building needs adequate ventilation to dry out the moisture that seeps in. If a good ventilation system isn't present, the moisture will continue to seep through and not dry, leading to problems.

> **Notes from the Field**
>
> Make sure your façade is water tight by hiring a construction engineer to do an inspection. He should look for open water joints, cracks, or missing caulking.

When water gets into the exterior, it can rust the steel frame. A little Science 101: When rust forms, it results in water and oxygen, so 1 inch of steel will result in 10 inches of rust. The rust needs room, so it pushes out on the building.

Consequences

Holding off on any needed repairs can cause repair costs to multiply. For example, a $100,000 roofing problem now costs three times that amount to fix later. It may also be a legal requirement in your state, and not following the law can lead to financial penalties. For example, New York City's residential buildings must comply with New York City Local Law 11, which was signed into law in 1998. This law requires that buildings undergo preventative maintenance inspections on a regular basis—buildings with more than six stories must be inspected by a licensed professional every five years—and imposes stringent requirements for repairing deteriorated conditions.

In addition, holding off on a repair can destroy a historic building, which requires more attention to detail during repair, and ordering parts may take much longer. Finally, and most importantly, not making a repair can actually put your building and your tenants at risk if something were to go wrong.

In the end, your building's façade is more than just the pretty face it shows to the passersby on the street; it's an integral component of the structure and it needs to be maintained like the roof or foundation. With a regular inspection schedule and a sound maintenance program in place, your building's façade will remain solid and secure for many decades to come.

Lush Landscaping

When you drive up to a property, one of the first things you notice is the landscaping. Attractive curb appeal—green and colorful trees and flowers—will draw residents and visitors into the building, while brown and dry greenery will turn them away. It's important to keep the lawn looking lush and healthy.

Notes from the Field

The Professional Landcare Network says that 95 percent of perspective home buyers will not even get out of their cars if a property's landscaping isn't attractive. Good landscaping has benefits beyond simply making the building more attractive—it actually improves the building's bottom line, keeping vacancies low and property values high in both residential and commercial properties.

Taking care of the landscape is about much more than watering a lawn. It's about mowing, weeding, pruning, and so on. In some buildings, the super is responsible for caring for the lawn. But if your building has a larger property, it's best to have your super take care of much more pressing issues than watering the lawn and leave that to a professional who can determine exactly how much water each foliage needs. A landscaping firm can take care of mowing, weeding, weed control, fertilizing, tree removal and maintenance, insect control, snow removal, and annual spring maintenance and winterizing plants and flowers. They can also suggest new designs and recommend more environmentally friendly landscaping alternatives (more on that in Chapter 7). If there isn't room in the budget for a landscape maintenance company, it might be best to invest in an in-ground water sprinkling system, or at least routine tree maintenance.

Tree maintenance should occur about twice a year. The number one consideration is safety. Trees with dead limbs can fall and cause accidents and damage to the property and to the tenants. Trees should also be examined for disease, such as Dutch Elm, and other fungus problems. They should also be annually pruned and winterized. Landscapers spray needles with an antidesiccant to prevent water loss during frigid winter months, when trees lose nutrients.

Alarm Systems

On any given day, hundreds of people—residents, customers, contractors, staff, and others—walk in and out of your building. Alarm systems—such as fire and security—are vital to protecting your building and the lives of your tenants, and they must be kept maintained and in good working order. The last thing you want to hear about your building in an emergency is, "it had an alarm, but it didn't go off." You want enough alarms to protect the building, but not so many that people feel unsafe and unwelcome. It's a fine balance, but today's security applications provide both security and comfort. Some examples of security systems include:

- **Access controls:** Access controls restrict building access to residents and their guests. It tracks who is entering and exiting by cards, electronic keys, or keyless entries. Need to know who was in the laundry room at a particular time? Just look at the records of key entries.

- **Cameras:** Video cameras are still a great way to keep your building safe. Cameras have come a long way since the grainy videotape from years back. Now, digital recording has allowed for much better quality pictures and the ability to zoom in and out of recordings.

- **Text messaging:** Want to reach tenants in a hurry during an emergency? Text them. Similar to what college campuses do now, you can broadcast an emergency message to the residents' phones. More on this in Chapter 16.

Things to Avoid

Any security system should be in code compliance with the National Fire Protection Association and the International Code Council.

Security systems are changing and upgrading all the time, so check with an expert before deciding what the best kind of security system is for your building and property.

Laundry Facilities

Properly maintained, laundry rooms can be a great source of revenue. If you don't want to set up or maintain them yourself, laundry vendors can provide the equipment and furnishings as well as the insurance. They also conduct repairs and pay the building a rental fee. The more people use the laundry room, the more revenue the building makes.

If you hire a firm to handle the laundry, the contract should outline the expectations of both parties, including maintenance, service, and payment. There are three types of agreements with laundry companies: the laundry lease agreement, the license agreement, and the management agreement.

- **Laundry lease agreement**—Five to ten years in length, this term is driven by equipment cost and the return that the laundry company can expect from the collections.

- **License agreement**—This agreement provides similar terms to a lease agreement, but some laundry companies do not want to enter into license agreements because it may not afford them adequate security.

- **A management agreement**—This agreement is primarily used when a building is subject to the 80/20 tax law.

No longer are laundry rooms dark and dingy. Today, laundry rooms are well lit and offer residents a way to sit back and relax while they watch their laundry go around. And forget the quarters. Today, smart cards—like debit cards—are used. Need a machine? Residents no longer need to leave their apartment to find out if one is available. They can simply call the laundry room and an automated system will update you on availability.

Productivity Tips

For your information, when a contract with a laundry company ends, you can either purchase the machines from the vendor or the vendor can take the machines back (and only the machines). The plumbing belongs to your building, not the company. See more about negotiation in Chapter 9.

Hidden Dangers

Some building hazards—cracked sidewalks, broken windows, or crumbling masonry—are obvious to even an untrained eye. Other building hazards—such as lead, asbestos, radon, carbon monoxide, and mold—are tougher to detect. Some can't be felt or smelled, and can be hidden away inside walls, seep into basements, or even be imbedded in paint. When it comes to these "hidden" dangers, often nobody knows they're there until the damage is done—and sometimes the results are tragic.

Things to Avoid

If you or anyone in the building smells gas or begins to complain of headaches, nausea, or other illnesses, immediately shut down the unit, call 911, and evacuate the building. You may have a gas or carbon monoxide leak.

Lead

If the building you are managing was constructed before 1960, there is a distinct possibility that the paint on the walls contains lead. In 1991, the Environmental Protection Agency (EPA) named lead the number one environmental threat to the health of all children in the United States. The danger comes when this lead is removed or disturbed—usually by scraping, sanding, or burning—and high concentrations of lead are released into the air and inhaled. Young children can also ingest bits of lead paint by biting on a surface (a windowsill, for example) covered in lead-based paint.

Lead exposure can cause a host of health problems in both children and adults. It can affect the brain, central nervous system, blood cells, and kidneys. Lead exposure has also been linked to birth defects and developmental delays in children. (See Chapter 10 for more information on lead laws.)

def•i•ni•tion

Remediation is the removal of a contaminant to protect human health and the environment.

Companies can test for lead in a building or apartment with x-ray fluorescence, which isn't destructive and doesn't release any lead into the air. Results can be returned in 24 to 48 hours. The cost for basic lead testing depends on how many units are being tested. If lead paint is found, the *remediation* process will begin.

On March 31, 2008, the EPA issued a rule requiring the use of lead-safe practices and other actions aimed at preventing lead poisoning. Under the rule, beginning in April 2010, contractors in all states performing renovation, repair, and painting projects that disturb lead-based paint in homes, childcare facilities, and schools built before 1978 must be certified and follow specific work practices to prevent lead contamination.

Carbon Monoxide

Carbon monoxide (CO) is the worst of the hidden dangers simply because it's highly toxic, it's ultimately deadly, and it can sneak up on anyone in a building without any warning. It has no odor to warn you that it's leaking, it has no taste, and it doesn't irritate your skin. CO is the product of the incomplete combustion of fossil fuels such as oil, natural gas, gasoline, and coal. It can come from building systems that burn fossil fuel, such as furnaces, water heaters, fireplaces, and parking garages. The warning signs of CO poisoning are headaches, dizziness, tiredness, and nausea. All of these symptoms can be easily mistaken for a virus or the flu. The affected person may choose to lie down and sleep, which can be deadly. To reduce the risk of CO exposure, every building must be equipped with at least one approved carbon monoxide detector installed within 15 feet of the primary entrance to each sleeping room. Landlords must provide and install at least one approved CO alarm within each dwelling unit. It's up to the property managers and superintendents to make certain that any detectors in the common areas are working properly at all times. It's also important that you educate your residents about checking their CO detectors regularly.

Asbestos

Asbestos is the name given to a number of naturally occurring, fibrous silicate minerals mined for their useful properties such as thermal insulation, chemical and thermal stability, and high tensile strength. It can be found in any area of the country, in many older homes that have been built with products that contain asbestos, such as pipe and furnace insulation materials, roofing shingles, millboard, textured paints, and floor tiles.

Asbestos can cause serious lung disease, which can lead to disability and death. Asbestos tests can begin at $300, but the final cost depends on the size of the building and what you want to have tested.

Radon

Radon comes from the breakdown of uranium in soil, rock, and water. It seeps into a home or building through cracks in the foundation and through well water. Like CO, you can't see, smell, or taste it. Radon can build up to dangerous levels, and breathing it in over a period of time can lead to lung cancer. Radon is a leading cause of lung cancer in the United States, claiming approximately 20,000 lives each year.

Radon tests can be purchased and used in any building, or can be conducted by a professional tester. The amount of radon in the air is measured in picoCuries per liter of air (pCi/L). The EPA estimates that 1 in 15 homes has a radon level of 4 pCi/L or more, which is considered high. If your building scores that high, there are ways to fix the problem.

Every state has a radon contact (you can find yours by visiting epa.gov/iaq/whereyoulive.html and clicking on your state) and specific requirements associated with providing radon measurements. A venting system can be installed to exhaust the radon, and the area should be retested once the changes have been completed.

Mold

Mold can be visible in bathrooms and in leaky areas of a building—or invisible, hidden behind walls. It's a very serious issue that may lead to myriad health ailments. It's another problem that is caused by water damage (which you, as property manager, really need to stay on top of). When mold is disturbed, spores are released into the air and produce chemicals called mycotoxins. When ingested or inhaled, mycotoxins have been linked to adverse reactions in people who are particularly sensitive to them or who are exposed to them in large amounts or over a long period of time. The symptoms of mold exposure include chronic runny nose, eye irritation, cough, congestion, and aggravation of asthma.

Mold is not the same as mildew—which is the discoloration caused by molds. You or your super cannot simply sponge off or cover up a mold problem. Mold needs to be removed by a properly trained professional with experience performing microbial investigations—especially if HVAC systems or large occupied spaces are involved.

Professional mold remediators use several methods of testing including inspecting, air testing, and physically removing samples with a sterile swab or piece of adhesive tape. Then, they test the sample for spore counts. If there is contamination, all tenants should be notified and an expert should be hired to verify the situation and take remedial steps to fix it. The two most important things you must do are to communicate with your tenants and be responsive to any issues that may arise.

It's your job to be mindful not only of the hazards you can see, but also of those you can't see. By being aware of the various risks and implementing a regular testing regimen for your building or association, you can make sure that your community is protected from the harm these hidden hazards can cause.

Hiring a Pro

When you need to hire a professional contractor to maintain, fix, or upgrade any of your building systems, it's best to check with your local trade organizations for referrals. For example, if you are hiring a builder or contractor, check with your local builders' association. Hiring a landscaper? Check with your local, state, or national landscaping trade associations for referrals. Once you have a few names, it's time to check them out:

- How long has the company been in business?

- What's their philosophy?

- What are their goals when it comes to accomplishing the work you hired them to do?

Ask for references and make sure to visit the job sites. Were those jobs the same as that which you require? If you have a larger job but the contractor has only worked on smaller jobs, will they be able to handle yours? Do they have a current job you can look at? If so, ask the company or association that has hired them what they like and don't like so far about the contractor's work.

Also, make certain they have their required licenses and insurance, workers' compensation, and so on. You don't want to be liable for any accidents.

- Low doesn't mean good. The contractor with the lowest bid isn't necessarily the best contractor for the job. Ask yourself why the contractor has underbid. Could they be desperate for work? Could they be inexperienced? You can always negotiate a higher bid down, but lowball bids are often a troublesome sign.

- Check warranties. Is the company guaranteeing the work they are doing? Most contractors provide a long-term warranty that shows the work they are doing will last for a minimum period of time. If anything were to happen with the item before then, they will cover the cost of the replacement or repair.

Some larger property management companies come with their own maintenance company within their management company. This can include employee maintenance coordinators, licensed contractors, and more for this department. This is a plus—it prevents having to hire outside contractors, and it keeps costs under control.

The Least You Need to Know

- A little knowledge about all the building systems goes a long way.

- Not all problems are things you can see—stay alert by using all your senses.

- If you know anything, it should be how to turn off the systems in an emergency.

- When hiring a professional, check out their previous work and make sure they worked on a similar job in the past.

Eco-Friendly Property Management

In This Chapter

◆ Discovering it's good to be green

◆ Being green saves green

◆ Getting a lesson on energy efficiency

◆ Incorporating water conservation methods

Everywhere you turn, experts are telling you what to do to protect your health, conserve water and energy, and protect the environment. Changing your way of thinking comes at an ideal time when energy costs—fuel, gas, and oil—are out of control. There is also a grave concern regarding our water supply. In addition, poor indoor air quality is a major health concern. Incorporating green strategies and systems into your building can help save money—financial experts even stress that tax breaks are available. This chapter will show you how implementing green strategies actually reduces your long-term building maintenance and upgrade costs, benefitting the environment, the tenants, and your building's bottom line.

Green Is the New Black

The biggest misnomer about becoming more environmentally friendly is that it costs more of the other green—big bucks. Yes, there is an initial financial outlay. Solar paneling, for example, can cost tens of thousands of dollars or more to install, depending on the size of your building(s). With each green improvement, however, you will get a bigger return on your investment. For example, solar panels—installed at the right time—greatly diminish your building's heating costs.

In addition, it has been proven that having a green building—commercial and residential of any size—attracts premium tenants who are willing to pay top dollar for such features.

Notes from the Field

According to the McGraw-Hill Construction Research and Analytics, the value of green building construction is projected to increase to $60 billion by 2010. Over 4.2 billion square feet of commercial building space is involved with the LEED green building certification system.

(Source: McGraw-Hill Construction Research and Analytics. *McGraw-Hill Construction SmartMarket Report: Key Trends in the European and U.S. Construction Marketplace.* Columbus, OH: The McGraw-Hill Companies, Inc., 2008.)

The ABCs of LEED and NAHB

The Leadership in Energy and Environmental Design (LEED) Green Building Rating System is a voluntary, consensus-based national standard developed by the United States Green Building Council (USGBC) for developing high-performance, sustainable buildings (www.usgbc.org). Building owners can have their building LEED rated and achieve certification ranging from "certified" to "platinum," depending on how many green features are incorporated and the building's energy efficiency. Each feature is worth a number of points on the LEED chart and that number adds up to a certification level. Platinum is the top certification.

The National Association of Home Builders, or NAHB (www.nahb.org), also has a voluntary standard for sustainable buildings and homes, with each feature worth a number of points to apply for certification.

In existing buildings, a LEED rating means that the green building systems help to minimize the negative impact that the building has on the environment. LEED encourages developers to incorporate green features that reduce water usage by 50 percent, use alternate sources of renewable energy, optimize energy performance, and use green power. New construction projects also have to meet several point requirements during the planning and building phases, like using material that is harvested and manufactured nearby and maintaining a small building site to reduce damage to surrounding property.

Zocalo Community Development Inc., in Denver, Colorado, chose to pursue LEED certification for two of their mixed-use multifamily projects: the six-story, 60-unit RiverClay Condominiums, and the eight-story, 60-unit 20/20 Lawrence condominium projects. In an article in *Multifamily Trends,* Zocalo says that in an otherwise tough market, the units quickly sold out, and one sold out before the ground was even broken.

That's not surprising, especially when the article also states that green buildings boost occupancy rates by 3.5 percent. The USGBC also shows that green buildings have a 3 percent higher rental rate than conventional buildings, and a 6.6 percent return on investment. Green buildings also see an average increase of 7.5 percent in building values compared with conventional buildings, according to a 2006 study by McGraw-Hill Construction.

Things to Avoid

You do not have to apply for LEED or NAHB certification to implement green strategies into your building. There are fees involved with certification that may not fit your budget. However, if you're interested in greening your building, LEED and NAHB can still guide you.

One Step at a Time

Making your building greener and more energy efficient is a new aspect of the property management, building construction, remodeling, and real estate development industries. Almost all industry members are on a learning curve—even veteran builders are still being trained on the newest green technologies and methods. So take the process one step at a time. There's new information every day, but trade organizations such as the USGBC and the NAHB and their respective trade publications have resources to help you.

Start Small

When it comes to incorporating green into your building, think small, especially if your budget is a concern. For example, if your building's heating bills are off the charts, start by having the super caulk any holes around the windows and doors, repair cracks in any walls or foundation, and add extra insulation to drafty areas. You might be thinking, "Why not just invest in new windows?" While that's a sound idea at some point, installing new windows without caulking the holes and cracks where air escapes is literally throwing money out the new windows. You can install new windows once you've corrected other problems first.

Perhaps its high water bills that are affecting the budget. An affordable idea might be to replace each tenant's showerheads and faucets with low-flow fixtures. It's an affordable first step that will show some immediate return in savings. You may also consider planting foliage on the property that doesn't require watering, versus a once-a-week wasteful hose down. Even using grasses and plants that are native to your area can tremendously reduce expenses, and they still look great. Once you've implemented one change, the money saved from that improvement can be moved over to fund the next project, and so on, and so on. Eventually you can move on to bigger projects, including door and window replacements, and finally (if needed) solar panels or more energy-efficient boiler replacements.

Productivity Tips _____

Installing energy-efficient systems—windows, doors, HVAC units, air conditioners, appliances, etc.—can not only save your building or association money, but they also may be eligible for tax breaks. Ask your property's financial advisor or accountant for information—there are many factors involved, including what state you are in, the product, the date of installation, etc.

Wait for Replacement

A common misconception about being green is that you should rip out everything and start anew. For example, you should rip out the lobby's five-year-old carpeting simply to put in an environmentally friendly bamboo floor. Or you should replace a slightly older boiler simply because a new, more energy-efficient one came on the market. False! Replacing anything when it doesn't need to be replaced is wasteful and contradictory to green goals. In both cases, unless the carpeting needs to be replaced or the boiler is on the fritz—or if it's more than 20 years old—it's best to wait until it needs to be replaced. With any product that needs replacing, ask yourself, "How can we choose a more energy-efficient, greener product for the building?"

Reduce Energy Use

In the last chapter, you learned that your tenants can use a lot of energy powering appliances, computers, televisions, and so on. The more energy the tenants and your building systems use, the bigger the bill. Conserving energy means reducing how much energy your building uses, thereby reducing the bill. For example, educating tenants and staff to cut back on using electricity by turning off lights when they leave a room is a great place to start. When energy is reduced, the bills decrease and you'll save money. From an environmental standpoint, reducing the amount of energy your building uses also helps to reduce the amount of greenhouse gases that your building is emitting into the air and reduce your building's *carbon footprint*.

def•i•ni•tion

When it comes to energy savings, however, the best bang for your building's buck is through an energy audit.

A **carbon footprint** is the effect that activities have on the climate.

Complete an Energy Audit

Before you consider any energy conservation changes, it's important to conduct an energy audit. The audit assesses your building's water and energy use and provides a rating for that usage. A professional auditor will walk through the property, inspect metering equipment, and provide suggestions on energy-savings measures you can make. The more efficiently you run your systems, the quicker the return on the investment will be.

The ENERGY STAR program (www.energystar.gov), founded by the Environmental Protection Agency (EPA), is a voluntary labeling effort that identifies energy-saving products, including major appliances, office equipment, lighting, home electronics, and residential heating and cooling equipment.

The ENERGY STAR program evaluates the energy efficiency of commercial buildings, including grocery stores, office buildings, and residential buildings. ENERGY STAR offers a portfolio manager, an interactive energy management tool to help you see how much energy and water your building is using. Visit: www.energystar.gov/index.cfm?c=evaluate_performance.bus_portfoliomanager.

Notes from the Field

According to ENERGY STAR, if every American home replaced just one lightbulb with an ENERGY STAR–qualified bulb, enough energy would be saved to light more than 3 million homes for a year, save more than $600 million in annual energy costs, and prevent greenhouse gases equivalent to the emissions of more than 800,000 cars. Inspired?

This software evaluates a year of energy bills, the building's location (small town versus big town), and the number of occupants. When an evaluation is complete, the building is assigned a number from 0 to 100, depending on its overall energy efficiency. If the building rates between 75 and 100, it is in the top 25 percent of energy-efficient buildings and is therefore eligible to earn an ENERGY STAR label. To earn the label, a professional engineer must visit the building and verify the score. To date, more than 600 buildings have earned the title of ENERGY STAR Approved. To maintain the label, buildings must recertify annually, which is based on the building's energy bills.

Up on the Roof

The roof is meant to fend off the elements, but it can be a huge contributor to high energy bills. Because most roofing material is dark-colored, it absorbs the sun's heat and can escalate the roof temperature to 170°F to 200°F, increasing energy costs because it takes more power to cool the building down. To help cool down the roof, thereby reducing your energy costs, consider converting it to a "green" roof.

According to the Green Roof for Healthy Cities (GRHC) in Toronto, Canada, a green roof is the creation of a contained live garden space on top of a human-made structure. This can reap both economic and environmental rewards for your building by:

- Conserving energy
- Improving air quality
- Conserving water

Adding plants helps cool, insulate, and shield the roof from the sun. Cooler roofs mean less air conditioning costs and more savings. Having plants on the roof also plays an important part in *storm water management*. The plants absorb water that would have otherwise run off in a storm, filtering pollution from rainwater.

def•i•ni•tion

Storm water management is controlling rain that runs off buildings or into driveways. By controlling where the storm water goes, it reduces the risk of flooding as well as other negative environmental impacts, including eroding streams and lakes.

The roof simply isn't strong enough to bear the weight of plants in soil, especially when you add water. The green roof system involves a special waterproof and root-repellant membrane, a drainage system, a filter cloth, a lightweight growing medium, and plants.

Intensive green roofs, also known as roof gardens, are pricey gardens that are accessible to residents. They may include lawns, flowerbeds, shrubs and trees, and even water features like waterfalls or fountains. They also require a great deal of maintenance, including routine inspection and upkeep.

On the other hand, extensive green roofs are not accessible to residents, require minimal maintenance, and usually include low-key vegetation like mosses, succulents, herbs, and grasses. Extensive green roofs cost more than traditional roofs because they require more material and labor for installation. Pricing will depend on the roof's complexity, the design, and the size, but it will provide a return on investment over time.

Things to Avoid

Your roof may not be suitable for a green roof! If it's steeply sloped, is part of a historic building, or is old and can't handle the additional weight, consider other energy-saving methods. Consult with a structural engineer and landscape design firm to see if your roof is a candidate.

If you can't commit to the garden roof, there are mid-level alternatives—for example, "white roofs," which are roofs painted with a specialized white covering that reflects the sun and reduces roof temperatures.

Energy-Saving Appliances

Another great energy-saving measure is to pick the right appliances—dishwashers, air conditioners, dehumidifiers, refrigerators, and more. As property manager, you can suggest to your residents a list of preferred ENERGY STAR appliances for replacement in their units.

You can explain to your tenants that when they are buying an appliance, they should look at the price tag and see two numbers. One number is the amount that the appliance costs. The other number indicates how much energy and water the appliance will save. ENERGY STAR appliances use 10 to 50 percent less energy and water than standard models.

Submetering

Submetering is a technology that forces the tenants to take responsibility for their own electrical, furnace, and water charges. It has been proven over and over again that if tenants are responsible for the bill, they are more responsible with their usage. When it comes to heating the building, sensors can be installed throughout the building to test temperature. Once the building's inside temperature drops below 70°F, the heat turns on. This is quite opposite of how the system traditionally worked. Older systems turn on depending on the temperature on the outside of the building, or they are manually operated regardless of the temperature.

Teach residents that they pay more for energy use when the price is high and supply is scarce (during the day). When supply is abundant, they pay much less. For example, residents should wash dishes after 10 P.M. and on the weekends, not after dinner.

Water Conservation

Water, water everywhere … not! The goal is to reduce water usage in the building, thereby reducing water costs. Incorporate various water-saving strategies and technologies. Water can also be submetered. You can attach sensors to toilets, baths, and showers and bill the resident for their actual water usage. These products force each unit to control their own water costs and remove the financial responsibility from the building. Usually, tenants will tighten the belt when they have to foot the bill. The cost of installing submetering products can range between $800 and $1,000 per unit, but will depend on where you are located. The return on investment should be within two years.

Fix the Drips

If smart technology isn't in the building's budget, then the number one thing you can do to conserve water is fix drips. One drip every five seconds from just one faucet equals 50 to 100 gallons of water a day! After repairing the leaks, retrofit with high-efficiency showerheads and faucet *aerators*. The cost? As little as $10 to $200 or more per fixture.

def•i•ni•tion

Aerators combine water with air to increase water spray velocity, which reduces splash, saves water, and conserves energy.

Laundry Rooms

According to the Multi-housing Laundry Association (MLA)—the North American trade association of companies offering professional laundry systems and services to the multi-housing industry—common laundry areas actually conserve more water than washing machines in the units. The study compared washing machine water usage rates in rental units versus coin-operated machines in common laundry rooms. The result: in-unit washing machines used an average of 11,797 gallons of water per year, while coin-operated machines in common laundry rooms averaged only 3,270 gallons per year—clearly a huge difference. What does this mean to you as property manager? Significant savings! There's also the extra added environmental bonus of conserving water.

Productivity Tips

Want to save even more money and conserve more water? When it's time to upgrade washers, convert to ENERGY STAR–approved models. When negotiating a laundry contract, adding ENERGY STAR–approved washers can reduce water usage even further and ultimately improve your building's bottom line.

Clean Green

Don't forget about greening the cleaning products that your staff uses. Green products should be non-petroleum-based and made from biodegradable, renewable resources. Not all "green" products are really green, so make sure you check for a Green Seal Standard.

There are many green products on the market from which to choose. Look for water-borne, nontoxic, pH neutral, nonhazardous products that contain no solvents, volatile organic compounds (VOCs), alcohol, ammonia, harmful oxygen-based bleach cleaners, or citrus-based products that may dissolve rubber or plastics. These products work just as good as your old cleaner, but they do it with green in mind.

Indoor Air Quality

It should be home *sweet* home, not home *sick* home. But unfortunately, the EPA has classified poor indoor air quality as one of the top five most urgent public health risks. The EPA also stated that the level of air pollution inside your home can actually be higher than outside your home!

In the 1970s, air quality was a big concern when buildings were sealed up to conserve energy. Sealing a building without proper ventilation, however, actually traps toxic pollutants such as mold, tobacco smoke, pest control products, dust, fireplace emissions, formaldehyde from furniture and cabinets, and more. When homes were tightened back in the 1970s, there wasn't an understanding of the importance of ventilation. When you trap the pollutants in, you need to provide a way for them to escape and be replaced by good air.

Side Effects

Poor indoor air quality can cause many physical side effects, such as the following:

- Eye irritation
- Headaches
- Dizziness
- Fatigue
- Respiratory diseases
- Heart disease
- Cancers

Too much moisture can also become a building contaminant. Too much humidity and your building becomes a breeding ground for bacteria, mold, and mildew. Mold can reproduce and cause headaches and/or fever, coughing, wheezing, runny nose/sinus problems, flulike symptoms, skin rashes, diarrhea, hypersensitivity, asthma, and other health problems.

Formaldehyde is a VOC that comes from particle board, plywood, adhesives, paints, varnishes, carpets, and other products that are made with materials that off-gas, which is the release of toxins into the air. With no adequate ventilation, the chemicals linger. The off-gassing can continue for years after a product has been installed.

Today, manufacturers are developing low- and no-VOC alternatives in flooring and paints that meet environmental standards for indoor air quality.

Carpets and the adhesives used to secure them emit VOCs into the air. In addition, carpeting is considered a dust and chemical trap that can cause eye, nose, throat, and skin irritation; headaches; shortness of breath; fatigue; and other symptoms.

Productivity Tips _____

In 1992, the Carpet & Rug Institute launched its Green Label program that tests carpets, cushions, and adhesives to identify those that are very low-VOC. Today, it's also possible to purchase recycled carpets, which have fewer emissions than regular carpeting.

Ventilation

Buildings should have a well-working, efficient ventilation system that allows the good air in and the bad air out. As air naturally leaks out of the building through cracks and other openings, it should be replaced by filtered incoming air. Ventilation systems balance the air by circulating it in and out, which is called air changes.

The best ventilation strategy is a combination of spot and whole-building ventilation. Spot ventilation is in individual units, and includes properly sized fans, exhaust fans, or ventilation hoods. Unfortunately, most older buildings use older HVACs that do not ventilate the entire building as well as the newer models. If your building has an older unit, make sure it's regularly serviced or upgrade if the system is just too old.

The American Society of Heating, Refrigerating and Air-Conditioning Engineers (ASHRAE) came up with a standardized rating system for air filters. It's called a Minimum Efficiency Reporting Value (MERV) rating, and the higher the MERV rating, the smaller the particles it will remove. The Lung Association's Healthy House guidelines require a MERV rating of 10 or higher.

Garbage and Recycling

There's tons of garbage, especially when you are managing an apartment building or office space. Families are cooking and cleaning, and trash chutes and garbage rooms can get clogged and filthy over time. In today's world, the goal is to cut down on garbage for environmental reasons and for personal reasons as well—garbage, debris, and allergens build up in the airways and passages, contributing to smells and potential health problems for tenants. HVAC systems, garbage chutes, and collection areas should be kept clean and sanitary.

Once the garbage and recycle areas are kept neat and tidy, focus on teaching the three R's: Reduce, Reuse, Recycle. Some states offer a recycling program for apartment buildings. For example, in New York City, there is an Apartment Building Recycling Initiative, or ABRI, which is offered through the Department of Sanitation. Check with your local government about what it takes to set up a recycling program if you don't currently have one. It might require training for your staff and tenants.

Motivate Residents

If you want to green your residential or commercial building, you need to get everyone involved. Motivating your tenants will help make the process easier. You can …

- Communicate through building newsletters, e-mails, or online portals about your goals and ideas. Start a "green" tips section. For example, tip #1 can be to take shorter showers or change one lightbulb to a high-efficiency compact fluorescent.

- Donate one compact fluorescent lightbulb per unit! Explain how effective making one change can be.

- Make them aware of what they are already doing that's environmentally friendly (such as recycling).

- Provide how-to information. Not everyone understands the greening philosophy, so a little tutorial might go a long way.

You can turn to many "green" websites and organizations for more information. You can also look for green organizations in your state to help you.

The Least You Need to Know

- The future in property management now includes being environmentally conscious.

- Start off slowly by fixing cracks and holes that are allowing air to escape. Work up from there.

- Your building might qualify for tax breaks, depending on what green initiatives you include.

- Talk to tenants and get them involved. The more people participating, the better your results will be.

Chapter

The Low-Down on Renting and Leasing

In This Chapter

- ◆ Marketing properties and finding quality tenants
- ◆ Interviewing prospects and perhaps rejecting them
- ◆ Understanding leases
- ◆ Collecting rents and evicting tenants

Every property manager wants good tenants. Good tenants pay their rent on time, don't break leases, keep the property clean and maintained, notify the landlord about all problems—including repairs that need to be taken care of—and leave the property in good condition when they leave.

There are plenty of good potential commercial and residential tenants and, if screening applicants is one of your responsibilities, it will be up to you to weed out the good from the bad. This chapter will show you how to find good tenants using today's cutting-edge technologies, how to thoroughly examine an applicant's background to help avoid tenant nightmares, how to reduce your building or property's tenant turnover, and how to create a happier and more successful environment for all of your tenants.

Video and Internet Marketing

Do you know that YouTube is for more than just watching the newest, cutest baby videos? Do you Twitter or have a Facebook or LinkedIn page? Do you post on Craigslist, blog, vlog, or podcast? If these online technologies sound like a foreign language to you, then you're missing out on one of the most successful methods of marketing your properties and finding terrific tenants. It's all about exposure.

Gone are the days when you just placed an ad in the Sunday edition of your local newspaper or hung a "space for rent" sign in the window and waited for applicants to come to you. Yes, those methods are still used today, and they still work, but they are used in conjunction with other methods, too, especially the Internet. Today, the Internet puts your property in front of potential commercial and residential applicants from all over the world.

A successful property manager stays on the cutting-edge of technology to help reach clients and promote properties. You don't need to be a tech-geek to work these technologies either. They are easy-to-understand and affordable marketing techniques. It's all about exposure.

YouTube

YouTube (www.youtube.com) is a Google-owned video sharing website where users can upload, view, and share video clips. Whether you are publicizing your property or your services, all you need is a digital camera or camcorder and a video-editing program that is usually included on most computers. You can use your video camera to walk viewers through a virtual tour of the property and the community.

The cool fact about YouTube is that someone in, say, New York can see your Texas-based property and then "link it" to someone else in another country through e-mail or a cell phone in seconds.

Websites

Websites are like online business cards. Just about every business has one, so if yours doesn't, get on it right away. Websites can show pictures of the property and list everything an applicant may need to know about living there. There are affordable, user-friendly web design sites to help you start. Include all of your marketing materials—photos, pamphlets, architectural plans, community information, and so on—so your potential tenants can get a complete view of your property.

Hiring a website design firm can cost upward of $10,000, and can often cost even more—and that's not even taking into account system administration, hosting, maintenance, and updates. If that's out of your budget, consider a basic website design company such as GoDaddy (www.godaddy.com) or Network Solutions (www.networksolutions.com), where you can monitor the site yourself for less than $20 per month.

Productivity Tips

Websites provide traffic counters so you know how many visitors the site has had in a given day or week. The site counter also tells you where your viewers are located. This will help you to market your properties better.

Blogs and Vlogs

Think of blogs as online diaries and vlogs as online video diaries. How can you use these to market your property? They are actually easier to update than websites and can be used to provide day-to-day information on your properties. For example, your website may include the above information, your blog may also include personal day-to-day notes about your management company, your personal feedback on an important community situation, and more. Some management company bloggers have talked about what events are being held at the property that day or a change in garbage pickup schedules.

Things to Avoid

Remember that blogs and vlogs are for business and not personal use. Don't include your personal opinions or personal information about tenants.

Podcasts

No, a podcast isn't something directly out of the 1980s thriller movie *Alien*. Podcasts are a series of audio or digital media files that you make as a *podcaster* and are distributed over the Internet. Viewers can download them and put them on their iPod or other portable media player, as well as on their personal computers. They can e-mail them to others, too. If you choose to do more than one podcast, viewers can subscribe to them. In other words, blogs, vlogs, podcasts,

def•i•ni•tion

A **podcaster** is someone who hosts or creates podcasts.

and so on, all allow you to gain a regular audience and help you market and spread the word about your property.

Marketing and advertising are vital to the success of your building. One of the first things to go when times are tough are those budgets, but what a mistake! It's important to keep business coming in during the tough times—without advertising and marketing your properties, it's like crawling into a hole where nobody knows your name. You should always be thinking of affordable marketing and advertising opportunities.

Residential Tenants

Your techniques have attracted applicants, and now they are interested in becoming a tenant. If screening applicants is your responsibility, your first contact with them will probably be on the phone after they have responded to an ad. Ask basic questions first: name, telephone number, reason for moving, when they want to move in, how many people are moving in, and pets. (You cannot ask how many children they have, so be careful about this!)

Let them know the cost of the unit up-front. If they can afford it and are interested in seeing it, now is the time for an in-person visit, application, and interview. If you have applications on your website, let the applicant know ahead of time so they can fill it out before visiting the property.

Interview

Be careful, fair housing laws are tricky and an interview process can get you into trouble if you say the wrong thing. Generally, you should give the details on the unit for rent and talk about the security deposit, move-in date, lease length, and more.

If you conduct an interview, make certain you have a written criteria form on you to show the applicant, and use a tenant screening form that has the same questions for each. Verify their basic information—previous employment history and where they used to live—so you know that all the information is current and accurate.

- Examine the applicant's behavior. Are they uneasy or anxious? Are they well mannered and respectful?

- How is their appearance? Are they neatly groomed or disheveled? Often, what you see in person will be what you get when they are in the unit.

- Ask why they want to live in your building or rent the unit.

◆ Ask why they are leaving their current residence.

◆ Ask how long the prospective tenant plans to live at the residence.

If you listen, really listen, to the answers, you can determine whether they are the right tenant for your building. For example, let's say that you ask a tenant if they like the place. An interested tenant might say something like, "It's so much better than my last place." That's a good sign. Tenants that may not be as interested might say something like, "It's not quite what I was expecting, but it's nice."

Don't give up. Follow up. Ask them what they were hoping for. Perhaps you can fix it, or not. But you won't know until you try. Body language can also give out clues. Keep in mind that you always have the option to hire a professional screening company who knows all the laws and procedures.

At the time a prospective tenant is given a rental application, provide the potential tenant a written notice of the tenant selection criteria and the grounds for which a rental application may be denied.

You should also have the applicant sign an acknowledgment indicating that they received the selection criteria. It should say something like:

> "Signing this acknowledgment indicates that you have had the opportunity to review the landlord's tenant selection criteria. The tenant selection criteria may include factors such as criminal history, credit history, current income, and rental history. If you do not meet the selection criteria, or if you provide inaccurate or incomplete information, your application may be rejected and your application fee will not be refunded."

Check References

The next step in qualifying your tenant is to make sure they have good references—credit, employer, and personal. When calling personal references, ask if the tenant was trustworthy and responsible. When contacting their previous landlord, make sure they paid their rent on time and find out if they have caused any damage or problems. Verify their employment and check your applicant's credit by running a credit check through the three credit reporting agencies.

Once you have completed these tasks, it's time to make a decision. If there are multiple tenant applications for one unit, you need to decide who you think is the best possible tenant.

Rejecting a Tenant

You've completed the interview and, unfortunately, decided that this person isn't a good fit. In Chapter 10, you will get additional information about the Fair Housing Act, but you need to know about this act now if you're going to reject someone.

Notes from the Field
Once your tenant expresses interest in leasing, the negotiations have begun. See Chapter 9 for tips and suggestions on negotiating leases so that both parties are content.

The Fair Housing Act prohibits you from discriminating in the sale, rental, and financing of any housing-related transactions. Basically, this means you can't tell your applicant "no" because of their race, color, national origin, sex, family status, disability, or religion. As long as it's not one of those reasons, you should be okay and not in any legal hot water. If you're unsure, contact your lawyer and ask first.

Commercial Tenants

An application for commercial tenants is slightly different than residential tenants, but it's just as important to check the background of commercial tenants as it is residential tenants. You want to make certain that the commercial business is a viable one that can afford to pay the rent. There are several methods of checking the background of a commercial tenant:

- Dun and Bradstreet (www.dnb.com/us), the world's leading source of commercial information (its database contains more than 140 million business records)

- Credit reports

- Better Business Bureau

- Local Chamber of Commerce

Before leasing out commercial space, it's vital that property managers, especially those that manage a mixed-use property, consider the type of business that is moving in. For example, residents may not be interested in having a restaurant underneath their building due to risks of fire or because the restaurant is open late, causing noise and traffic.

Selecting Mixed-Use Tenants

When choosing a commercial business tenant for a mixed-use building, it's important to pick a tenant that matches with the building.

◆ Is the tenant the right fit? For example, a building with mostly older tenants may not want a pub downstairs that is open late hours and that can be rather loud at times. This may result in conflicts between the tenants and the business. Does the building emit odors that may be offensive or unhealthy to your residents? Does the business require large trucks for deliveries?

◆ Will the tenant add to the overall goals of the building?

◆ Can the tenant pay the rent? Mom-and-pop businesses are great for that small neighborhood feel, but they may not be as reliable as a larger franchise. Research the corporation or business to make sure it's a viable, money-making venture or you may end up with bigger problems.

◆ Will the business require ample parking spaces? Is it a hair salon that has customers coming and going, or is it an insurance firm that usually has less traffic? Can you accommodate the extra traffic?

◆ Will the business require additional needs, such as more air conditioning or heat, than the rest of the building? Will they need storage space for supplies or inventory?

◆ Do your local zoning ordinances prevent certain businesses from moving in?

As a property manager for any property, you need to know your market to attract and keep tenants. When you are marketing a mixed-use property, however, you need to know your local commercial and real estate market. You also need to know which types of businesses are successful in your community and which ones are struggling.

Understanding Leases

Once you have a tenant, it's time to sign a lease. A lease is the contract between the management company and the tenant that protects both sides. It gives the lessee a place to live or to run their business for a specified amount of time at a specified amount of rent per month. It's also a legally binding agreement and spells out everything that both sides needs to know—length of the lease, restrictions, how much the rent and other fees are, the payment due dates, late fees, and more.

Residential Leases

Residential leases are binding agreements between tenants and landlords. Usually, residential leases are signed for one year at a time, but in some cases, you might not want to have the tenant sign a one-year lease. Instead, you may make the lease a bit longer, or even a bit shorter, to avoid it ending in November or December. There are several types of leases:

◆ **Fixed end date:** This is a lease with a certain date that ends the lease. During the lease, the landlord can't raise the rent unless the tenant agrees.

◆ **Periodic:** This type of lease can just continue to renew as long as the landlord or the tenant doesn't want to end the lease. The landlord can raise the rent by contacting the tenant.

Commercial Leases

A small business that is just starting out may sign a lease of only a year or two. This is to protect both sides should the small business not make it. Other commercial leases can run for many years, depending on the business. There are also special clauses in a commercial lease, such as the Use Clause (tells a tenant how the space can be used), the Exclusive Clause (limits a competing business from opening up next door), and the premises (exactly what does your rental include).

There are several types of commercial leases:

Things to Avoid

Keep the completed lease applications for the entire time that your tenant is in your building. You should also keep a rejected application and note in red why you declined the applicant. This is to protect you should a tenant or a rejected applicant come back later and accuse you of discrimination.

◆ **A single net (Net or N) lease** requires the tenant to pay some of the property taxes in addition to their rent.

◆ **A double net (Net-Net or NN) lease** stipulates that a tenant is responsible for real estate taxes and building insurance.

◆ **A triple net lease (Net-Net-Net or NNN)** is a lease agreement in which the tenant pays all real estate taxes, building insurance, maintenance, and so on, in addition to rent. The tenant is responsible for repairs and replacements of the building structure. These rents are usually much lower than other forms of leases.

♦ **A gross lease** requires the tenant to pay a set amount of rent and expenses, which the landlord can use to pay whatever. If more than one tenant leases, those tenants share the expenses, determined by the square footage of the tenant's business.

Productivity Tips

When leasing a commercial space, be certain that all parties are correctly listed on the lease. This is especially important if a married couple opens a business together (and possibly divorces later).

Also included in a lease can be an Escalation Clause, which states the landlord's or owner's right to increase the rent to reflect any changes in the real estate taxes that the landlord is paying or based on the economy.

Collecting Rent and Fees

The lease has been signed, the tenant is moving in, and all is right with the world. Or so it seems. Now it's time to collect the rent. To be a successful property manager, this should be your mantra: "collecting rent is a business." It's what pays the building's mortgage and maintenance.

Depending on your tenants, collecting rental payments and other fees can be simple or it can be the juggernaut on your path to staying a successful property manager. When someone is late, you'll hear strange and true stories about why. They'll appeal to your emotions and friendship. Bottom line: it's your business to collect rent and fees—get the job done.

Outline Expectations

The best way to collect rent and fees is to outline what your payment expectations are when the lease is being signed. Say it to the tenant, so that if they have any questions or concerns they can be addressed at that time. Tell them when the rent and fees are due, the *grace period*, and the method of payment. After all, not everybody reads the fine print of all important papers.

def•i•ni•tion

> A **grace period** is a time period after the rent is due—usually just a few days—that allows the tenant to get their money in to you without being penalized. It's not an obligation, although some managers and landlords provide a courtesy grace period. If the grace period is met without payment, the tenant will be charged a late fee.

Encourage your tenants to let you know if the rent is going to be late. Sometimes, a tenant only needs a few days for one reason or another. They should feel comfortable coming to you and talking about why. Remember, however, that it is a business and you need to work out a plan for payment. If a tenant has asked for an extension a few times, this is a red flag that the situation might worsen.

Billing

Residential rent collection is much easier than commercial rent collection. Most residential collection occurs on the first of the month, and tenants have a few days grace period.

Commercial rent collecting is more complicated. Commercial leases, which include taxes and insurance, may have various billing dates. Additional rent provisions may require the landlord to bill taxes quarterly and insurance upon receipt of the bill. Others may get billed on a monthly basis. Years ago, property managers would go knocking on their tenants' doors to collect the rent. Although some smaller properties might still depend on this method of collecting rent, most property managers utilize software programs and website applications that automatically remind tenants to pay and provide a safe online method of payment.

Rent Increases

Nobody wants to hear it, but it's inevitable that rents will be raised at some point, especially if the economy and the real estate market aren't doing well. Of course, once word spreads among the tenants about rents being increased, the grumbling and the mumbling will start, so it's best to approach your tenants directly, explain the situation, and have backup materials to show why an increase is necessary.

Eviction

Nobody likes the idea of evicting a tenant, but you'll have to do it at some point if a tenant gets behind in the rent or becomes troublesome (which we'll discuss in Chapter 12). How you evict a tenant depends on whether they own or rent the space and whether they live in a condo, cooperative, or commercial space.

There are several reasons for eviction. The tenant may not have paid his rent, he hasn't left even after his lease has expired, or you're evicting him because he breached his lease contract and won't leave. There are also times when a tenant is not in compliance with the terms of their lease, such as getting a pet in a no-pet building or disturbing the neighbors. You would then serve a notice stating what action they must take to correct the violation or else face eviction.

The approach to evicting a troublesome residential tenant depends largely on whether you're dealing with a co-op or a condo tenant, because co-ops can have subtenants and condos can have tenants who are leasing directly from the unit owner.

- ◆ **Condominium:** If the troublesome tenant owns the unit, it's impossible to evict them, although they can be sued. If the tenant leases the unit, you can start eviction based on what the bylaws say needs to be done.

- ◆ **Cooperative:** Again, the eviction of a shareholder or renter depends on what the bylaws say. If the problem is with a subtenant, however, the bylaws may state that the eviction can name both the shareholder and their subtenant. How you evict also will depend on whether it's a rent-stabilized or rent-controlled building.

To evict someone, however, there needs to be a petition requesting a court hearing. That notice must be served to the tenant. The tenant then must respond and show up to court, and the court decides whether the landlord can evict a tenant. Every state can be different, so follow your state laws when serving a notice.

Things to Avoid

Never take food stamps as rent payment—it's against the law!

If you win, don't think that you can just hire a moving van, pack up the Hatfields, and kick 'em to the curb. You must give them a warrant of eviction, and only a sheriff or marshal can do the actual evicting. And remember, you are not allowed to keep a tenant's personal possessions. However, depending on your state, you might have to keep any possessions that are left for a certain period of time.

Things to Avoid _____

A commercial or residential tenant falling behind in rent payments may also file for bankruptcy. As a result, the lease is considered "frozen" during the bankruptcy process, and the eviction can be stalled. Contact your attorney to find out what you can do in this situation.

Commercial Tenants

Evicting a commercial tenant can get a little more complicated and may depend on your state laws. Commercial tenants must be given a three-day notice to correct any violation of a lease and avoid being evicted.

Overcoming Obstacles

When the economy started to suffer a few years ago, property managers began to worry. How would tenants pay their rents? Then, businesses began to go bankrupt and tenants were laid off from their jobs. Of course, the common scenario would be to simply evict the tenants who are behind on their rent.

But successful property managers must face obstacles all the time, and it's smart to find out-of-the-box solutions. For example, shopping malls that house hundreds of stores don't want tenants behind on their rent payments, but they also don't want to be facing a high vacancy rate, so they have come up with several alternatives for their tenants, such as:

- Deferring rent to the end of the lease

- Temporarily reducing rent

- Reviewing leases and offering shorter leases to keep the facility occupied

The bottom line is to work with your tenants when they hit obstacles, as early as possible, before things get worse.

The Least You Need to Know

- When you're marketing your business and properties, step out of the box and spread the word in creative, unconventional ways.

- Not every tenant is going to be a right fit for your property, but make sure you say "no" in a very professional—and legal—way.

- Always follow the state and federal fair housing guidelines for rejecting, interviewing, and evicting a tenant.

- Collecting rents is part of your business, so make certain you have outlined the process to the tenants from the beginning and have provided them with several convenient payment methods.

- Remember that your job is a business—from collecting rent to evicting tenants who don't pay—so don't take it personally.

Chapter 9

Negotiations, Contracts, and Bids

In This Chapter

- ◆ Understanding the art of the deal
- ◆ Negotiating all types of contracts
- ◆ Working with vendors and contractors
- ◆ Hiring a middleman to decide

Real estate tycoon Donald Trump wrote *Trump Style Negotiation: Powerful Strategies and Tactics for Mastering Every Deal* (Wiley, 2008). Why an entire book on negotiation? Because negotiation is a skill that needs to be learned and then fine tuned with each experience you have. Successful negotiation isn't nervously entering a room and hoping to come out with some sort of compromise. Successful negotiation is confidently entering a room prepared with offers and counteroffers and coming up with an agreement that satisfies both sides.

Trump's book opens with an amusing tale of a father with 10-year-old twins—one who is too pessimistic and one who is too optimistic—and he'd like each of them to change just a little bit. So, for their birthday, he buys the pessimist a bicycle and the optimist a pile of horse manure. The pessimist tells his dad he hates the bike because he'll get hurt on it or some big goon at school will beat him up for it. The father then watches the optimist play in the horse manure. The father questions him and the boy says, "There has to be a pony in here somewhere!" The point? A good negotiator will go through poop to get what he wants.

This doesn't mean that each time you enter into negotiations with a potential tenant or contractor you will have to go through a metaphorical pile of manure. Not all negotiations are so difficult. Either way, Trump's story shows that a good negotiator—and successful property manager—is optimistic and determined to negotiate until each side is happy with the outcome. And, like an up-and-coming ball player who practices so one day he'll be a pro, you'll get better each and every time you're up to bat.

During your property management career, you'll be negotiating …

- Purchases and leases with prospective and current residents.

- Purchases and leases with commercial tenants.

- With property owners, vendors and contractors, and governmental agencies.

This chapter will show how each type of negotiation comes with its own set of challenges and criteria. But first a little basic information on preparing for these negotiations and then we'll break down the types of negotiations you'll be doing.

Preparing to Negotiate

Enter a negotiation without being prepared and you've lost before you've even begun. You can start by asking yourself some key questions. The answer to these questions will help you to complete your preparation:

- What's the agenda? There should be an agreed-upon list of things that both sides want to be done or discussed in a particular order during a meeting or negotiation.

- What results do you want out of the negotiation? Do you want a tenant to renew their lease? Do you want a rate increase? Do you want a laundry machine vendor to lock in a price? Knowing what your goals are ahead of time is vital to your negotiation success.

- What does the other side want? Do they want their rent to stay the same? Not sure? Play all possible scenarios in your head so you're prepared with answers and counteroffers for each one.

◆ Are you prepared with the financials you need to back up your decision? For example, do you know your tenant's rent paying history? Are they notoriously late or perfectly on time? Have other tenants complained about the noise that the tenant makes? Do they want to keep their rent stable and negotiate paying for repairs and remodeling to their store or unit? Have they asked for this before? How will you respond?

◆ What are the going rental rates in the neighborhood?

◆ Do they have particular strengths or weaknesses that you can use to your advantage?

◆ Do you need to talk to a member of your team before negotiations? Will a conversation with your accountant, lawyer, or developer help you?

Once you have the answers to these questions, you can then contemplate the possible outcomes to your negotiation.

Understanding Possible Outcomes

You win. You lose. Seems like those might be the only solutions to a negotiation, but it's a little more complicated than that. First, let's say you won. Congratulations! You got a great deal. The tenant signed or you got a great vendor deal. That's your perfect outcome. Or, you got the tenant to sign but you had to make some concessions. That's okay, too. You got the tenant to sign and the tenant made the concessions—still good. Maybe you walked away from the negotiations and left with a vacant apartment, storefront, or office space. Believe it or not, that could be a good thing, too, since the tenant might not have worked out under the contract that you were negotiating.

Think through about what the consequences are for every negotiation. What are you going to win? What are you going to compromise on? What will you lose? Knowing this ahead of time helps you make the right decisions.

Keeping Your Emotions in Check

Don't bring your emotions to the negotiation table. It doesn't matter if you don't like Mrs. G in Apartment 5A, or maybe Mr. Smith who runs the pizza shop just grates on your last nerve. But they pay their rents on time and they don't bother anyone. You can't bring your emotions to the negotiations when it's time to discuss their new lease. Your job is to work with them and come up with an agreement. Whether or not you like them is irrelevant.

In the same vein, there should be no name calling, yelling, or accusations from either party. Be assertive and professional, but understand that your current tenant or applicant is concerned about keeping their unit at a fair price. They will do what they can—including prove to you that they have been a good tenant and list problems they've had with the unit—to stop the rent increase.

Listening

Negotiating doesn't mean that you, or the other side, do all the talking. Listening is a huge part of a successful negotiation. Are your tenants complaining about repairs or building problems? Don't look at it as a personal attack on you or a ploy to get something they want. Instead, listen to their concerns. Don't just think they are complaining. Instead, they may be stressing that they want to stay in the building, but they just need some assistance. The best negotiators are those who listen, don't interrupt, and let the other side go first.

Remembering to Give and Take

Once a prospective tenant expresses interest in leasing a unit, it's time to move on to negotiations. All terms of the lease must be agreed upon. As property manager, you need to understand that your tenant is going to come to the table with the same goal that you have—to get the best deal, whether it's a first time negotiation or a renewal.

Negotiation is about give and take. It's doubtful that you or your tenant will give in without wanting something in return. What concessions can you make so that you get what you want? Know what those concessions are before negotiations begin. Perhaps the budget allows the tenant's rent to remain the same for the next year in exchange for having them do minor repairs in the store.

Here are some things to keep in mind when negotiating a good residential lease.

Check Payment History

For first-time residential leases, you should check out past rental history and ask if the tenant has paid their rent on time at their former building. Were there any complaints filed against them? Did they leave the unit in good condition when they left? If it's a renegotiation, what is your tenant's payment history? Checking references is only one part of the process.

Know the Market

Whether you are negotiating a new or current lease, be familiar with the rental prices in your area. This is especially important if you are going to increase a tenant's rent or if a new tenant suggests they can get the same type of space for less money somewhere else.

If you are increasing a current commercial tenant's rent, be able to explain why—they *will* ask. You might explain to them that the average rate for equivalent commercial space is $25 per square foot and you're currently charging $20, so a slight rental increase to $23 is still a savings for the tenant. The tenant should know they are still getting a discount compared to other going rates, and yet the new rate still brings in additional income for the building. Perhaps you are charging the tenant more because the corner apartment has an amazing water view? Explain the amenities they are paying for compared to other apartments.

Rent increases should be proportionate to inflation rates. For example, if you are increasing a tenant's rent from $450 to $550, it may not sound so bad when you explain that it's only a $100 increase. When you do the math, however, it is really a 22.5 percent increase, and the resident may balk. Perhaps a $50 increase will be economically suitable for the tenant and profitable for management. It also keeps the tenant in the building and lowers your vacancy rate.

Take Care of Business

If a tenant expresses that they have had problems with the unit and management hasn't been responsive, look into the complaints. If the negotiation is the first time the tenant is complaining about insects or other problems, it might be a ploy to get you to forgo the rent increase. If they have, however, complained before and the problem hasn't been fixed, it's best to look into it before further negotiations.

Free Rent and Other Concessions

There are plenty of opportunities to offer new tenants some incentives to get them to sign the lease. For example, "Rent and get first month free." In a slow market, that free month might be increased to a two- or even three-month incentive. Other management companies offer a lower security deposit for applicants with great credit, free Internet access, free cablevision, and even free rent for the twelfth month. These are powerful marketing tools that are used to encourage tenants to sign and extend leases. In turn, it reduces your building's vacancy rates and turnover.

Personality Roles in Negotiation

Believe it or not, personality can play a big part in negotiations. Just think about it. If you're negotiating with someone who is a bit more aggressive and demanding, they may not be flexible in their give-and-take. If you're negotiating with someone who's timid, they may not react with a counteroffer and walk away. Knowing how to negotiate with a particular personality makes you a very successful property manager.

If you're negotiating with a strong personality, it's best to focus on what amenities they will be getting. For example, they may show concern about the rental fee, but when you continue to express that they have the unit with the best view or a store connected to the best area of the parking lot, they may bend. Make them feel like they've won already.

If you're negotiating with someone who has millions of questions and can't seem to come to an agreement, be patient. The best way to handle this personality is to assure them that these items are being taken care of, answer their questions, and see what happens. Pushing this personality to make a decision is bound to push them away. Don't make them feel bad about their concerns. On the flip side, you may encounter a get-to-the-point tenant. Follow his lead and seal the deal.

Most importantly, keep your personality out of the negotiations. This isn't about you; it's about the building and the tenant. It doesn't mean you should be uncomfortable; it just means you need to make some adjustments to get the contract signed.

Commercial Leases

Negotiating a commercial lease is different than negotiating a residential lease. There are additional things to consider, including operating hours, signs, store design, length of the lease, and more.

Term

The lengths of most commercial leases vary from 1 year to more than 10 years. Some startup businesses—for example, restaurants or beauty salons—may sign a shorter lease of only a few years until they determine the success of their business. What you don't want, however, is cycles of empty space in the building, because that leaves you with a shortfall of income. An alternative might be to offer a startup business a lease with an option to renew. It provides the tenant with an option, but ensures a possible rent increase at renewal time.

Productivity Tips _____

If you are negotiating a commercial lease for a residential building (mixed use), it's best to hire someone who specializes in retail contracts. They will understand the criteria of commercial leasing better than someone who specializes in residential leasing. You may also need an outside consultant if the lease terms are complicated.

Operating Hours

If you are negotiating a lease for a mixed-use building, you need to consider the operating hours of a 9-to-5 business versus the operating hours of a pub or restaurant, and the business hours' effect on the residents. On the other hand, leasing the space to a loud dance studio that plays music at night and that has late rehearsals might be a bad mix with the quieter administrative office next door.

Signage

Signs are needed to advertise businesses, but signs that are too big or distracting can become a nuisance to tenants and customers. This is a hot topic of negotiations. Without the right signs, the business can claim that their customers can't find them. The contract should include detailed instructions on how signage should be handled. Local zoning laws might determine signage requirements, but include clauses that explain what can be put on the windows and on the building's exterior, doors, and walls. Neon signs are popular, and must be considered prior to negotiation.

Notes from the Field

A signage story from leasingprofessional.com: One attorney for a chain store retailer: "I have seen several deals hung up on signage alone. This was after all other business and legal issues had been resolved—we were at loggerheads over the size of a particular letter in our trade name because it determined the size of the other two letters. This also had a big impact on the whole graphic appeal of the store. The attorney on the other side laughed and said, 'I can't believe that the size of a letter will blow this deal.' The retailer prevailed, but the deal nearly fell out of bed on that design issue alone."

Remodeling/Repairs

Businesses that want to repair or remodel the space will negotiate to have those expenses deducted from their rent. This is especially true if what's repaired will stay with the building when the business leaves—for example, plumbing and windows. In addition, the tenant will negotiate for unforeseen repairs. For example, they begin working on plumbing for their baths and find a water leak that needs to be repaired.

Keep in mind, however, that if the item that needs to be repaired needs to be done because of a safety or maintenance issue, it's best to just examine the situation and ultimately repair it now. Another option would be to have the tenant repair it and deduct the costs from the rent.

If the tenant is asking for either more money or more repairs than have been deemed necessary, it's important to assert your authority.

Rent

What's the bottom line? A net lease requires that the tenant pay rent, utilities, taxes, and assessments. Net-Net leases require that the tenant pay rent, real estate taxes, utilities, assessments, and insurance. There are other versions of this Net-Net arrangement, too. It's also important to add in a percentage rent increase each year, or you'll be stuck with the first rental fee for the duration of the lease.

A triple net lease (Net-Net-Net or NNN) is a lease agreement where the tenant pays all real estate taxes, building insurance, and maintenance in addition to rent. The tenant is also responsible for repair or replacement costs for the property.

Vendors and Contractors

As a property manager for commercial and residential properties, you'll be dealing with a lot of vendors and contractors—painters, pest control companies, equipment vendors, and janitorial services—and you'll be negotiating contracts at least once a year:

- Do you represent more than one building? If so, you should be able to buy in bulk—and even negotiate a discount—from one vendor to take care of all buildings.

- In co-ops and condo associations, boards should not be handling the negotiations. Management should conduct the negotiation, but report the changes back to the board.

◆ Some items that should be included in negotiation are: costs, equipment, invoices, timeliness of deliveries and repairs, insurance, repairs and communication, and access to the building and units.

Laundry Room Contracts

There are three main reasons that properties elect to renegotiate laundry room contracts: money, modernization and updated equipment, and beautification. Modernizing the laundry room allows the management company to charge more money for the services and return bigger revenue. Beautification is when the laundry room is "prettied up" with new lighting, air conditioning, additional televisions, and so on. Read the fine print on the contracts, as many automatically roll over for five years at a time.

Also, be aware that laundry contracts may have clauses that transfer when there is a sale of the contract to another company.

Laundry companies will start negotiating at least a year before the contract is up. Good service should be just as important as the bottom line, so be careful when negotiating. Not all renegotiation leads to a contract renewal. The new rates may be too low for the building or too high for the vendor, or perhaps the building was not satisfied with the service they received from the vendor.

Things to Avoid

Some companies use boilerplate agreements with "right of first refusal." Right of first refusal gives the building's current vendor the right to match any bid that a prospective vendor has provided to the building when it comes time for renegotiation. The building is then locked in to using the current vendor again.

Owners and managers want to maintain a laundry room that is safe, operational, and comfortable, and that generates revenue and makes the residents happy—and that's the ultimate goal of the negotiations. Otherwise, both sides are all washed up.

Maintenance Contractors

A contractor will maintain, repair, or replace something when it needs it. They work with architects, engineers, plumbers, carpenters, and electricians to come up with a bid for the project that needs to be done.

In some cases, as property manager, you will hire the contractor to complete the job. In other cases, such as with a co-op or condo association, you will obtain bids and present your findings to the board. The board will make the final decision on who to hire, based on the bids you received and your input.

Negotiating contractor bids starts with obtaining competitive bids from several contractors for the same job. This is especially important with the more expensive jobs. Get references and ask the contractor's previous customers about their experiences with that contractor. Once you have accepted a bid—and the lowest isn't always the best—it's important to make sure the contract includes what you need.

For example, if one bid is lower than another, is it possible that they are including different parts and accessories? Are these parts sufficient for the job at hand? Is the lower bid an indication that the contractor is cutting corners? Do some homework on the particulars of the bid before making a final decision. You may be able to negotiate the higher-bid contractor down to a more affordable price when you find out he is including top-of-the-line everything—including items you may not even need.

Negotiating Employee Contracts

Employment contracts are agreements between your firm (employer) and your staff member (employee). This agreement outlines what the staff member's role at the firm will be over a period of time, as well as salary, perks, benefits, health insurance, and any possible severance package.

Staff …. You've hired your staff and, eventually, you're going to have to renew their contracts. When it comes to staff renegotiation, it's best to talk a few months in advance of the contract's end. It provides time to go over the issues and time for both parties to come to an agreement.

Some building staff members may be part of a union—for example, many New York City superintendents are members of Service Employees International Union (SEIU) Local 32BJ, which represents 70,000 building service employees, from cleaners and porters to superintendents and security guards. Whether or not a staff member is a union member doesn't determine whether they'll do a better job.

There are some unique aspects, however, to having unionized employees. First, having to fire a union member can be difficult because they can rely on their union defender to come and negotiate on their behalf. Second, a unionized employee for one job can't do another job. But you may be able to ask a nonunionized super to do a job outside his initial job description. It's important for all property managers to follow the rules that are found in union contracts.

Union labor contracts are generally negotiated every few years—in New York, for
example, negotiations occur every three years.
Collective bargaining occurs at this time. Both
management and union are trying to avoid
the picket line. To do so, it's all about communication.

def•i•ni•tion

Collective bargaining is the process whereby workers organize
together to meet, converse, and
compromise on the work environment with their employers.

Legal Help

For some negotiations, you are going to need legal counsel. Your attorney should be
aware of any particular issues that are arising with negotiations so they are prepared to
step in and help you solve the situation. It's also important that your attorney review
the documents before both parties sign them, just to make sure that you haven't
missed anything. While you are a strong, successful property manager, your experience with real estate law and negotiation may be limited and the knowledge and experience of an attorney will help you.

Your attorney can also help in settling any disputes you may have over contracts,
finances, or otherwise. A successful property manager turns to an expert when it's
needed.

Signed, sealed, and delivered! Once an agreement has been reached in any negotiation, an attorney will formalize that agreement in writing.

Closing the Deal

Closing the deal is the hardest part of the entire negotiation process. Why? Because
the prospective tenant may second guess himself before signing on the dotted line. In
his book, *The Art of Closing Any Deal: How to Be a Master Closer in Everything You Do*
(SP Books, 1989), James W. Pickens describes two main reasons why customers won't
sign or buy:

1. An objection

2. A condition

He says, "An objection can and should be overcome by the seller. There should be no
excuse for not overcoming a legitimate honest objection from a customer." It is the
closer's job to provide answers, get the agreement, and close the deal. A condition,

however, is something that you can't change. For example, the customer can't afford to match your price. If you can't come down in price, then it's something that's not going to change because the customer can't make more money.

The following are some other reasons why a potential tenant may not sign a contract:

♦ **Timing:** Sometimes negotiations fail because of timing. For example, an office negotiating on September 10, 2001, might have changed their mind on September 12, after the terrorist attacks occurred.

♦ **Economy:** Potential deals fell through after the government announced the nation was in a recession. Scared about moving into a new apartment or starting or expanding a business, tenants chose to stay where they are, hold onto their deposits, and wait it out. Another tenant could've lost a job before signing the lease or a business could've hit a snag with their product that halted the rental of a bigger facility.

Mediation

Of course, it would be ideal if there weren't any problems during negotiations or they were easily resolved. But you know as well as we do that not all negotiations are going to be picture perfect. So, when both sides come to a standstill in the negotiations, it might sound like the next logical step should be to head to the courts so a judge can decide on the outcome.

Fortunately, there is an alternative that attempts to solve problems and minimize the need to step into a courtroom. It's called alternative dispute resolution, and the concept is simple: All parties first meet with a *mediator* and try to solve the problem. If mediation doesn't work, the disgruntled residents meet with an *arbitrator* (similar to a judge), who will render a verdict. Still at a standstill? The next step may be litigation.

def•i•ni•tion

A **mediator** is someone who acts as a neutral party, listening to both sides in a dispute and making a decision. An **arbitrator** is a private, neutral person chosen to arbitrate a disagreement, as opposed to a court of law. An arbitrator could be used to settle any noncriminal dispute, and many business contracts make provisions for an arbitrator in the event of a disagreement. Generally, resolving a disagreement through an arbitrator is substantially less expensive than resolving it through a court of law.

(Source: www.investorwords.com)

Alternative dispute resolution has been gaining popularity in recent years as an effective problem-solving method, with one reason for its popularity being the abundance of court cases already in the system.

The process is a confidential one in which parties can talk freely about their issues. The mediator uses various techniques to help to negotiate an agreement. The first step is to select a mediator.

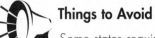

Things to Avoid

Some states require that parties enter into mediation and arbitration before going to court to resolve problems. Make certain you know ahead of time what's required in your state.

Any party or parties may voluntarily initiate a mediation under the auspices of the American Arbitration Association (AAA, at www.adr.org), or they may work with a private alternative dispute resolution (ADR) company. Through the AAA, there is no filing fee to initiate a mediation. Nor is there a fee to request the AAA to invite parties to mediate. The cost is based on the hourly rate on the mediator's AAA profile. Private mediation companies charge differently, so be sure to ask.

The mediator reaches out to the parties—individually or together—to learn more about the subject matter of the dispute. In some cases, the mediator requests brief written positions from the parties. The next step is for the actual mediation to take place with the parties and their lawyers, if any. The mediator's job is to listen to both sides and to come up with a mutually agreeable resolution.

If mediation doesn't work, the parties continue to a quick arbitration process. Arbitration is an informal hearing in which the parties meet before an arbitrator who hears their arguments and decides what a judge would say. Arbitration is binding, which means that you must do what the arbitrator has decided, but you have 45 days to appeal.

The Least You Need to Know

- Keep a level head in contract negotiations, and don't let your personality get in the way. Almost all contracts can be negotiated if you remember how to handle the other side's personality.

- Remember that all leases—residential and commercial—can be negotiated.

- Decide if your tenants are going to pay rent that covers utilities, taxes, and maintenance or if those items will be charged separately.

♦ Whether you have 1, 50, or 200 employee(s), have an employee manual in place that addresses all of the possible staffing concerns.

♦ When at a standstill, arbitration and mediation lets someone else stand in and decide.

Legislation

In This Chapter

- ◆ Understanding the law
- ◆ Making buildings accessible
- ◆ Dealing with state and local laws, too

As a property manager, you might feel like you need a law degree to understand all of the legal mumbo jumbo that gets thrown at you. There are bylaws and proprietary leases and house rules, oh my! There are federal, local, and state laws—such as the Americans with Disabilities Act, Fair Housing Act, Equal Credit Opportunity Act, and more. You do need a thorough understanding of these laws to do your job well. Violating these laws can result in serious consequences, including hefty financial penalties. The good news is you don't need to head to law school to figure all this out. In addition to reading this chapter, consult your building's attorney when in doubt about a particular legal matter.

Discrimination Laws

Title VIII of the Civil Rights Act of 1968 (Fair Housing Act), as amended, prohibits *discrimination* in the sale, rental, and financing of dwellings, and in

def•i•ni•tion

Discrimination is unfair treatment of a person or group on the basis of prejudice.

other housing related transactions. Prohibited actions include discrimination based on race, color, national origin, religion, sex, familial status (including children under the age of 18 living with parents or legal custodians, pregnant women, and people securing custody of children under the age of 18), and handicap (disability).

Several federal laws have been enacted to prevent discrimination against and help improve the living environments of disabled tenants. These are ...

◆ Section 504 of the Rehabilitation Act of 1973.

◆ The Fair Housing Act of 1988.

◆ The American Disabilities Act of 1990.

We'll look a little closer at each one, but first it's important to understand what is classified as a disability.

The U.S. Department of Housing and Urban Development (HUD) defines a person with a disability as "any person who has a physical or mental impairment that substantially limits one or more major life activities; has a record of such impairment; or is regarded as having such an impairment."

In general, a physical or mental impairment includes the following:

◆ Hearing.

◆ Mobility and visual impairments.

◆ Chronic alcoholism.

◆ Chronic mental illness.

◆ Autoimmune deficiency syndrome (AIDS) and AIDS-related complexes.

◆ Mental retardation that substantially limits one or more major life activities. Major life activities include walking, talking, hearing, seeing, breathing, learning, performing manual tasks, and caring for oneself.

In other words, if someone uses a wheelchair, a cane, crutches, or a walker; has a hard time seeing, hearing, speaking, lifting/carrying, using stairs, and/or walking; or has difficulty with activities of daily living in or out of the home—such as bathing, eating, going to the bathroom, dressing, and keeping track of money, housework, and medication—they may be classified as disabled. If someone has a learning disability, developmental disability, or some other mental condition, they can also be classified as disabled.

To thoroughly examine discrimination against the disabled, we'll first look at it in relation to being a residential property manager, and then look at it in relation to being a commercial property manager.

Section 504 of the Rehabilitation Act of 1973

When it comes to housing and other basic necessities, many disabled residents receive federal funding or live in federally funded buildings. In 1973, to foster economic independence and prohibit discrimination against the disabled, Section 504 of the Rehabilitation Act was passed.

This act prohibits condo and co-op property managers and boards from discriminating against any disabled tenant who receives these federal funds and who requires reasonable accommodations and changes in rules and policies. For example, let's say that the building you are managing was once a widget factory. Today, it's a bunch of apartments, and it's not handicapped accessible. A disabled individual wishes to live there, and needs the board to modify a unit to make it happen. According to Section 504, this request must be honored, as long as it's reasonable and financially possible.

Notes from the Field

Federal law is the body of law created by the federal government. There are several important federal laws that you need to know to be a successful property manager. Some of these laws pertain just to a residential property manager, and some pertain to both residential and commercial property managers.

What Is Reasonable?

The key to understanding Section 504 of the Rehabilitation Act of 1973 is understanding the meaning of the word "reasonable." Reasonable means that what the tenant is asking for is not excessive or extreme—it's fair. A tenant asking for a ramp for wheelchair access? Yes, that's reasonable. A visually impaired tenant asks that you allow a seeing-eye dog on the premises, but animals aren't permitted in the building? Yes, that's reasonable. A temporarily disabled resident had back surgery and needs a ramp? Yes, that's reasonable.

If the request is deemed reasonable, you must comply with it and foot the bill. If your building's insurance policy doesn't cover it, a *special assessment* can be made.

def•i•ni•tion

A **special assessment** is a one-time fee collected from homeowners by the board or management to pay for something that regular monthly dues did not cover. It's usually reserved for emergency purposes only.

Unreasonable Requests

On the other hand, an unreasonable request is not fair—it's excessive and extreme. For example, a disabled tenant who asks you to do their grocery shopping. That is an unreasonable request.

How do you handle unreasonable requests? First, it's very important to listen to the request and analyze it according to the Americans with Disabilities Act (ADA), which we'll discuss in this chapter. Unsure what your answer should be according to the boundaries of the law? Consult with your attorney. If you do not follow legal procedure, you may face penalties and lawsuits.

Second, if you must say no, be kind. "That's not something I can do for you," should be nice enough, but you can also provide the tenant with a letter of explanation. Finally, if the tenant persists, explain in writing that while you would like to help, the request goes beyond the boundaries of the law, is too expensive, and so on, or have the attorney respond.

The Fair Housing Amendments Act of 1988

The Fair Housing Amendments Act of 1988 expanded on the last act, Section 504, to include all disabled persons. It bars discrimination in the sale or rental of housing on the basis of a disability. In other words, you can't stop a wheelchair-bound tenant from wanting to lease a unit. The act also requires that any new construction of multifamily buildings meet certain adaptability and accessibility requirements.

EQUAL HOUSING OPPORTUNITY

Things to Avoid

When you steer someone, you take them somewhere or guide them in a direction you think they want to go. In real estate, it's against the law, and it's covered by the Fair Housing Act. "Steering" means showing potential home buyers homes that are only in certain neighborhoods. For example, it's against the law to only show a black couple homes that are in predominately black neighborhoods.

The Americans with Disabilities Act of 1990

On July 26, 1990, President George H. W. Bush signed into law the Americans with Disabilities Act of 1990—the world's first comprehensive civil rights law for people with disabilities. The ADA prohibits discrimination against people with disabilities in employment (Title I), public services (Title II), public accommodations (Title III), and telecommunications (Title IV).

Title I

Title I of the ADA relates to employment. It prohibits discrimination in all employment practices, including job application procedures, hiring, firing, advancement, compensation, training, and other employment terms, conditions, and privileges. As a property manager in charge of hiring staff—a janitor, a concierge, a super, and so on—you cannot discriminate against a *qualified individual* because they have a disability.

def•i•ni•tion

A **qualified individual** with a disability is a person who has the skills, experience, education, or whatever other requirements a person must have to do the job you are hiring for, but who is not hired based on their disability.

Title II

Title II pertains to state and local governments. Among other items, according to the ADA, Title II says that you may not refuse to allow a person with a disability to participate in a service, program, or activity simply because the person has a disability. For example, a city may not refuse to allow a person with epilepsy to use parks and recreational facilities. A second example: a city office building is required to make an exception to the rule prohibiting animals in public areas to admit guide dogs and other service animals assisting individuals with disabilities. Title II also says …

◆ Public offices must furnish auxiliary aids and services when necessary to ensure effective communication, unless an undue burden or fundamental alteration would result.

◆ Public offices may not place special charges on individuals with disabilities to cover the costs of measures necessary to ensure nondiscriminatory treatment, such as making modifications required to provide program accessibility or to provide qualified interpreters.

Commercial Properties and the ADA

Title III pertains to public accommodations and commercial buildings. It basically says that nobody may be discriminated against—by any person who owns, leases (or leases to), or operates a place of public accommodation—because they are disabled, and should have the same opportunity to enjoy the goods, services, facilities, or accommodations of any public place. These public accommodations include inns, hotels, recreational facilities, transportation, educational facilities, restaurants, stores, care providers, and places of public displays, among other things. Bottom line? If you are a commercial property manager, make sure your building is accessible to everyone.

What this means is the ADA requires that you eliminate any architectural and communication barriers so individuals with disabilities can enjoy the same use of the goods and services that others can. Barriers must be removed when it's "readily achievable." This depends on the cost of the accommodation and what the business can financially handle. There are exceptions to this rule, including those properties on the National Register of Historic Places, so know the law.

Accommodations

Just some examples of accommodations that a commercial building must have for their disabled customers and employees include the following:

- Automatic entry doors

- Wheelchair ramps

- Grab bars

- Braille or raised letters on buttons

- Bathroom stalls with wheelchair access

There are many more aspects to supplying accommodations, and there are other Titles of the ADA, so it's best to read up on the act and be sure you know how it pertains to your job as a commercial or residential property manager.

Many businesses won't sign leases in buildings that do not comply with ADA requirements.

The Americans with Disabilities Act Amendments Act of 2008

On September 25, 2008, President George W. Bush signed the Americans with Disabilities Act Amendments Act of 2008. It made some changes to the definition of "disability." It keeps the ADA's basic definition of disability, mentioned earlier. It made some changes, however, including how "major life activities" are defined. The new changes took effect on January 1, 2009.

If a property manager or developer/owner fails to comply with the ADA requirements for either residential or commercial buildings, the Department of Justice (DOJ) may be waiting to lay the smack down. The DOJ is the federal agency that enforces the ADA. When the act is violated or ignored, they settle through lawsuits and settlement agreements. A lawsuit may be filed in federal court to enforce the ADA, and courts may order compensatory damages and back pay to remedy discrimination if the lawsuit prevails.

The penalties can be severe. According to the ADA, remedies may include hiring, reinstatement, back pay, court orders to stop discrimination, and reasonable accommodation. Compensatory damages may be awarded for actual monetary losses and for future monetary losses, mental anguish, and inconvenience. Punitive damages may be available as well, if an employer acts with malice or reckless indifference. Attorney's fees may also be awarded.

For example, Under Title III, the DOJ can obtain civil penalties of up to $55,000 for the first violation and $110,000 for any subsequent violation. The DOJ, however, may not sue a party unless negotiations to settle the dispute have failed.

Notes from the Field

When I wrote about the ADA for *The Cooperator* (www.cooperator.com), a trade journal for New York co-op and condo owners and managers, an attorney told me of two cases in which the board denied the tenant's reasonable request. Case 1: They wouldn't build a ramp. The disabled tenants proved they needed it, and won. They won $220,000. The cost of the ramp would've been cheaper. Case 2: A tenant needed an animal for healing and was denied. This tenant received more than $200,000.

If you have a disabled shareholder or unit owner who believes their rights have been violated, have them write a letter to the board. This letter should be answered within a few weeks. If not, HUD is ready to help with any problem involving housing discrimination. Refer the tenant to www.hud.gov for further information on how to file a housing complaint.

Uniform Residential Landlord and Tenant Act

The Uniform Residential Landlord and Tenant Act (URLTA) was created in the 1960s during the civil rights movement. The goal of this federal act was to make residential landlord and tenant laws more fair to all parties. Some states follow this act while other states follow a variation of it. Some of the items this act includes are …

- **Preventing landlord retaliation.** A landlord may not retaliate against a tenant by increasing the tenant's rent, by decreasing services that are due to the tenant, or by bringing or threatening to bring an action for possession of the tenant's premises because the tenant has complained to a governmental agency, has complained to a landlord that they violated the lease agreement, or has organized or become a member of a tenant's association or similar organization.

- **Providing landlord rights.** A landlord may bring an action for possession if the tenant is in default on rent; if the violation of a building, housing, or fire safety code was caused primarily by lack of reasonable care by the tenant, by a member of the tenant's family, or by another person on the premises with the consent of the tenant.

It's important to know this act since property managers act as or on behalf of landlords.

Fair Credit Reporting Act (FCRA)

The Fair Credit Reporting Act (FCRA) is another federal law that regulates the collection, dissemination, and use of consumer credit information. It was originally passed in 1990, and is enforced by the Federal Trade Commission. Property managers look at a prospective tenant's paycheck stubs, W-2 forms, cancelled checks, and credit file to make certain they have the ability to pay their rent on time. By obtaining a copy of their credit report, property managers can evaluate a tenant's background, including delinquent credit accounts.

If you are simply verifying information that your prospective tenant has given you on an application, you do not need to give notice to the tenant that you are reviewing the credit report. However, if you refuse to rent to the person or require a co-signer, a deposit, or a larger deposit compared to other tenants, you must let the consumer know why in writing. Failing to do so can result in severe penalties, including having to pay damages, costs, and attorney fees.

Why would a consumer need to know if you peeked? Because if the information you're looking at is incorrect, they need time to challenge the credit report and either correct, modify, or delete the item(s) in question within 30 days. If you are rejecting the applicant, you must inform them of ...

◆ The name, address, and phone number of the credit agency that provided the information.

◆ How they can obtain a free copy of their credit report so they can see the mistakes.

> **Notes from the Field**
>
> Let applicants know they can visit www.freecreditreport.com to get a free copy of their credit report once a year, before they apply.

After it's corrected, they may return to you, show you the amended credit report, and ask you to reconsider.

Lead-Based Paint Act

In Chapter 7, we discussed the hidden dangers of lead paint. If painted walls are disturbed—by scraping, sanding, or burning—high concentrations of lead are released into the air and inhaled. Because lead can cause a host of health problems in children and adults, there are laws regarding the proper removal of the substance, as well as required disclosures that must be followed.

For example, New York City's Local Law 1 of 2004 requires the following:

♦ **Annual notifications.** Managers or owners must notify all occupants about lead if there are children younger than six years of age residing in the unit. Owners must include a notice with each lease about owner responsibilities under the law and must provide a pamphlet informing occupants about lead. Owners must also physically inspect the units of those occupants who do not respond to determine whether there is a child under the age of six residing in the unit.

♦ **Examination of units and common areas.** Owners must investigate units in which children under the age of six reside, as well as common areas on the property, to find peeling paint, chewable surfaces, deteriorated subsurfaces, and friction and impact surfaces. This investigation must be conducted at least annually, or more often if the owner knows about a condition that may cause a lead hazard or the occupant complains about such a condition.

♦ **Correcting the problem.** The property manager must ensure remediation of lead hazards, using safe work practices and trained workers and making apartments lead safe upon turnover.

♦ **Using safe work practices.** A property manager must use safe work practices for all repairs and renovations performed in a unit in which a child under the age of six resides and in the common areas of buildings with such units. When removing lead-based paint hazards, the contractor must post signs that stay for the duration of the job. The signs must say, "Warning: Lead Work Area. Poison. No Smoking or Eating." Tenants must also be warned to stay out of the area.

State and Local Laws

Not only must a successful property manager know federal laws and legislation, but you must also be up to date on your own state's laws and regulations. This includes any state building codes.

Megan's Law

Megan's Law is a law requiring law enforcement authorities to make information available to the public regarding registered sex offenders. Each state decides what information will be made available and how it should be disseminated. Usually this information includes the offender's name, picture, address, incarceration date, and nature of their crime. The information is often displayed on free public websites, but can be published in newspapers, distributed in pamphlets, or provided through association websites or e-mail.

Megan's Law is also known as the Sexual Offender (Jacob Wetterling) Act of 1994 and requires persons convicted of sex crimes against children to notify local law enforcement of any change of address or employment after release from custody (prison or psychiatric facility). The notification requirement may be imposed for a fixed period of time (usually at least 10 years) or permanently.

Building Codes

Your state's building codes will dictate every point of construction, remodeling, and maintenance for your building, including systems, elevators, walls, and so on. Although you might think that only contractors need to know this information, it's vital that property managers have an understanding of state building codes or know where to obtain the information when it's needed.

You will need to know codes when making building alterations and repairs. State codes may govern fire prevention and sanitation codes as well.

Codes are often amended or added when something happens (often something tragic). For example, when reliable carbon monoxide detectors came on the market, the New York City building codes were changed to require that they be installed in each building. To keep on top of the most recent building codes, contact the Department of Buildings for your state. Just use the search phrase "(your state here) Department of Buildings."

Notes from the Field

If you'd like to be kept in the loop about all building code changes, create a "Google alert" for yourself. Go to www.google.com/alert and put in the term you would like Google to follow, such as "Montana building codes." Choose how often you would like to get this information. Google will search the web for all Montana building codes references and send them to you via e-mail. You can also ask your state builder's association for information.

Just like federal laws and regulations, don't violate the state and local codes either. The penalties for failing to correct any code violations can be hefty. Some states offer a grace period for correcting any violations before being fined. Violations after the grace period can result in fines ranging from several hundred to several thousand dollars.

It might sound like it's getting a little complicated, but think of local and state laws and regulations as ways to keep your building and your tenants safe and protected.

For example, one building owner failed to pay attention to local fire codes, using electric space heaters to warm the tenants instead of fixing the building's gas heaters. Tragically, a tenant died when an electric space heater that was on top of an entertainment center caught a piece of furniture on fire.

The Least You Need to Know

- ◆ A successful property manager doesn't need a law degree, but does need knowledge of some important federal, state, and local laws.

- ◆ A successful property manager knows to check with an attorney when in doubt about a legal situation.

- ◆ If you need a refresher course on legal matters, see if you are eligible to take a continuing education course.

- ◆ If you're concerned about a situation with a tenant ending up in court, make certain that you get everything in writing to avoid disputes.

Part 3

People Management

This part delves into the key skills you need to communicate with your tenants, staff, contractors, and pretty much everybody you meet each day. And because not all relationships are a bed of roses, this part teaches you how to handle conflict. You'll learn how to manage that one tenant that drives the other tenants crazy and how to evict that tenant if the conflict cannot otherwise be resolved. You'll learn how to create a better environment for tenants who are fighting like the Hatfields and the McCoys.

Finally, being a successful property manager means balancing many responsibilities and keeping the tenants and your property safe and secure. Most importantly, you'll learn how to handle emergencies—from evacuating tenants in a swift manner to talking to the press and keeping everyone informed.

Chapter 11

Personnel

In This Chapter

◆ Establishing a great team

◆ Learning personnel roles and responsibilities

◆ Hiring the best

◆ Handling problem employees

It may take a village to raise a child, but in the world of property management, it takes a team to run a building. Do you have the right players on your team? Your team may include your staff members—superintendents, concierge, janitors, housekeepers, security guards, other property managers, and more. If you manage a smaller building or property and you don't have any additional staff members, you may work with other outside team players—accountants, lawyers, contractors, and others.

Just like in football, each of you has an important position to play. But remember, you're the quarterback and the captain of the team! A captain's job is to get your team members to work well together, do their job, and do it well.

Working together, you and your team must take care of the building and its tenants. Have all of your team members been trained properly on the building's plays and strategies? Are they all working efficiently? Does everyone work well together? Do they know what is expected of them? Are you all working toward the common goal of having a well-run building and happy tenants?

This chapter explores each of your player's responsibilities, and shows you how to create a positive working environment and how to effectively communicate with your employees. And as much as you'd like to think you have the perfect team members, it's inevitable that something is going to go wrong. In this chapter, you will learn how to handle some of the problems that might arise and, as Donald Trump likes to do, learn how to say "You're fired."

Superintendents

The superintendent (also called the "super") is the person responsible for a building's day-to-day repairs and maintenance. He can also be called a porter, a caretaker, or an apartment manager. When something goes wrong—a pipe or window breaks, for example—the super is usually the first person a tenant calls.

Years ago, the super was more like the property manager. Remember Schneider from television's *One Day at a Time*? He made all the repairs, did all the paperwork, and took care of the residents' needs (including flirting with Mrs. Romano). Today, in most buildings, the super reports to the property manager and focuses on the repairs and maintenance of the building. The super's job often comes with a nice perk: most supers and their families live in the building in a free (or low-cost) nonbasement apartment. In some areas, a super is legally required to live in a building with more than 10 units.

Responsibilities

There's no one-size-fits-all job description for supers. What he does on a daily basis depends on his experience and education and your needs. It's best to have the responsibilities written out, however, just in case there are any disputes, such as "It's not my job" or "It's not in my job description." The job description should include what the super is responsible for and what he can and cannot do for a tenant or resident.

Some of the super's responsibilities may include, but aren't limited to …

- ◆ Managing and training other building staff members, including porters and housekeepers.

- Keeping the heating, ventilation, and air conditioning (HVAC), and plumbing and other mechanical equipment operating efficiently.

- Cleaning the building, both inside and out.

- Organizing and scheduling repairs, renovations, and new construction, and making sure they stay within budget.

- Supervising these repairs, renovations, and new construction projects to make sure all are done correctly and according to what was requested.

- Maintaining records of all work completed.

- Responding to any tenant complaints and requests.

- Supervising all maintenance contracts (such as lawn mowing and snow plowing).

Some management companies have a maintenance company within the management company, which includes employee maintenance coordinators, licensed contractors, and more for this department.

Skills and Education

A super doesn't need a college diploma, but some post-high-school education might be beneficial. For example, in a large building with more sophisticated HVAC systems and equipment, a super should have additional training—perhaps from a trade school—in fire safety and HVAC repair. In New York, for example, the Certificate of Fitness is required in areas that include standpipe and sprinkler systems and low-pressure oil burners.

An ideal super is experienced in, or has taken courses in, carpentry, electrical work, and HVAC maintenance and repair, and has some knowledge of local building codes. In today's high-tech world, being computer savvy is beneficial, too. Someone who wants to be a super but has less education or experience might be better suited to a smaller property as a porter, janitor, or handyman. They can gain experience and then move up the ranks. Bigger buildings and luxury properties should be left to the more experienced supers.

During their careers, supers also have opportunities to expand their knowledge by taking courses through the local builder's or real estate associations, trade organizations, trade schools, or unions. Some courses provide certificates of completion.

It's also important that your supers have people skills. They deal directly with tenants and staff every day, so having a super who's personable, friendly, patient, authoritative, and understanding is vital to your building's success. Most importantly, they need to be trustworthy because they will be gaining access to a tenant's home, store, office, etc. Later in the chapter, you will learn how to conduct a thorough background check on a potential employee.

Doormen

A doorman is the first impression of a building's personality. They are usually the first staff person that anyone encounters and often talks to when they walk through the front door. Having the right person in that job is essential. Just imagine if Mr. Smith the doorman was gruff and rude to a guest. Would anyone really want to become a tenant or resident in the building?

Responsibilities

A doorman or doorperson, because many are now women, doesn't just open doors. Like supers, one description doesn't really fit all. The job description depends on what you need to have them do. For example, they can accept packages, hail taxis, shovel walkways, greet guests, and more. Some late-night doormen are more like porters and take care of nighttime cleaning as part of their responsibilities. A doorman is also the first level of building security. They prevent unwelcome visitors, monitor security cameras, and maintain logs of delivered packages.

Some buildings also have relief doormen to cover when illness strikes or the doorman needs a day off. This is especially important because the lobby needs to be covered at all times.

Skills and Education

Being a doorman doesn't require any special education or degree, although some doormen attend security classes. They are privy to personal packages and information, so candidates' backgrounds must also be thoroughly checked before they are hired. A good doorman should be nice, have good communication skills, be attentive, and have a sense of humor. They should also be alert, reliable, and have a great attention to detail.

Notes from the Field
Peter Grech, a veteran New York doorman, says wintertime is the doorman's hardest and busiest season. Not only do they have to assist with snow removal, but also there typically are more residents home during the winter in comparison to the summer. It's the season where tenants may complain about heat, and most tenants will contact the superintendent via the doorman.

Concierge

A doormen and concierge are not the same job. The difference? A desk. A concierge sits behind the desk and directs the lobby from the chair. A doorman doesn't sit behind a desk. A concierge can handle luggage and mail, make dinner or theater reservations, and address any other requests from guests or visitors. This job definitely needs a sense of humor, especially when tenants will ask just about anything.

Responsibilities

Concierge help tenants do things they don't have time to do, or don't have the resources to do. For example, in a high-end luxury residential building, a busy executive may ask the concierge to pick up dry cleaning and make dinner reservations.

Skills and Education

This is another one of those people-person positions. A concierge should—like the doorman—be polite, friendly, and chatty. They should also know how to manage their time. It's a position that doesn't require a license or diploma, but a concierge should have extensive knowledge of your area. They should also have contacts, so they know how to quickly get the people what they want. Some concierge start as doormen and work their way up.

Notes from the Field
A concierge definitely needs a sense of humor. John Turiano, managing editor of *Westchester Magazine*, interviewed concierge and writes, "… a resident complained about birds cawing too loud outside his window. The resident expected the concierge to stand outside the window and play scarecrow … a number of residents who don't want their dogs to get wet when it's raining leave their pet with the concierge, leash looped around his/her wrist, while they run across the street to CVS or the bank."

The Hiring Process

Want to hire the best? You need to go through a thorough hiring process for each of your employees. It's important to have an effective hiring process that allows you to select the best applicants for the job. Remember, a successful property manager surrounds themselves with a bright, qualified, and efficient team.

Resumé Review

When you're hiring your staff, a resumé is your first impression of who an applicant is. It can tell a lot, both positively and negatively. What are you looking for? Job stability. Do they stay at their jobs or hop from job to job?

Things to Avoid

Has your candidate skipped years of employment? Find out why. It could be that they went back to school, decided to travel for a time period, or some other explainable reason. Then ask why they want this position. It might give you some additional insight into the type of person they are.

Background Checks

You want to hire good, trustworthy employees. Sounds simple, right? Well, you need to dig around in their backgrounds before offering them the jobs. Why? These potential employees can get into the residents' homes and into businesses, and they have access to private information, packages, and building systems.

You have a duty to provide to your tenants the best people for the job, and that means putting potential employees through a rigorous screening process to weed out candidates with records of termination or disciplinary action, or with criminal histories. How do you check someone's background? Make certain she is eligible to work in the country? Qualified?

- Call any schools the applicant listed as well as previous employers to confirm the applicant attended those schools and worked at those businesses.

- Complete a credit report check. The Fair Credit Reporting Act (FCRA) sets the standards for screening for employment and defines a background check as a consumer report. You can't get the credit report without telling your applicant.

Bad credit? Find out why. Perhaps a divorce or medical issues? If your applicant has no credit, it might be a red flag to a bigger problem.

If you choose not to hire your candidate because of the findings on the credit report, you must tell him or her and provide the applicant with a copy of the report. It gives the candidate a chance to fix the report.

Notes from the Field

Some employers are surfing the Internet and checking on Facebook and MySpace to get an idea of their possible new hires' hobbies, personal lives, and former employment and schooling (although using personal information from these sites, which is otherwise illegal to know and use against the applicant, may open the employers up to liability issues). One report in *Workplace Management* showed that 40 percent of employers are now using these sites to gauge their candidates.

♦ Criminal checks are vital. Just imagine hiring a super who enters a business after hours and assaults a young woman working overtime. It comes out later that you didn't do the criminal check on him and didn't know he had previous arrests. Your *liability* is huge. Make certain you do the same background check on all employees for the same position.

def•i•ni•tion

Liability is the state of being legally obliged and responsible. In other words, it's your fault the young girl was assaulted if you didn't do a criminal check on the employee.

Criminal checks, including restraining orders for domestic abuse; civil cases for violent incidents; and military, federal, and court records, can be completed online or by professional security companies. What if you uncover a red flag? Consider the nature of the situation. How old were they? What happened? Were they upfront about it? If so, perhaps reconsider. If not, you may want to take a pass.

What NOT to Ask

There are questions you simply cannot ask an applicant during an interview because the questions may be considered discriminatory and can land you in some major legal hot water. For example, you can't ask the applicant questions about race or color. Your limitations can get tricky. For example, you can ask someone for their date of birth, but you can't ask them their age. So, be careful.

Drug Tests

Drug tests are a test of either urine, sweat, blood, or other body fluids to determine if the applicant has recently been using any drugs. Drug tests can be a part of a successful employee background check.

Other Team Players

Throughout your career, you'll also be relying on outside experts—architects, engineers, attorneys, and accountants—to help you do your job. It's important to nurture those professional relationships in the same way you would treat your staff.

> ### Notes from the Field
>
> "Not everything runs smoothly or easily with contractors, but I do find that contractors are a lot happier to hear from you and work with you if you pay them quickly. I usually get a check out for the invoice within a couple of days. They're used to chasing after their money so this just makes them happier to do business with you—and hopefully more responsive and cooperative!"
>
> —Carol Hodes, Deerwood Farms Homeowners Association, Old Bridge, New Jersey

Architects

Whether you're remodeling a common area or planning a complex commercial development, an architect helps turn the vision into reality. Architects are working more with property managers and developers, especially when it comes to incorporating new green technologies. Bringing an architect on board early and effectively telling them what you're looking for is the key to a successful project.

Attorneys

From time to time, you'll need to consult with an attorney about various legal concerns, such as lease negotiations, dispute settlements, and contract reviews. It's important to have a qualified attorney or law firm on your side. Attorneys can be set up on a monthly or annual retainer, which may cover payment for reading contracts, making telephone calls, and attending board meetings. Attorneys can also be hired on a case-by-case basis. It's best to compare prices before deciding on which way to go.

What's the best way to maximize your professional relationship with your attorney? First, use judgment when calling. Attorneys are costly, so try to resolve some problems before reaching out. If you're noticing that a situation is getting out of hand, however, don't wait too long to call for advice. That could backfire as well. Also, consider whether your attorney needs to attend each and every meeting. Instead, can you forward them a copy of the meeting minutes or can you have them on the phone for a conference call?

One thing you shouldn't do is sign any contracts with vendors or contractors without having an attorney review them. You don't want to be legally bound to a contract that has dire consequences.

Accountants

Remember that we discussed the importance of accountants in Chapter 5. They are hired to partner with you or take care of the fiscal responsibilities of the building or association. These responsibilities may include completing tax returns, budgets, and financial statements, and providing regular financial information and advice. Accountants also keep on top of any tax law changes.

Communication is important with all staff and team members. An accountant helps you spot financial problems and shows you ways to cut costs, so it's important to let them know as soon as something unexpected arises that might shake up the budget.

Troubleshooting

Solving problems is a large portion of your job. Whether it's a building issue, tenant concern, or contractor situation, you'll have to find solutions. When troubleshooting staff problems, it's important to understand why the problem is happening in the first place.

When it comes to your staff, the goal is to prevent turnover. You want your staff to stay and work with you. It's a time-consuming process to hire, train, fire, and hire again. You therefore need to think of your staff as an investment. It's also important to have satisfied, motivated employees working for you.

Retraining

Jane does most of her job, but seems to forget to complete several responsibilities. Is it possible that she doesn't understand those tasks at hand or hasn't been adequately trained? Have you talked to Jane and asked her what the problem is? If she doesn't understand the problem, train her or have another staff member train her. Check in with her and see if she's doing okay.

Improving Morale

When the economy is suffering, staff members may be going through personal crises and morale may be suffering. A good solid team may suddenly be tense and irritable. The solution? How about team-building activities? Some sort of a special surprise break—something to ease the tension? It's important for a manager to recognize when their staff members may be feeling the pressure and to find a solution to ease it.

Really Listening

Most importantly, your door (figuratively and literally speaking) should always be open. Employees should feel comfortable talking to you and sharing their problems. Instead of saying, "Not now!" or "This is NOT a good time," tell your employee "I really want to be able to focus on what you're saying … can we talk on Monday?" And, when you do meet with the employee, turn off your BlackBerry and the "you've got mail" computer guy and LISTEN.

Motivating Employees

Roxana Hammock, regional manager of Guardian Management LLC, considers motivating her employees to be one of her most important duties. She says when her team members are motivated and driven they are more productive and successful. She encourages them to act as owners and not as employees and treat the properties as if it were their own.

Before motivating them, she asks herself some basic questions about the employee:

◆ What are his or her career goals and expectations?

◆ Does she want to be in the current position for the next 10 years, or is she looking to grow?

The best way to motivate someone, she says, is to empower them to make decisions in their work. When someone calls me with an issue, she asks, "What do you think we should do?" It makes them feel they are important and helps them to brainstorm solutions, so that next time this happens they already know what to do. She also …

◆ Offers praise. "I recognize team members' successes either through public recognition (a little personalized card telling them how excited and pleased I am with their specific accomplishment), taking them to lunch, or awarding a few hours off at the end of the week."

◆ Leads by example. "One time, the staff was down because the grounds weren't in good shape and they never seemed to have the time to catch up. So, I scheduled a clean-up day and we spent the entire day cleaning the outside and talking about challenges and successes. We accomplished several things: a better-looking property, team building, a good workout, and motivated employees. I received comments from all the team members telling me how motivating the day was. They know that I understand the challenges, that I am there to help them succeed, and that—no matter how difficult it gets—I believe in them."

◆ Sets S.M.A.R.T. goals. "Setting specific, measurable, attainable, realistic, and timely goals and agreeing on those goals is crucial to our success and their motivation."

Language and Immigration

Your employees can come from a vast array of ethnic and sociological backgrounds, which can often pose its own distinct challenges. In some cases, staff members speak other languages, and their English isn't good or is nonexistent. There's a learning curve involved. Employees need to speak the same language as you do, but the good news is bilingual staff members can help when incidents arise with residents that speak other languages, too.

When dealing with a diverse staff, get to know the employees not as an ethnic group but as people, and appreciate the differences.

Managers and superintendents should work together to develop effective training strategies, promote consistent messages, and build communication skills between staff and residents.

Productivity Tips

If your staff consists of diverse ethnic backgrounds, consider hiring a management company to provide diversity training. The companies often help diffuse any potential animosity.

Firing an Employee

Donald Trump isn't going to be the only one who utters the words "You're fired!" to an employee. Eventually, you may have to let someone go. But, like everything else in this job, you have to do it right, or you could be facing a wrongful termination lawsuit.

If you've already talked to your employee regarding the problems—perhaps poor performance or attitude—and the employee hasn't improved, it's time to let them go. It's not easy to do, but it can be done professionally, legally, and respectfully. Here is an example:

Jane Smith is your building concierge and has been repeatedly late for work, isn't completing her daily tasks, and just isn't working out. You know you need to terminate her. So what do you do first? The best thing to do first is to document everything. Are you giving her another chance and have expectations about her performance? Have her sign a document stating so.

> **Things to Avoid**
>
> If you are terminating an employee, make certain to get all keys or cards that provide access to the building or property. If they are familiar with security codes, look into having the codes changed.

If you have given her warnings about her performance, document those warnings and the dates and responses from the employee. When you meet with her or make the decision to terminate her, have another employee or manager on hand as a witness. Again, document it all, including any severance pay the employee will receive.

It's Against the Law

There are state and federal laws that will prohibit you from firing your employee for certain reasons. Make sure you are familiar with these reasons before you let the employee go.

Discrimination

Federal law states that you cannot fire an employee because of their race, gender, national origin, disability, religion, or age (if the person is older than 40). You also can't fire someone because they are pregnant or have given birth. Check with your state laws as well for additional antidiscrimination laws.

Refusal to Take a Lie Detector Test

Money is missing and you want your employees to take a polygraph. James refuses. You can't fire him. He's covered under the federal Employee Polygraph Protection Act, which prohibits you from firing an employee who refuses to take it.

Alien Status

If your employee is legally allowed to work in the United States, you can't fire them because they are an immigrant. The federal Immigration Reform and Control Act prohibits it.

Retaliation

Tom, your employee of three years, has been at jury duty for a few weeks now and the case shows no signs of ending. Work is piling up and you'd really love to fire him and find someone new. Hold on … you can't do it. It's illegal to fire someone for retaliation simply because they are exercising a legal duty, such as jury duty. You also can't fire someone because they are exercising their statutory right—for example, filing a workers' compensation claim or complaining that their work space doesn't meet federal health and safety rules.

There are many other reasons why you can't fire an employee—for example, if they refuse to commit something illegal—so the best advice is to contact your attorney before letting your employee go, so you are not sued for wrongful termination.

The Least You Need to Know

◆ Think of your staff as your team—you are captain and it's important to make it work or get rid of the players who aren't doing their job.

◆ Ask the staff for suggestions on improving the workplace.

◆ If an outside team player—such as an accountant or a lawyer—isn't doing his job, it's okay to replace him with someone who better fits the job.

◆ Keep yourself up to date with hiring and firing practices by reading online articles geared toward human resource specialists.

Chapter 12

Tenant Relations

In This Chapter

- Creating a happy building
- Complaints, complaints, complaints
- Handling the Hatfields and the McCoys
- Evicting when necessary

Ideally, you want tenants who don't cause any trouble. They get along with each other and with you, pay their rent on time, and don't cause any conflicts. But no matter what you do, some of your tenants—and it doesn't matter if it's a commercial or residential property—are going to butt heads with other tenants and with you. The problems can range from simple noise issues or late-night parties to problems that are far more serious, throwing building harmony into a tailspin or even putting the physical or mental well-being of other tenants in jeopardy. How do you deal with tenants like these?

This chapter shows you several productive and effective steps you can take to improve the relationships between tenants and ultimately create a positive tenant atmosphere. These steps include complaint letters, effective communication practices, and mediation/arbitration for when problems between tenants just can't be resolved.

Start at the Beginning

Every relationship starts the same way—two people getting to know each other—and the tenant and property manager relationship is no different. To get things off on the right foot, the terms of the relationship should be established at the beginning. The tenant should know what is required on their part when they sign the lease or move in. It's your responsibility to see that the tenants understand, because tenants do not carefully read their leases. Let them know verbally what rules they need to follow and what they should do if they have any problems with another tenant. Communication is key to any successful relationship.

Communication

One of the most important techniques you can use to create a positive tenant relationship is good communication. The Internet and other technologies have changed the face of property management; you can now have faster access to your tenants, the ability to respond quickly, new options for e-mailing bills, and more. Unfortunately, technologies have taken away from face-to-face meetings—many managers depend on a quick e-mail to solve the problem and stay in contact with tenants. It's okay to use these technologies, but tenants also need to know who you are. Every once in a while they need to see your face.

Personal Touch

Of course, if you are a manager of thousands of units or hundreds of stores, you probably won't have time for face-to-face contact with every tenant on a regular basis. When the opportunity presents itself, however, perhaps while examining a particular repair problem or attending a tenant social event, chat it up a bit and let the tenants know you care about making them happy.

But, remember that Isaac Newton had it right: for every action, there's an equal and opposite reaction. This is especially important when you are dealing with upset tenants. Say Mr. Jones, a tenant in unit 1A, calls you yelling, screaming, and cursing that he can't take the behavior of Mr. Johnson and his family, the next-door neighbors in 1B. You arrange to meet face-to-face so you can try to calm him down. In this scenario, one of two things can happen. First, he can be pleased that you cared enough to take time out of your day to stop by and help him solve the problem.

Second, he can become enraged and launch a personal attack on your ability to manage. If he does this, a successful property manager doesn't react with anger and hostility toward Jones. Instead, you should find another method of dealing with the hostile tenant and helping him to resolve a problem. If you engage in a verbal battle, nothing is going to get solved on either side and your reaction is likely to cause a bigger explosion of his temper. In a situation like this, it's vital to accept any responsibility of the situation that might be yours and then offer to find the tenant some solutions.

Association Websites

In the past, tenants would contact you by either leaving you a message on your answering machine or leaving a note at the office and waiting for a response. Today, online portals are a great way to keep the lines of communication open between residents, board members, staff, and management. An online portal is a website where tenants can log in and post maintenance requests, complaints, and comments, and find out about upcoming social events, chat with each other, and leave messages. By having multiple ways to reach you, a tenant can feel comfortable that you'll respond in a timely, efficient manner to their request or concerns. (On the flip side, however, tenants may expect their e-mails answered almost as quickly as they send them. Make sure you set up guidelines so residents know how quickly they can expect a response.)

Two companies that provide these websites are Association Voice (www.associationvoice.com) and BuildingLink (www.buildinglink.com). Both companies offer such features as the following:

- Preformatted websites

- Archiving

- Newsletters

- Discussion rooms

- Spreadsheets

- Record keeping

- Special sections for the board of directors

- Section for doormen to note deliveries

- Section for requested maintenance tasks

Productivity Tips

To save time from repeating answers to tenants' questions over and over again, set up a Frequently Asked Questions (FAQ) section on the community website. Residents can search and find answers to their most commonly asked questions.

◆ Ability to add signatures and pictures for identity

◆ Secure payment sections for fees and rents

Management companies or associations can rent these websites for a small monthly fee, the cost of which is divided and added into the resident's monthly management fees. One common concern residents have about websites like these, however, is identity theft and Internet "phishing" scams in which identity thieves use bank logos and attempt to con consumers out of credit card numbers and other financial data. These websites protect passwords, so educate tenants on using the sites. Also, let them know not to respond to any e-mails (or click on any links in the e-mails) that ask for passwords or bank account numbers.

> **Productivity Tips** _____
>
> Remember that not all residents have computers or cell phones, so make certain that you're using communication techniques that reach all tenants.

Handling Disagreements

The reality is there are many different personalities that live, work, or volunteer under one roof or on one property. Disagreements are bound to happen. Some of the most common complaints between tenants include excessive noise, smoking, leaving belongings outside the unit, stealing laundry, not locking doors after exiting or entering, and subletting.

How you handle a complaint is going to depend on a variety of factors. For example, handling a dispute between residents of a co-op or condo will depend on what's written in the bylaws. A dispute at a single family homeowners' association or between two commercial residents will be handled differently. Regardless of how it's handled, the goal is to solve the problem before it gets to litigation. Once lawyers become involved, it costs the building money, so litigation should be the last thing on everyone's mind.

Stay Out of It

The first step to solving a problem between two tenants should be to step back and see if the tenants can solve the problems on their own.

If you notice that's not going too well, don't wait too long before stepping in. A champion property manager tries to solve the problem before it gets out of control. Keep on top of the situation and listen to both sides. For example, you may find out that one tenant comes home from work and blasts his music clear through the dinner hour. The other tenant has repeatedly tried to talk to the first tenant about lowering the music, but the first tenant doesn't stop. The first tenant approaches you to help the situation, especially since the second tenant isn't breaking any rules (a certain level of noise is usually allowed until later in the evening). Don't wait until the anger bubbles over from the tenants to do something.

Remember, when a situation arises, you have a job to do. Of course, it's inevitable that you may become friendly with some of the tenants, but do not give anyone preferential treatment, even if a tenant asks for it because of your friendship. Your priority is to remain professional and ethical.

Things to Avoid

If a tenant poses a potential threat or presents a danger to the tenants' or staff members' safety, call the authorities immediately.

By keeping on top of the music situation mentioned previously, you find out that the second tenant didn't know that the first tenant works nights and sleeps days, or has young children who go to bed early. Or, you may find out that the second tenant is new to the area and didn't read the rules closely for playing music. Problem solved.

Complaint Letters

Tenants may write complaint letters (or complaint e-mails) to you to tell you about a situation. It could be a tenant-to-tenant situation or something else they want to complain about. If they have taken the time to write to you about a tenant-to-tenant situation, chances are they've already tried to approach the tenant with their complaint and have been unsuccessful. Do not ignore these letters/e-mails. Get in touch with the tenant who is complaining as quickly as possible to rectify the situation. If you cannot offer then a quick solution, at least acknowledge their letter and let them know when and how you will be handling it.

You may also be the one who sends complaint letters. For example, if you have approached both sides of a complaint and the problem has not been resolved, sending a letter of complaint to the person causing the problem is usually the next step. (This complaint letter is usually from the board of directors or building attorney.) This is especially important so you can keep written documentation of how a complaint has been handled. Written correspondence is especially effective if the tenant is in violation of the building's bylaws or proprietary laws or house laws.

Mediation/Arbitration

Still no change to a problem? Oftentimes, tenants who don't see a quick resolution will begin to get frustrated and threaten legal action. But forget Judge Judy for now. There is another method to help parties resolve problems before stepping in any courtroom. It's called alternative dispute resolution (ADR), and the concept is simple: both sides meet with a neutral party mediator, who will try to work things out. The ADR process is a confidential one in which both parties can talk freely. Commercial mediators are also available to meet each side in a caucus. During the caucus, each side speaks confidentially. The mediator listens to both views and comes to a solution that both sides agree on.

If mediation doesn't work, it's time to bring in an arbitrator. An arbitrator is as close as the parties will get to being in front of a judge without actually stepping in a courtroom. The arbitrator hears both sides and can render a binding verdict. Still no solution? Now it might be time for litigation.

> ### Notes from the Field
>
> Find a mediator and start the process rolling for mediation by visiting the American Arbitration Association (www.adr.org) or working with a private ADR company. With ADR, there's no filing fee to initiate a mediation or fee to request that the AAA invite parties to mediate. The cost is based on the hourly mediation rate published on the mediator's AAA profile.

Let your tenants know that arbitration and mediation are available, and work closely with the tenants to get any and all problems resolved as quickly as possible. Dealing with a disruptive, unpleasant, problem resident is hard on everybody—including the neighbors, the board of directors, and management. That said, everyone should work together to efficiently and effectively resolve problems. Like any argument, the more it festers, the worse it's going to be. The tension will then spill over to other tenants.

Noise Control

Noise complaints are probably the number one reason tenants have problems with one another. It could be someone having a party into the wee hours of the morning, blasting their favorite Aerosmith album, trying to console a crying newborn baby, or even fighting with their children or their partner. In a commercial building, there could be complaints about noise from factories, machinery, construction work, alarms, radios, and other irritants. How can you quiet things down?

Tenant Education

If you're getting more than your normal share of noise complaints, it might be a good time to educate your tenants about local noise laws or any noise reduction requirements that are in their lease or bylaws. For example, in Milwaukee, Wisconsin, you can send a copy of the Milwaukee Nuisance Noise Ordinance flyer from the Department of Neighborhood Services (DNS). It includes such suggestions as the following:

- If you receive a Notice of Noise Violation from DNS, discuss it with your tenants. If the lease is month to month, consider serving a 14- or 28-day notice to end the lease due to a lease violation or warn them that the next such incident will result in eviction.

- If the lease is greater than month to month, give a five-day notice to cure and explain the consequences of a second noise violation.

- If you receive a second notice, consider an eviction action as an alternative to you being assessed a tax lien for police and administration costs.

You can also regularly remind tenants about their noise laws through e-mail, newsletters, or on the association website.

Write a Letter

This is one of those situations where a short letter could solve the problem. The letter should address the noise complaint, point out the noise laws, and ask the tenant to correct the situation as quickly as possible. As said before, when there is a complaint, write a letter to the tenant and save a copy for your records should it be needed as evidence if the case ends up in court.

Contact the Authorities

If the tenant still won't respond to a complaint letter, the tenant doing the complaining may contact the authorities, who can issue a noise violation notice. The tenant should tell the authority what the complaint is and when it occurs, and provide their name and phone number. Most areas allow noise complaints to be filed anonymously to protect the tenant. Contacting the authorities is usually enough pressure to stop the person in violation from continuing.

Special Circumstances

From time to time, when dealing with tenants, you're going to have problems that aren't your typical run-of-the-mill problems, and there's no handbook that describes how to handle the situation. For example, there are special considerations with the elderly and illegal activities. Remember, a successful property manager handles any circumstance from the norm to the ridiculous ethically and professionally.

The Elderly

Mrs. Jones is a 75-year-old woman who has lived alone since her husband of 20 years passed away about 5 years ago. Until a few months ago, Mrs. Jones was a sweet, healthy, independent woman, but lately she's been exhibiting signs that her mental health may be deteriorating. There have been several occasions where Mrs. Jones has been wandering alone at night and has been found dirty and hungry.

In this case, Mrs. Jones may no longer be able to take care of herself. She may not be a risk to you or your other tenants yet, but that can change. If you believe she may be a risk to herself or to other residents, you may have to contact her family and explain the situation or contact protective services.

Illegal Activity

If you suspect that your tenants are engaging in an illegal activity—drugs, stealing, vandalism, big-scale gambling (not a weekly poker or blackjack game) etc.—in the building or on the property, it's vital to contact your local police department or drug enforcement agency as soon as possible. Illegal activities such as growing or selling drugs can spread very quickly, and it's important that you put an immediate stop to it. Landlords and property managers are required to make sure the property is secured for the safety of your tenants. This is important if you know that crime activity has previously occurred on the property. For example, if the property has been broken into before, you must provide the building with better security systems, including locks, lighting, and deadbolts. You have a duty to keep your tenants, your staff, and yourself safe.

Effective Eviction

You can evict a tenant for several reasons:

- A tenant does not pay rent on time.
- A tenant is being destructive to the property.
- A tenant poses a risk to other tenants.
- A tenant won't leave after the lease has expired.

In the book *Secrets to a Successful Eviction for Landlords and Property Managers* by Carolyn Gibson (Atlantic Publishing Company, 2008), she says that—believe it or not—there is a positive side to eviction (for property managers anyway). You'll send a message to other tenants that you're serious regarding the rules about rent and behavior. Keep in mind, however, that it's important to follow the rules and regulations of effective eviction.

Co-Op and Condos

In a co-op, there are special rules and regulations that must be followed when evicting a tenant. A co-op tenant must be given a notice of eviction, and once this has been done they have three to five days to answer the complaints that are forcing the eviction. If a shareholder does not answer the complaints within five days, the co-op can obtain a default judgment (they are evicted by the default of not answering). You can then obtain an "order of eviction" or a "writ of possession" and have the tenant removed by the local sheriff or marshal. You cannot remove the tenant's belongings from the apartment.

Things to Avoid

A tenant can overturn an eviction decision if the board didn't follow the rules or acted outside their authority.

Condominiums

It's very hard to evict someone who owns a condominium. Owning a condo is similar to buying a home; a condominium owner actually owns the unit they live in (not the shares). Even if the homeowner doesn't pay their common charges, they can't be evicted—or it would be extremely difficult. Instead, this would call for a foreclosure action to begin or a lawsuit to try and win back those charges. A condominium rental, however, can be subject to eviction, but check with your attorney.

Commercial Evictions

Commercial tenants can be evicted for not paying their rent. Once they are given a notice of eviction, commercial tenants must fix any violations within 5 to 10 days.

A commercial tenant really doesn't want to be evicted. Eviction can be detrimental to their business—they have to move, set up a new location, and pay the costs of the new location. In addition, they are still forced to pay the costs of their eviction. As a result, some commercial tenants are more eager to settle the problem and not be evicted.

In some cases, however, it may be in the building's best interest not to evict, but to work with the tenant and settle any differences instead. For example, thanks to the harsh economy, customers are cutting back on their dry cleaning. Johnson's Dry Cleaners is feeling the pinch and has fallen behind on their rent payments. But the company has been a good tenant, and they really don't want to close up shop.

After a long conversation with them—good tenant relations—you find out that they can afford to pay a lower monthly rent, on a temporary basis, until things turn around. Without talking to them, you might have lost a good tenant. As a result, they sign a new agreement to pay the new rent for six months, then review the payment situation. Although you lost a little financially on the rent, it's nothing compared to the court costs that would have been paid, the paperwork that needed to be filed, and the time lost spent on the eviction process.

Counter Claims

When evicted, some tenants may file a lawsuit against the landlord, demanding that the eviction proceedings be stopped. They may put in a claim that management didn't follow procedures or didn't make repairs that they requested. In other words, they will do what they need to do to blame someone else and have the eviction removed. An eviction doesn't look good on the tenant's record, especially if they try to move to another building.

Some legal websites recommend to tenants that, due to the heavy financial risk that comes with eviction, it's better to stay and sue the landlord than risk eviction.

Going to Trial

If your tenant has gone through any of the other steps—mediation and arbitration—and is finally at litigation, you should have all of your ducks in a row (although in many cases it's the landlord that is taken to trial). Make sure you have documentation (and copies of documents to provide the court and the jury).

Obtain counseling. In most areas, there are lawyers who handle evictions on a regular basis for landlords of large-scale buildings. If you don't know how to find an attorney, consider asking a major landlord in the area who they use.

After the Eviction

Once you receive a writ of possession to evict a tenant, the tenant has a few days to evict on their own, depending on local and state laws. If you need assistance, you could have a sheriff or a constable help with the eviction. The sheriff can physically remove the tenant and lock the tenant out of the unit. He can also take all of the tenant's belongings that have been left in the unit. Management cannot enter the unit until the tenant is gone.

The Least You Need to Know

◆ It's all about communication—open lines of communication keep you informed of what your tenants need and what problems might arise.

◆ Rules and regulations exist for a reason. As property manager, you'll have to follow them when evicting someone.

◆ When in doubt about eviction, consult with your attorney.

Chapter 13

Board Communications

In This Chapter

- ◆ Learning the basics of boards
- ◆ Holding productive meetings
- ◆ Working through communication problems

If you manage a cooperative or condominium association, you'll be dealing directly with a board of directors. A board of directors, as has been mentioned before, is a group of volunteers who are unit owners that devote their time to the association. They act as a governing body for the condominium and, thanks to the Condominium Act, they have powers to control what is permitted to take place and not to take place in both the individual units and the common areas.

As property manager, your responsibility is to work with the board as a team. This means being accessible to the board members, talking to them about building concerns, and handling any and all concerns or emergencies they have told you about. Working with a board is like having multiple bosses to whom you must report, who will analyze and comment on your work and performance and who will make decisions and prioritize certain tasks.

Unfortunately, this relationship doesn't always go smoothly. Boards and managers can bicker over many things. Managers aren't happy when members contact them about nonessential items during off hours, or harass them with minor concerns that could wait until the next day or the next meeting. In addition, board officers can change each year, making it difficult for you to adjust to a variety of styles and personalities. This chapter will discuss the various roles of the board and the relationship between you and the board. In addition, it will provide several strategies for creating a successful working environment with the board of directors.

Meet Your Board

It's time to meet your fictional board of directors. There's Mr. Johnson, a sweet 61-year-old man who has been a resident and member of the association for 20 years. He knows the neighborhood and has been through many board changes. He's also held many positions on the board—treasurer, vice president, and president—and has headed several committees. He is currently serving as treasurer, a time-consuming position that involves detailed management reports and invoices, reviewing financial matters, and reviewing the budget. Volunteers with a financial background are often asked to serve as treasurer; Mr. Johnson has a banking background, so he is qualified to see where the building is financially and make monetary decisions. He doesn't like confrontation, but he speaks up when he feels that something isn't going right.

Next, there is Ms. Appleton, a young, fresh-faced 25-year-old woman who just purchased her first home and is excited about making a difference on the board. She has a great heart and a lot of ideas, although she doesn't really have a lot of board experience yet.

Mr. Chan is a hard-working doctor who is always late for meetings. But, after working 72-hour shifts at the hospital, the board members try to understand and schedule meetings around these shifts.

Mrs. Curry is a stay-at-home mom with three children and is the secretary of the association. Her job is to take the minutes of the meeting and keep track of paperwork.

Finally, the president of your association board is Mr. O'Malley, who works hard at his day job as the office manager of a local dentist practice and attends various association meetings and functions at night. He's stressed out, but he's done a lot of good for the association and you and he have a straightforward, easygoing professional relationship.

You're lucky. You'll be working with a very talented, hard-working cooperative board. But it doesn't always work out that way. Some property managers have had to deal with some really interesting characters. In some cases, these are selfish, power-hungry people who want to get themselves elected to a board simply to push their own agenda, or to get a rule passed that means something personal to them. Then there are those board members who have even resorted to breaking the rules, and sometimes even the law. For example, here are a few true stories:

◆ The president of a condo association was arrested after allegedly taking ballots from under the neighbor's door. The president was running for reelection and wanted to guarantee her victory (she didn't count on her competitor installing a surveillance camera because of past election fraud concerns).

◆ A board president and board member were not paying their assessments, while everyone else was … for the past decade.

◆ A board treasurer repeatedly put his hand in the "kitty" and helped himself to much of the association's money. He was eventually busted.

Know Your Responsibilities

What you are responsible for and what the board is responsible for should be outlined in your contract. One of the biggest obstacles in creating a successful working environment with the board, however, is that the line can often be blurred as to who does what. For example, a tenant may go to a board member to discuss a building issue instead of to you, or vice versa. Make sure the responsibilities are outlined from the beginning and, if a concern arises, address it at your next meeting with responsibilities in hand.

Your responsibility to the board is to provide them with the information they need to make their decisions. Their job is to take this information and use it to make those decisions and to also carry out whatever goals the board has set for the association regarding the building, the staff, financial issues, and so on.

Board Complaints

Your board may be doing a good job, but occasionally there will be complaints about them from the tenants. One of the biggest complaints is that board members do not respond promptly to shareholder or owner complaints, or worse, they don't respond at all. Polite inquiries and even urgent problems are all met with silence, and repeated requests for action seem to fall on deaf ears.

It's been said before, but it must be said again: good communication—between managers, agents, shareholders, and board members—is the key to running a successful, solvent co-op or condo building. When the lines of communication break down at any point in this group, problems and animosity are almost unavoidably the result. Why do the lines of communication break down? It could be any number of reasons, including:

- The board is busy and overwhelmed.

- A board member has a personal crisis that has interfered with the work that the board needs to do.

- The board is waiting for answers from outside parties, who have yet to return their calls.

Board Relationships

How a board responds to a tenant when approached should be written in a protocol. All tenants and members should be familiar with the protocol and follow it.

For example, if a tenant has a broken pipe that needs to be fixed, they should know if they contact the super, the board, or the property manager (who may then delegate the responsibilities to the super). This chain of command can be different in every building, although the typical protocol in this situation is to call the super about the broken pipe first. If it's not taken care of by the super within a reasonable amount of time, the tenant should then contact you. If, however, you fail to complete your responsibility to the tenant, he has the right to complain to the board of directors.

Board Communication

Sharon Williams has been a shareholder for seven years in the MyHome Condominiums in Dream, USA. She has asked the superintendent to make several repairs. Unfortunately, the large association's only super is backlogged with repair orders. Williams talked to her property manager next—the third manager that the board has hired in three years—to take care of the problem, and he is also swamped. Williams, who becomes extremely frustrated with the situation, writes a letter of complaint to the board of directors. The board's responsibility is to answer her letter and then take steps to resolve her complaint.

If a tenant like Williams has a concern and goes straight to the board to complain, it should be your responsibility to step in and help alleviate a shareholder's concern. You can do this by improving the board's response time to shareholder complaints.

Shareholder Response

If the shareholder has followed the protocol and notified the appropriate person (for example, the super), the complaint should be immediately acknowledged. If the shareholder doesn't receive a response from the super and files a complaint with you, the manager, you should respond to it immediately as well and let the tenant know what the status is. It should *not* get to the board of directors, unless it is something that directly falls under their responsibility.

If you cannot respond to the tenant within a few days, the shareholder should at least be told why. Drop her an e-mail—the preferred method, just to keep a paper trail of complaints—or call her and let her know exactly why her complaint will take a few days to resolve. Perhaps you need additional information, or you need to contact an expert, or the person you need the information from is away on vacation. Just let them know.

Keeping Up to Date

Not only should the tenants be kept informed, but the board should be, too. You are generally responsible for providing the board with a weekly report that states what is happening in the building and on the property and what projects have been accomplished. These reports should contain any invoices that have come in, checks that need signatures, and any correspondence they need to see. You can also assist the board by drafting reply letters or, if you have already responded to a particular problem, you can show them a copy of your reply. Be prepared with anything the board needs to know when you sit down for your regular meeting.

The Costly Price of Silence

Believe it or not, the board doesn't have a legal responsibility to respond to its shareholders. What it does have, however, is a political responsibility because, if shareholders are upset at the board's lack of response, the board can eventually be voted out by the shareholders. If you are part of this silence, shareholders can complain to the board and you can lose your job.

As scary as it sounds, some disgruntled tenants have taken their complaints about their building's board and management to the Internet. On various trade journal or community websites, tenants post questions, concerns, and complaints, looking for assistance. Unfortunately, some comments include the real names and/or addresses of their buildings. These comments can be extremely detrimental to your building's reputation. A future tenant searching the Internet for information on the building may read these comments and decide not to become a tenant.

Things to Avoid

Want to know what's being said about your company or building on the Internet? Create what's called a Google Alert. Go to www.google.com/alerts and follow the directions. You'll insert your building or company name and decide if you want notifications as they come in or on a daily basis (daily is better). Google will provide you with a list of entries when your name, your management company's name, or your building name has been found.

For example, this real-life comment was found on a trade journal website before going to press: "Help! Our property manager is taking advantage of us. She hasn't shown us any financials, budgets or anything else. Our board members continue to obey whatever she says, and she attends their private meetings as well as running the shareholders meetings, taking the minutes and answering for the board members during the meetings."

Productivity Tips

If there is no system in place for how shareholders or tenants should complain to the board, develop one. Notify the tenants by using e-mail, websites, flyers, and so on.

The complaint goes on to say that the manager charges the tenants a fee to view their own documents, doesn't allow the tenants to see contracts, and is friends with both the attorney and accountant. At the time of this printing, the building's location was listed. Not good.

Rules of the Game

It's 11:30 P.M., and you've just settled down after a long day at work. You're cuddling with your spouse, the kids are in bed, and you're enjoying the *Tonight Show* … when the phone rings. It's a board member who is sorry to bother you, but who just has a quick question. You—the utmost professional that you are—answer his question, but make a mental note to discuss the rules of the game at the next board meeting.

Okay, it's not a game, it's your career. But, even though you are available to the board 24 hours a day, it doesn't mean they should call you at all hours to discuss minor things. Unless there is an emergency in the building, a board should respect your time away from the job unless absolutely necessary. It's important to establish some ground rules so both sides play fairly. For example, board members should only call you at home or off hours in certain situations:

- The building is on fire. That's a given.

- A building system breaks down. If the building is without heat or hot water, it's okay to call. (But, depending on the building, it may be suggested that the board member call the superintendent first. The super can then contact the property manager if they see a need.)

- There is a leak. If the hot water system has not only broken but is also leaking all over the basement, it's okay to call. But, again, depending on your building's protocol, the board member may want to reach out to the super first.

- A staff member quits. If your superintendent has suddenly packed up his tools and quit, it's okay for a board member to call you.

Then there are situations that can wait until you get into the office the next day. Those situations are:

- Bookkeeping. If a board member has a question about a deposit or a financial report, or a concern about an upcoming expense, it can wait until the next day and, in some cases, the next weekly or monthly meeting.

- Personal favors. Board members really shouldn't be asking for personal favors. But, if there's something they want to discuss with you privately, they should do so during regular working hours.

- To check on a request. If it's an emergency request, it might be suitable that the board member calls you after hours. But, if they are checking to see if you looked up the names of a new landscaping company, it can wait until you're in the next working day.

Make it clear to the board—in an authoritative, but not demanding tone—that repetitive calls over a short time period are stressful and not very productive. If the board needs to contact you off hours, they can try via e-mail, so that you can respond to them at a time that is convenient for you.

Board Meetings

As manager, you will be attending many meetings, including monthly (or sometimes biweekly) co-op or condo board meetings and committee meetings. These meetings are generally held at night because the volunteers usually have day jobs. Your presence at these meetings is very important because you—and the board—need to stay up to date on what's happening.

Boards make decisions and vote at these meetings. For example, they may vote on a remodeling project that needs to be completed, an assessment to pay for a new roof, or a new policy. Of course, you can read the minutes of each meeting to know what's going on, but it's much more effective if you attend all of the meetings (it might also be a job requirement). You may have input or suggestions that may be pertinent to that vote. It is also a good idea to have something spelled out in your contract as to how often you meet with the board. Specify time limits for these meetings, too. Board meetings can drag on, but limiting them can get the meetings moving quicker and more effectively.

Depending on the building, the meetings can be run quite differently. Some buildings use a more formal approach to meetings, while some—usually the smaller buildings with only a few board members—use a less formal approach. Condo or co-op bylaws will typically specify what rules the association must follow during meetings. Following your own rules or Robert's Rules (see the following sidebar) keeps meetings running systematically and in control.

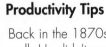

Productivity Tips

Back in the 1870s, Henry Martyn Robert attended a meeting and it didn't go very well. He didn't want that to happen again, so he created a series of laws to help run meetings more efficiently. Those were called Robert's Rules of Order, which were introduced to the general public in 1876 and have been used in meetings ever since.

Visit www.robertsrules.com for more information. There is also a shorter version of the rules you can order to have on hand.

Board Meeting Conflicts

Board meetings can get very heated. Different ideas, differences of opinion, and different agendas can cause much stress in a meeting where people want to give opinions, solve problems, make decisions, vote, and get back home to their families. As a result, board meetings should also have a protocol or policy in place for when things get a little tense and tempers start to flair out of control.

For example, your board member Johnny has just gotten home from a long day at work. His boss is annoyed with sales figures and he took it out on Johnny and another salesman. Johnny worked overtime, caught the train home, and ran to the meeting. He was on time, but he's frustrated, hungry, and would rather spend some time with his wife and kids. At this point, he's ready to vote on anything, but he gets testy when Sallie Doright wants to discuss some of the issues in more detail. The meeting lasts even longer when Johnny and Sallie start to argue.

Of course, it might have helped if you had known what Johnny's day was like before the meeting, but board meetings need to be run in a professional matter with personal situations and opinions kept out of it. Although most board members are friendly and there will be some chit-chat, there really is work to do and it's important to stick to the business at hand. You should have Sallie and Johnny focus on the tasks at hand and leave the personal attacks out of the room.

Get Ready!

So, Johnny had a hard day at the office, but honestly other board members work hard, too. And, because the positions are voluntary, it's important to have a stress-free meeting that runs smoothly for everyone. Well-run meetings respect the time commitments of everyone who attends. To help defuse situations like the one between Johnny and Sallie, a detailed agenda should be prepared ahead of time and sent to the board members so they have time to review them before the meeting starts. Johnny might have been able to read the agenda on the train ride home, and therefore, have been more prepared for what was going to be discussed.

The agenda might look something like this:

- ◆ Meeting start time: 7 P.M.
- ◆ Review and approval of previous minutes
- ◆ Board President report and discussion
- ◆ Property Manager report and discussion
- ◆ Committee reports and discussion
- ◆ Voting on implementing an emergency assessment

- Adopt resolution to change bylaws

- Discussion of new social activities director

- New business

- Announcements

- Adjourn 9 P.M.

Get Set!

To help get Johnny out of the meeting faster, you should also have your property management reports ready to go—even days ahead of the meeting—and provide them to the members beforehand. Johnny and Sallie could have time to digest the information and formulate a list of any questions and concerns to be discussed instead of just winging it at the meeting. It also gives time for the board to send you any questions and concerns ahead of time so that you have time to research any additional information that you may need.

Productivity Tips _____

Because board members are volunteers, understand that they have separate lives and may not remember meeting times. Drop them a reminder e-mail or phone call and let them know when and where the meeting will be held.

Go!

All meetings need to have minutes recorded. The minutes of the meeting will show you, minute by minute (get it?), what happened during each meeting. It's the secretary's responsibility to make certain that the minutes are accurately taken. Therefore, if there are any questions about decisions that were reached or comments said, you can refer to the paper trail. Remember, from a legal perspective, this is very important.

After the meeting is over, the secretary must send copies of the minutes to you and any manager to whom you report, the building's attorney and accountant, etc. These team members can and should attend the meetings, but if they don't, they at least have a written record of what's gone on.

¿Que Pasa?

America is a melting pot of ethnicities; millions of residents are culturally and economically diverse. In almost every community, building, and association, there are people with different ethnic and sociological backgrounds. Managing co-op or condos that are home to residents from varied backgrounds, language groups, and cultural perspectives can sometimes pose distinct challenges.

Language and cultural barriers are some of your biggest obstacles when it comes to communicating with your tenants and board members. You might find yourself talking with a Japanese couple who just opened up a new restaurant and barely speaks English. Or, you might be a property manager in a predominately Hispanic community, where Spanish is spoken more often than English.

Breaking Down Barriers

The first step to breaking down language barriers is to evaluate your building or community and look for solutions. For example, if your residents are predominately Hispanic, it might be a good idea to offer important documents—for example, Emergency or Evacuation Procedures—in both English and Spanish. If only one of your tenants is fluent in Japanese but speaks little English, it would still be a smart move to have the documents translated into Japanese, for your tenants' safety.

At holiday time, the cultural differences of your tenants may come up more often. Many buildings are decorated in Christmas décor, but perhaps your residents are predominately Jewish. What to do in this type of situation? Discuss it with your tenants and board early enough for a decision to be made on what decorations will be used.

> **Things to Avoid**
>
> Do not stereotype your tenants! Make sure you and your staff treat them all equally. Do not to make jokes that could be misunderstood or considered off-color.

Bias

Occasionally, you may have to deal with a comment from one tenant about another tenant that is racially or culturally offensive. Comments like this can create tension between residents. Your job is to evaluate each conflict and try to come up with a solution that works for both sides. For example, an article in the association newsletter or on the website might explain a culture in more detail, which may open dialogue between the residents.

Unfortunately, not everything you do is going to work. Some residents won't budge when it comes to their racial intolerance, no matter what suggestions you make. Although your tenants are entitled to their own opinions, the tenant cannot cause problems or become verbally abusive, or you can have them removed.

Celebrate

Celebrate the fact that your building is so diverse. It might be a great way of bringing your tenants together. For example, if your building is socially active, create a monthly event based on a resident's particular culture. For example, you could host a Hispanic day or Chinese day that includes food, music, and celebration. Just remember that what you write in the ads, newsletters, or websites to promote these events can be misconstrued as discriminatory. If you're unsure what to write or if you think what you have written could be offensive, run it by your attorney first before posting.

The Least You Need to Know

- Don't overstep your boundaries when it comes to board meetings.
- If the board is trying to push you to complete responsibilities that aren't in your job title, let them know and explain who should complete the job.
- Never include your personal feelings into a board decision at a board meeting.
- Provide facts at the meetings and have statistics and information to back you up.
- It takes planning and effort to run a good board meeting and to have a great relationship with the board.
- Remember that you and the board are a team, making decisions for the building or association, not for the individuals.

Chapter 14

One Job, Many Hats

In This Chapter

◆ Utilizing different management styles

◆ Managing different staff sizes

◆ Knowing when to ask for help

When visiting different doctors, have you noticed that they all have different personalities? One doctor is friendly and talkative, but another is the polar opposite—he foregoes the chit-chat, completes a thorough examination, and says goodbye, matter-of-factly reminding you to make an appointment for your next visit. One doctor is timid and reserved while the other one is aggressive and loud. And they all have their own ways of getting the job done.

What kind of property manager are you? What is your work personality? How do you get your job done? Read any business management book and experts will tell you there are different management styles you can use to be successful. What style you use will determine how you treat your staff, tenants, vendors, and contractors. Your personality and your management style also help you to handle problems that you encounter along the way. Winston Churchill once said, "A pessimist sees the difficulty in every opportunity; an optimist sees the opportunity in every difficulty." For example, how many times have you heard a disgruntled employee say, "I can't handle this job," or "It's too much for someone to do," when confronted with difficulties at work? Do you think they will be successful? Think how different it would have been if they said, "I'll find out the answers," or "I'll find someone to help me." Same problem, different outcome.

Finding the right style for you can help you become successful in your career. The key idea here is that you have to find the right style. For example, if you are typically a quiet, reserved personality, managing a building with an assertive management style may not be right for you. You can still motivate your employees, keep tenants happy, and get the job done using other techniques. This chapter will review different personalities and management styles and how they can help you accomplish your day-to-day duties as property manager. This chapter will also encourage you to find a style that's comfortable for you and will help you become the manager and leader you want to be with your staff and with your tenants. Finally, a good manager never hesitates to ask for help, and this chapter will show you where you can turn to for help along the way.

Management Styles

According to the experts, there are many management styles, such as the shark, turtle, fox, teddy bear, and owl. You can manage like Donald Trump or Winston Churchill. You can manage in what's called a participatory or directing way. Some experts will tell you there are only three standard styles, while others will tell you that there are a dozen or more. It all depends on who is doing the talking or writing. If, after reading everything here, you're still unsure of your management style, search for management quizzes on the Internet that will help you identify your strengths and weaknesses.

Zoo Animal Management

Some business management experts drop the jargon and classify management styles according to zoo animals. Are you a shark—more forceful, aggressive, with the need to be the victor? Are you a turtle, who takes his time solving a problem or sits back and allows the others involved to work it out on their own? A dolphin style is more cooperative, while a lion is more competitive. Interestingly, these styles also have their negative sides. For example, a turtle might take too long to solve a problem and miss out on things because he is too slow. You can also be a combination of animal styles.

Laissez-Faire Property Manager

On the Internet there is a blog geared toward property managers, aptly titled www.propertymanagementblog.com. In it, the writer describes three management styles: laissez-faire, authoritarian, and democratic. A laissez-faire property manager "allows subordinates to work things out largely on their own with almost no direction from above." They say that this kind of property manager, "works best when group members are highly experienced, trained, motivated, and educated and when trust and confidence in group members are high." They say a strong leader is not really needed for the group to accomplish its goals, and believe that this is the least effective property manager.

Authoritarian Property Manager

At the other extreme, an authoritarian property manager gives orders and expects their subordinates to obey them simply because they are the boss (and who hasn't had this kind of boss during their career?). This manager manages with a style that makes employees (and even tenants) intimidated and afraid. This is not a popular type of management style, but they explain it can be effective in an emergency. An authoritative person will definitely evacuate the building quickly!

Democratic Property Manager

A democratic manager falls in the middle of both authoritarian and laissez-faire. A democratic manager is not as harsh as an authoritarian manager, but has more control than a laissez-faire manager. The blog writers, however, do not believe a democratic manager would be able to get everyone out of the building safely from a fire because, they claim, it would take a democratic property manager too much time to come up with an escape plan.

A + B = C

Just like you aren't one type of personality outside of your job, you probably aren't one type of management style either. Most people fall into more than one category. Say, for example, you are having a relatively run-of-the-mill day. Everybody is doing their job and there have been no surprises. In this situation, it's okay to have a democratic management style during the day. Then, when an emergency strikes—BAM!

Fire!—you become Authoritarian Man or Woman, able to react to an emergency in a single bound! You get everyone out of the building safe and sound and return to democratic manager once the emergency is over.

Your Staff

What type of management style you have also depends on the size of your staff. Do you have a small staff or a larger staff—where there is a higher chance for conflicts— or are you flying solo? Even someone who is flying solo as property manager needs a management style. At some point, you will be handling vendors and contractors and, of course, you'll be using this management style to deal with your tenants.

Managing a Small Staff

When you have a smaller staff, you may know more about their personal lives, and it might be easier to solve problems with less people. At the same time, a smaller staff that knows each others' business can lead to potential conflict. What management style you use with your small staff will depend on their personalities, too. For example, you might think that you should be more caring and understanding of your staff's personal problems since you are friendlier with them. That might backfire, however, as staff may ask for personal favors since you are "friends." You may actually need to be more aggressive with a smaller staff depending on the situation.

Productivity Tips

"Sure, you exchange polite chatter with your coworkers, and maybe even complain about clients, projects or your boyfriend—but save the gory details for your friends outside of the office. Bottom line: The workplace is not a place for idle chatter. Not only is it bad to spill details about your latest conquest, but you never know when that particular bit of shared titillation might be used against you."

—Rachel Weingarten, author of *Career and Corporate Cool*

Managing a Large Staff

Managing a large staff takes more organizational skills to keep on top of the work that they are doing. You are also dealing with more personalities than with a small staff, so the possibility of conflict is increased. With a large staff, you want to create a workplace where job responsibilities and behaviors have been clearly identified and defined.

You may find that you need to use various management styles with such a large group. For example, Morgan Miller worries incessantly about her job and checks with you on every detail. She does a great job, so the last thing she needs is an aggressive manager. Instead, you should reassure her that she performed her job well, the problem is taken care of, and move her on to the next task.

Notes from the Field

A suggestion from AllBusiness.com, an online media and e-commerce company: when you have a large staff, create a collaborative and friendly culture. Create a workplace characterized by mutual trust and respect. High ethical standards should be the norm, and those who cannot abide by company rules should face the consequences. Be consistent and firm—but respectful, too. Communicate what's expected, and demonstrate your commitment to that standard.

Five minutes later, you're managing Jose Sanchez, who needs to be pushed a little harder to take on new projects. You are impressed with the work that he has done, but he's afraid of failing when he takes on something new.

Ah, but the one employee you don't have to worry about is Anne Marshall, who does her work and does it well, reports to you, and doesn't miss too many days. What you don't know is that Anne feels lost among the crowd and doesn't feel that she will be able to move up. Morgan and Jose have your attention, but Anne is the model employee. In a large company, you need to make Anne feel like she has a place. That's a different management technique all together. So basically finding a management style isn't quite one-size-fits-all.

Managing a Young Staff

If you have a predominately young staff, they are eager to learn and eager to move up the corporate ladder. This may be their first job in the "real" world, and they may need more molding and teaching than a staff member who has been in the workforce for a while.

When you're training a young person, your management style—especially if it's more

Productivity Tips

If you just hired a new employee, pair her up with a mentor, someone who has been in the company a longer time. If the new employee has concerns or questions, she can ask the mentor—but assure her that she can still come to you when she needs to.

authoritative—may need to take a backseat until the young employee gets her feet wet. As the employee becomes more experienced, she will take on more responsibility and become more independent and confident in her skills and abilities. You can then resume your regular management style with her when necessary.

Micromanaging

When a manager micromanages, he basically stands over his employees' shoulders, watches their every move and controls what work they do and how they do it (this might be done figuratively or literally).

For example, you've given your superintendent a project that includes checking out various contractors for an upcoming remodeling job and reporting back to you with the information on prices, recommendations, and so on. You gave him the job on Monday, with a deadline of Friday. You checked in with him on Tuesday, Wednesday, and Thursday. Your super confirms each day that he's working on it and will have it for you on Friday. Why are you doing this? It is definitely not a productive management skill. If you find yourself micromanaging, you may need to analyze why you are doing it and come up with solutions to change it.

Your Own Insecurities

The last time you needed to present a remodeling project estimate and recommendations to the board of directors, you were late. Now you're overwhelmed and have no time to complete the job. You called on your super for help, but now you're nervous about meeting your own deadline and you're on your super's back to get you the information you need.

Is this the first time you are giving the super an extra responsibility? Are you nervous that he's not going to do it right? The good news is your super is probably thrilled that you trusted him enough to do something new, but the bad news is he feels you don't trust him enough to get it done. It's a double-edged sword, and micromanaging the situation isn't making it any easier for you. You gave him a deadline of Friday, so back off and give him until Friday to do the job. Along the way, you can ask him once if he needs any help or guidance and assure him that you are here if he needs to consult with you. Let him show you he can do the job. Next time, consider that something this important should be your responsibility and you could give the super something else to do in its place.

Poor Training

You've given Bob a repair job in one of the buildings, but you know that Bob has done some of his repairs wrong before. This time, just to be on the safe side, you stand over him and watch until he gets it right. He's frustrated, and tells you that this is how he was trained by the previous super. That should be the clue to solving the problem with Bob.

As you can see, Bob has expressed to you that the previous superintendent taught him how to do the repair. Therefore, the training manual (if there is one) should be reviewed to see whether there are mistakes and whether Bob hasn't properly learned the nuts and bolts of the system. If the manual shows there are mistakes, bring in an expert who has experience with that system to retrain Bob. Follow it up by making corrections in the repair/training manual so the mistakes don't happen again.

Changing Styles

After all of this talk about your personality and management styles, this next part might get a little confusing. It was briefly mentioned that you really shouldn't have just one management style that you depend on all the time, regardless of the situation at hand. The style you use for each situation depends not only on your personality and management style, but also on the personality of the other persons involved, whether it be a staff member, tenant, contractor, etc.

Other Personalities

Let's say you are a property management supervisor for a commercial management company. You supervise three property managers and check in with them to see what's going on. One manager hasn't been doing his job very well and the head honchos (your bosses) at the company are considering firing him. They have asked you to discuss his performance with him and give one more chance to correct the situation. If his performance isn't corrected, they will let him go.

The problem? Anthony, the manager, who has been with the company for five years, is quite temperamental. Approaching him with a very stern "do your job right, or else" might backfire. The result? He might become defensive and argumentative. The situation could escalate even further, and Anthony will find himself out of a job anyway, or you might exchange verbal spars that land you in trouble, too.

How should you handle this situation? Consider the type of person that Anthony is and use a management style that is more effective to that situation. For example, temperamental Anthony should be approached in a friendlier, calmer tone. Focus on the positive—perhaps you could tell him what he's doing right and how the management company wants to keep him onboard. Then, you could explain to him how he needs to improve. Suggest those changes and provide Anthony a copy of them in writing. Tell him that you'll be reviewing his progress at a given date.

Becoming More Effective

You're a laid back kind of manager. When you first took over as a property manager for a multifamily unit, the staff was delighted to see you. Their last manager was extremely difficult and intense, and he was constantly yelling at his employees. Your more relaxed personality is a nice change of pace. They enjoy coming to work now, and the stress—which was once very palpable—is gone. You're the "nice guy" and "nice guys finish first," right?

Maybe. Fast forward one year—you love your job, but you've realized that this same staff has now started to take advantage of your easy-going personality. Maria has arrived late to work on many occasions because she really doesn't think you would get angry with her. Mark, the doorman, has been caught "sitting down" on the job (so to speak) and not completing his daily tasks. The staff isn't feeling as motivated to do a good job because they do not fear the backlash they once did from the former manager.

There is a middle ground here. It's okay to be relaxed if that's what is comfortable for you, but you need to nip these problems in the bud. Your management style, in a situation like this, should be quick and assertive. Hold a meeting and let the staff know that, while you aren't as harsh as the last manager was, you won't tolerate staff members who aren't doing their jobs nor those who aren't working up to their potential. Do not let this situation fester or it will get worse. Make sure you immediately and assertively address any problems and concerns. They need to know you are the boss.

Back to Normal

Just know that in no way, shape, or form are we asking you to change who you are. It is important, however, to change how you react to a situation as it's happening. Once the situation is under control, you can return back to your more comfortable style of management. You may have to regularly do this back-and-forth juggling routine of styles, so be prepared. Knowing what management style to use at what time is a sign of a good manager.

Personality Management

So, we've established that there are different management styles. And we've discussed that what management style you will use for a particular situation depends on the employee's or tenant's personality. If Mrs. Jones in 4B is a quiet, reserved elderly woman with a sweet disposition, you're not going to approach her like a lion attacking your prey the first time you ask her about the conflict she is having with another neighbor. So how do you handle different personalities, such as introverts and extroverts?

Mrs. Jones in the preceding example could be classified as an introvert. According to research, an introvert is not someone who is shy. The concept goes back to the 1920s and the psychologist Carl Jung. Jung coined the concept back in the 1920s, and today's personality tests are used to determine whether someone is an introvert. An introvert typically wants to be alone, and often avoids social situations.

An extrovert enjoys being around other people. This is why many property managers enjoy their jobs—many are extroverts. Unfortunately, your management style and personality may conflict with your staff if they are the polar opposite of you. A good, successful manager learns how to work around that problem.

For example, your staff member Jake is an extrovert. He attends meetings all gung-ho and ready to get to the matters at hand, but gets upset when there is no time. Marsha, on the other hand, attends her staff meetings wishing she could go back to her post. She doesn't look forward to speaking in front of the rest of the staff. These meetings can become stressful for her.

How do you handle a meeting filled with employees or tenants who are a mix of introverts and extroverts? Easy: structure. Create an agenda that provides both sides opportunities to do what they need to do. For example, providing an agenda to the staff on Wednesday will give Marsha time to review what's to be discussed at the Thursday meeting. At the end of the meeting, you can add in time for Jake to discuss any new business or ideas.

Where to Turn to for Help

Remember that good communication with your employees and tenants is key, regard-less of your personality and management style. Without good, solid communication efforts on your part, there is going to be conflict. Throughout the chapter, you've been given guidelines on handling many problems and situations with tenants and staff. At this point, you should have an idea of how to quickly and efficiently handle a situation. But, like most things in life, the solutions aren't all neatly packaged for you. Sometimes, a problem can baffle even the most educated and experienced property manager. You're stuck with no answers and no solutions. Even an emergency room doctor sees a new case that wasn't taught in medical school, from time to time. So, where do you turn to when you need help?

Higher Ups

Start right inside your own company. If you work for a property management firm, is there someone you can talk to about a particular problem? It's actually best to bring your problem or situation to the firm before going to an outside source. They may not want particular issues being mentioned outside the firm. They may also have another property manager who might have gone through something similar and can offer first-hand advice or experience.

Your Dream Team

Remember that you should have already created a team of experts to turn to for advice. As a reminder, this team should include an attorney, a financial expert, and an accoun-tant. When you are having a problem, turn to them for advice and pick their brain on how to handle a situation. Remember, however, that you're the final decision-maker on the situation, so don't feel obligated to take their advice.

Peer Assistance

If you own your own property management firm, you might have networked with other managers in the area, perhaps at a trade show or business meeting. Can one of these contacts from another firm help you with a particular problem? Keep in mind, how-ever, that you are a competent (and successful!) property manager who simply needs advice or resources occasionally. It's important to limit how often you turn to your peers for advice or resources—it may make you look as if you can't handle your job.

Internet

Property managers and lawyers have turned into Internet advice columnists, often blogging (you'll learn more about blogging in Chapter 18) with readers who write in asking specific questions. In turn, these experienced managers offer advice, suggestions, and resources. To find these blogs go to Google.com and type your problem—say, "troublesome tenant"—in the search engine. You may find someone in another city or state who has gone through something similar and could share what they learned with you.

Things to Avoid

When you are getting advice from other property managers or attorneys on the Internet, remember that laws vary from state to state. If a specific law or regulation is mentioned, it's important to follow up and make sure it pertains to your situation. You don't want to end up in hot water.

Think Out of the Box

You can also search for landlord resources, such as www.LandlordAssociation.org, which is a site for landlords, real estate investors, property owners, and property managers. It is a free site that provides services related to news, information, ideas, knowledge, and resources. You can search under "landlord," "property management," "tenants," etc.

Tenant Resources

Tenant resource websites will also help you find information on various subjects related to your tenants. Some sites offer free explanations of tenant legal issues—such as leases, evictions, deposits, multiple tenants, environmental problems, rent increase and control, repairs, and discrimination—and may give you the answers you are looking for. Organizations such as Housing and Urban Development (HUD) also have information on public housing topics.

Trade Organizations

If you are a member of any trade organizations—such as the National Association of Residential Property Managers (NARPM), the Building Owners and Managers Association (BOMA), or Institute of Real Estate Management (IREM)—these organizations have resources, including back issues of their publication articles, which are available to members on their website. Perhaps there is a particular problem that someone in the organization has either experienced or can help you with. Trade organizations also offer online resources to make your job easier.

Productivity Tips _____

To learn more about renter's rights, try Law.Com. This National Landlord Tenant guide offers state specific legal information related to rental properties for both the tenant and the landlord. It also provides a search engine that locates properties for rent in specific locations. Membership is free, and it covers areas such as the following: normal wear and tear issues, renter's insurance, security deposits, section 8, housing vouchers, and evictions. This information can come in handy.

Real-World Example

Kimberly Smith is broker/owner of AvenueWest Corporate Housing. Her company specializes in monthly rentals of furnished corporate housing.

"We are all about the systems. We have twice as many details to take care of versus an unfurnished property, and our tenants expect a lot from us. We only work with specialized properties in the right condition in the right area. We also try and work only with educated investors.

I don't think you can be laid back and democratic. If you are dealing with an issue like bed bugs and you don't have the right procedures in place, one infested unit can turn into an entire unusable building! I am all about the manual, detailed records, and good communication with your property owner. We make an effort to touch base with them, and not just when something is broken and they need to approve the repair. We try and find positive reasons to communicate with them a couple times a year. I think, eventually, all property managers become callous because it is hard work. The tenants wear on you and the owners wear on you, but it can be lucrative if the system works. Remember, take a vacation!"

The Least You Need to Know

- You don't need to be a psychologist to figure out someone's personality—simply listen and watch.

- Management styles need to be changed depending on tenants, employees, and what's working.

- Management styles depend on the type of property you are managing.

- There's nothing wrong with asking for help when you need to solve a problem.

Safety

In This Chapter

- ◆ Keeping the tykes safe and sound
- ◆ Taking care of special needs
- ◆ Weather-related safety
- ◆ Maintaining fire safety
- ◆ Providing evacuation education

Ensuring the safety of everyone in your building is one of the most important aspects of being a successful property manager. The last thing you want to happen is a tragedy—a child who falls into an unfenced pool, a fire that started because of faulty electrical wiring, or a senior who died during a tornado because nobody was aware that they needed extra assistance during the evacuation.

This chapter focuses on safety—precautions you need to take both inside and outside of the building, how to be prepared when Mother Nature unleashes her wrath, and how to efficiently and effectively evacuate the building.

Nobody wants to think about any of these things happening where they live or work, but there is always a possibility that something could go wrong. A successful property manager thinks ahead, contemplates the worst-case scenarios, and then makes sure all steps are taken to reduce the risks when something does happen. Then, everyone who is living or working in your building will feel much safer knowing that you've done your job.

Common Areas

It is your responsibility as manager to make sure the entire property is kept secure and safe for everyone. Decks and railings should not be loose, where residents or guests can fall. There should be adequate lighting in all common areas as well to prevent injuries and discourage intruders. Tenants must also assume some responsibility when using the common areas to keep the area clean and safe when they are done.

Child Safety

Children are curious. They like to touch and explore and, while that's usually considered positive growth development, curious children can get into things they shouldn't and get injured. Of course, it's a parent's or caretaker's responsibility to keep an eye on a child, but it's your responsibility to make your building as child safe as possible on the playground, in common areas, and by the windows.

Playground Protection

Swing sets, jungle gyms, and teeter totters are nice amenities in some residential buildings and associations. These playgrounds can be located in the yard or on the fenced rooftop of a high-rise building. While kids love playgrounds, having one on your property creates three major concerns for you. First, you must make sure the playground is durable and lasts a long time. Second, if you're buying a new one, it needs to fit the building budget. Finally, and most importantly, you need one that's going to keep the little tykes safe.

If you're adding a new playground, remember that the choice of surface material is very important. If little Johnny falls from the monkey bars, he should land on something that's going to soften his fall. Today, there are certified play surfaces to choose from—such as poured or shredded rubber or wood fiber—that offer maximum protection. Poured rubber surfaces provide cushioning, shock absorbency, and durability. Shredded rubber is loose, but protective, and gives way when a child falls. Wood fiber is an engineered wood fiber, contains no waste wood, and is environmentally friendly.

Notes from the Field

According to the Consumer Product Safety Commission (CPSC), there are over 200,000 playground-equipment-related injuries each year, only a portion of which involve equipment in apartment complexes. To keep those stats low, the pros adhere to building guidelines from the American Society of Testing and Materials (ASTM) and the CPSC. Equipment must also meet the Americans with Disabilities Act (ADA) requirements so disabled kids can use these play areas, too.

An upgraded playground must be designed to meet your budget and the requirements by the Americans with Disabilities Act. A smaller budget might have basic swing sets, while larger budgets can include all the bells and whistles for kids of all ages!

Hire a licensed playground installer. If the company doesn't have professional install-ers on staff, make sure subcontracted installers are licensed. The company should per-form regular safety checks and maintenance. Make sure your building's liability insurance covers any injuries. But, to reduce liability, make shareholders and unit owners sign a hold harmless agreement—a waiver that protects the building and the board should a child get hurt (ask your building attorney if you're uncertain).

Productivity Tips

To help the children stay safe, teach residents about child-proofing their units or homes, or bring in a community expert and offer a free seminar.

Common Area Concerns

The property's common areas need to be child-proofed, too. Make sure hazards—such as electrical outlets and loose wires—are inaccessible to children. It only takes a sec-ond for a child to escape from a parent's hand and stick a foreign object into an outlet. Have a licensed electrician install ground-fault circuit interrupters (GFCIs). This electronic device protects individuals from serious injury by monitoring the electricity flowing in the circuit. Any imbalance and the GFCI will shut off the current flowing through it, preventing shorts, overloads, and serious burns.

Make certain that any construction areas are well secured so that children cannot get into them. Staff members should never leave any tools or machines unattended and plugged in. Fences should be locked, and doors to staff-only areas should be secured.

Window Guards

Children dream about flying like Peter Pan, Spider-man, or Superman, so it's important to protect them in case they want to try out their imaginary wings. According to The National Safety Council, a child can fall from a window that's open only a few inches. Make certain your building's windows are guarded and secure enough that a child cannot topple out. The CPSC estimates that over a dozen children under age 10 die each year from toppling out of windows, and more than 4,000 others are treated in hospital emergency rooms for window-fall-related injuries.

Many states have window guard laws, so check with your attorney regarding your state's requirements and make sure your building complies. For example, a New York City resident who owns a co-op or a condo and has a child under age 11 must have Health-Department-approved metal window guards installed on all apartment windows.

Pool Safety

If your association has a community pool, safety is a vital concern for all residents, but especially for children. Precautions such as pool alarms, self-closing and self-latching gates, and lifeguards are all necessary to keep the pool area safe and secure from tots and other unwanted visitors.

Things to Avoid

In Chapter 7, you learned about the dangers of lead. In Chapter 10, you read information on lead laws. Just remember that children are curious, so it's important to follow these laws and guidelines to reduce the potential hazards to the kids.

The most important legislation you need to know regarding pool safety is the Virginia Graeme Baker Pool and Spa Safety Act, passed by Congress, which requires all public pools and spas to cover the drains. This act was passed after several children were severely—and sometimes fatally—injured (often disemboweled) when they were sucked into the drain. Check your building's pool and spa to make sure they meet the most recent safety requirements.

Special Needs

A successful property manager makes sure all residents and occupants are taken care of in case of an emergency. Some tenants—such as the elderly, disabled, and "latch-key" kids—depend on others for help in an emergency. Planning ahead gives you and your residents a greater chance of survival. How do you find out who needs additional assistance? It's simple. Just ask. Send out a letter to all tenants asking for information on anyone who might need additional help during an emergency. Make sure you obtain their contact information. To prevent legal trouble, confer with your attorney to draft a letter with the correct wording.

Seniors, Disabled, and Special Needs

Some elderly, disabled, and special needs residents can fend for themselves in an emergency, but others can't. Talk to those that need additional assistance or to their caretakers. Find out about their physical limitations, communication difficulties, any special equipment that needs to be moved, and medication procedures. Plan on how you will alert those who are hearing or visually impaired or who cannot otherwise communicate.

Your responsibility is not to be a caretaker to a disabled or senior resident, but to know which residents may have difficulties. Elderly residents or those with disabilities can establish a buddy system with other residents or let their local firehouse know, so they can reach the person quickly in an emergency.

Latch-Key Kids

Every day after school, 12-year-old Suzie comes home, lets herself in the house, locks the door, and starts her homework while she waits for her working parents to arrive home at 5 P.M. Almost one third of school-age children in the United States are latch-key children like Suzie who come home to an empty house every day. Suzie was properly instructed by Mom and Dad not to open the door to strangers. Unfortunately, this makes your job a little harder. If there's a building or property emergency, Suzie might not let you in or evacuate with you. A good property manager needs to work with the parents to create a system of communication with their children.

It's likely that Suzie's parents feel uncomfortable telling you that their child is home alone. You could try to convince them that, in an emergency, it could save their child's life. The parents may provide you with emergency phone numbers and any language-barrier information. If Suzie still doesn't open the door during an emergency, have a uniformed firefighter or police officer accompany you to the door to explain the emergency.

Productivity Tips _____

Check in with the American Red Cross (www.redcross.org) for cardiopulmonary resuscitation (CPR), first aid, and automated external defibrillator (AED) training; injury prevention courses; blood-borne pathogens training; and community disaster preparedness education. They offer complete, flexible programs that help your company stay prepared for virtually any life-threatening situation. The Red Cross is a member of the Occupational Safety and Health Administration (OSHA) Alliance, which ensures your employees are receiving the highest quality information and training available.

Natural Disasters

Be prepared for anything Mother Nature is going to throw at you—tornadoes, hurricanes, and floods, oh my! Believe it or not, planning for a natural disaster is actually a little easier because most—for example, hurricanes—provide some warning. Others—such as earthquakes and floods—don't provide warning, but you can take steps to minimize the damage.

Of course, what you experience will depend on where your property is located. There should be a plan of action in place that outlines what needs to be done after any of these natural disasters occur.

Floods

There are several types of floods. First, there's the flood that occurs in the basement, thanks to a water leak (some buildings have roof tanks that could cause leaks and force an evacuation, too). Second, there are water and sewage backups that can also cause floods. Third, and potentially the most catastrophic, is the Mother Nature flood.

Heavy storms can bring lots of rain to rivers and lakes, which then flood the land and, possibly, the building and property.

Be forewarned: if you are not in a flood zone, your building may not be covered for flood damage. Check with your insurance company to see whether there is specialty insurance you can add to the building's policy. Should a flood occur, follow your prewritten evacuation procedures (we'll talk more about that later in the chapter) if needed.

Productivity Tips _____

Say cheese! Keep a digital camera—and extra batteries—on hand at all times to record any damage from floods, fire, vandalism, and so on. The camera can also be used to take pictures of parts that need to be repaired or replaced.

Hurricanes

If there's a hurricane in your area, it's important to be prepared. You may have days or even a week to prepare and batten down the hatches. Start by learning the weatherman's lingo. A hurricane watch means a hurricane is possible in your area. A hurricane warning is when a hurricane is expected in your area. Be prepared to evacuate. Monitor local radio and television news outlets or listen to NOAA Weather Radio for the latest developments. If local authorities advise you to evacuate, leave immediately.

Hurricanes are classified into five categories based on wind speed, central pressure, and damage potential. Category 1 and 2 hurricanes are dangerous, with 74- to 95- or 96- to 110-mile-per-hour winds that can cause building damage. If you are located near an ocean, these hurricanes can cause major storm surges. A Category 3 and higher hurricane is a major hurricane with winds starting at 111 miles per hour and reaching more than 150 miles per hour.

If there is a hurricane threat in your area, you need to secure your residential or commercial building, inform your employees of their responsibilities, make a decision about evacuation (if it hasn't been declared mandatory by the local government), and be sure to back up computer files and store other important paperwork in a waterproof container.

If your building is located in a hurricane zone, various supplies should be kept on hand at all times: heavy plastic sheets, duct tape, sandbags, an emergency generator, a chain saw, and plywood. To protect the windows during a storm, you can use the plywood and duct tape to cover them. After the storm, use the chain saw to cut away trees that have fallen onto the property.

The Disaster Handbook, Hurricane Preparedness for Commercial Type Buildings from the Institute of Food and Agricultural Sciences at the University of Florida, also recommends these preparation tips:

- Make arrangements to pay employees in cash because it may be some time before banking institutions are operational.

- Remove loose objects from the roof and the property, including trash cans and outdoor signs. Secure any loose items in offices and on desks.

- Move items away from the windows if you're still in the building.

- Move computers and other important equipment to safer areas.

- Disconnect all electrical appliances and equipment, except for refrigeration units.

♦ Close all windows and draw blinds or drapes. Cover items that can't be moved with plastic sheeting and duct tape.

♦ If you are leaving the building, turn off all electricity except for refrigeration units and lock all doors when you leave.

You can also teach your residents to make an emergency family plan for all possible emergencies.

Earthquakes

Earthquakes can be mild or extremely violent and may cause extensive damage to the buildings and property. They happen without warning, so it's impossible to plan for one. If you're in an earthquake zone (and hey, even New Jersey gets earthquakes from time to time, so don't think it won't happen to your geographic area!), your best bet is to plan for the unexpected—any potential hazards that can occur during an earthquake. The Federal Emergency Management Agency (FEMA) suggests repairing deep plaster cracks in ceilings and foundations, anchoring overhead lighting fixtures to the ceiling, and following local seismic building standards. Taking these steps will help reduce the impact of earthquakes.

In addition, building occupants should know what to do during an earthquake, including staying safe under a sturdy table or other piece of furniture and holding on until the shaking stops. They should be taught to stay away from glass, windows, outside doors and walls, and anything that could fall (such as lighting fixtures or furniture). You can also use a strong doorway if it's close to you. Most importantly, tell your occupants to stay out of the elevators during an earthquake and after until they have been cleared as safe.

Tornadoes

Although there might be some bad weather signs before a tornado strikes, in most cases you'll either have no warning or just a small warning of its imminent arrival. There should be a tornado emergency plan in place so all staff and residents know how to respond to tornado warnings the same way you have a plan of action for the other disasters.

Like earthquakes, some geographic zones are more prone to tornadoes than others. Either way, management should have an emergency plan that includes preparations and reactions to tornadoes. Occupants should know the safest places to hide—which should be underground, if possible.

Extreme Weather

Floods, hurricanes, and tornadoes cause damage, but other severe weather such as heat waves and extremely frigid temperatures can also be a concern to your residents. These extreme weather conditions can be especially harmful to the elderly, newborns, those with chronic illnesses, and other "at-risk" people. During these extreme weather days, it's important to check on your residents to make sure they are okay. Heat-related deaths and illnesses are preventable, but according to the Centers for Disease Control, from 1979 to 2003, excessive heat exposure caused 8,015 deaths in the United States. During this period, more people in this country died from extreme heat than from hurricanes, lightning, tornadoes, floods, and earthquakes combined. In 2001, 300 deaths were caused by excessive heat exposure.

Fire

Fire spreads quickly, so there's not much time to think and evacuate. Depending on your location, your building may also be near—or in the direct path of—a wildfire, and may feel its effects. There are special precautions these buildings must take against wildfires. For example, thick smoke may require the additional cleaning of building ventilation filters. If the situation gets dire, evacuation may be necessary. If you are a manager of a commercial building, it may be used as a clean-air shelter for evacuees.

Each year, more than 4,000 Americans die and more than 25,000 are injured in fires, many of which could be prevented. If your building was on fire, are you confident that everyone would be adequately warned, protected, and saved? If you're not adequately prepared to protect your building against fire, here are some steps you can take now to secure the building and keep the residents safe.

Up to Code

The number one fire prevention tip in all buildings is to make sure that the entire building is up to code and that all fire prevention equipment is in working order. Remember that fire safety building codes and laws differ from one municipality to the next and may include …

◆ No garbage blocking the doors or halls.

◆ No exits are blocked.

◆ Emergency lights are working.

◆ Regular inspections of boilers and heating and electrical systems.

To keep up to date with the latest research, technology, and safety practices, consider investing in a copy of the National Fire Protection Association (NFPA) *Fire Protection Handbook*. It includes information on premises security and on how to incorporate architectural, technical, and operational security elements into a comprehensive and effective security plan. It provides tips on increasing a building's resilience to such events, and includes strategies for evacuation. Visit www.nfpa.org and type "Fire Protection Handbook" into the search box.

Productivity Tips _____

Consider installing a knox box. Knox boxes allow firefighters to have a key to buildings after hours. The steel key boxes are extremely secure.

Sprinkler Systems

Sprinkler systems have been proven to save lives and reduce fire damage, so make sure yours are working properly. According to the NFPA, the Parque Central—a 56-story government office building in Caracas, Venezuela, and South America's tallest high-rise—had a faulty sprinkler system. Unfortunately, when a fire broke out, it caused more than $250 million in damage, burning the structure's contents from the thirty-fourth floor to the fiftieth.

The NFPA states that the original designers built a state-of-the-art high-rise fire safety system for the 1970s, which included fire detection and alarm systems, fire hose cabinets, and pressurized stairs. A wet pipe sprinkler system, utilizing copper tubes and designed following the pipe schedule method, was installed and connected to on/off sprinklers.

Bottom line? If your building's sprinkler system is faulty, it doesn't matter how state-of-the-art it is—the building will burn and people can die. The NFPA shows two examples of how a sprinkler system can work effectively:

◆ An elderly woman suffered first-degree burns and smoke exposure during a fire in the bedroom of her apartment in a 236-unit building for older adults. She escaped additional injury when her attempted escape by wheelchair came to a stop under an operating sprinkler, which controlled the blaze and kept most of the heat and smoke away from her.

◆ A single sprinkler controlled several fires set by an arsonist in an unoccupied movie theater. People were evacuated from the operating theaters in the multiplex before the fire department arrived. The two-story theater had concrete block walls with a protected steel frame. An operating smoke detection system covered all areas, including the duct work in the heating, ventilation, and air conditioning (HVAC) system.

To make sure you have the correctly sized sprinkler system for your property or building, check the International Building Code's requirements. There are different requirements for each type of building, the building's size, and the amount of occupants.

Get Residents Involved

Another effective fire-prevention strategy is to make sure your tenants are educated and involved in keeping the building safe. In residential buildings and associations, the bylaws and house rules outline what is expected of the residents to help prevent fires and what to do if one should start. You can send out regular reminders in newsletters and e-mails.

Fire Extinguishers

Fire extinguishers are your first line of defense against a fire, so it's vital that they are functioning properly. Extinguishers have a number that serves as a guide for the amount of fire the extinguisher can handle. The higher the number on the extinguisher, the better the ability to fight a larger fire. There are four basic types of fire extinguishers, each for fighting a different type of fire:

◆ Class A extinguishers are for fires that involve ordinary combustible materials such as cloth, wood, paper, rubber, and many plastics.

◆ Class B extinguishers are for fires that involve flammable and combustible liquids—such as gasoline, alcohol, diesel oil, oil-based paints, and lacquers—and flammable gases.

◆ Class C extinguishers are for fires that involve electrical equipment such as appliances, wiring, circuit breakers, and outlets.

◆ Class D extinguishers are for fires that involve combustible metals such as magnesium, titanium, potassium, and sodium.

◆ Class K extinguishers are for fires that involve vegetable oils, animal oils, or fats in cooking appliances. This is for commercial kitchens, including those found in restaurants, cafeterias, and caterers.

So, for example, a multipurpose, dry chemical Class ABC fire extinguisher would be considered the best choice for general home use (good for residents).

In commercial buildings, however, the type of fire extinguishers that are required depend on the type of building it is. Say, for example, the commercial building is home to a large department store. That building would need a Class ABC fire extinguisher. But, because it doesn't have a deep fryer, you wouldn't need to keep a Class K extinguisher on hand.

Class D extinguishers are typically found in manufacturing plants; sometimes, the extinguishing agent is a bucket of soda ash or bags filled with metals that interact with the burning metal compounds to cancel the chain reaction that is causing the fire. In such cases, chemistry is necessary—for example, if you put water on a burning pile of magnesium chip, you can cause a catastrophic explosion.

Smoke and Heat Detectors

A smoke detector or smoke alarm is a device that detects smoke and issues a high-pitched alarm to alert those in the area that there may be a potential fire. A heat detector responds to a change in temperature and releases another alarm if the temperature gets too high. Just like fire extinguishers, there are no national laws that require buildings to have smoke detectors. There are state and local ordinances, however, so make sure you check local guidelines and follow them exactly.

Notes from the Field

According to the United States Fire Administration (www.usfa.dhs.gov), direct property loss due to fires in 2007 was estimated at $14.6 billion. From 2002 to 2005, U.S. fire departments responded to an average of 3,900 reported hotel and motel structure fires per year. These fires caused an estimated annual average of 11 civilian deaths, 144 civilian injuries, and $64 million in direct property damage.

What you are required to have in your building varies from state to state, but they all conform to standard guidelines. Your building may still require sprinklers or standpipe hoses (standpipes are connections that are used to extinguish a fire). The sizes and fluids in each of these systems also can differ.

Defibrillators

It's not fire-fighting equipment, but it's definitely life-saving. Automated external defibrillators are electronic devices that administer an electric shock to restore heart rhythm. The machine analyzes the rhythm of the heart and lets you know whether or not you need to administer a shock. Buildings that have an AED must have a training program and a licensed physician to oversee training and reporting of any usage. According to the National Conference of State Legislatures, many states have passed legislation that requires the presence of an AED in such public buildings as schools and health clubs. Check their list at www.ncsl.org/programs/health/aed.htm to stay up-to-date on your state's required laws and training programs.

Productivity Tips

Be prepared! All tenants should have an emergency kit, which includes drinking water, flashlights, fresh batteries, a water-resistant battery-operated AM-FM radio, and a mylar emergency blanket. Residential tenants should also have an evacuation kit that includes their medical supplies (prescriptions, insulin, inhalers), flashlights, batteries, first-aid kit, a change of clothes, important phone numbers, car keys and house keys, etc.

Evacuation and Escape Plans

At some point, you may need to evacuate the building. Although every person is truly responsible for her own evacuation, management, you and your staff should be the guiding force to make certain the evacuation goes smoothly. In any emergency situation, residents and occupants will look to you and your staff for leadership. They'll want to know what's wrong, what to do, where to go, and how to get there. Evacuation procedures should be conducted using at least two or three alternate routes, and drills should be practiced regularly with your staff and tenants.

Here are some tips for you and your staff to keep in mind during an emergency and evacuation:

- Before an actual emergency exists, practice regular evacuation and fire drills with your staff and with your residents/tenants.

- Review your information regarding who may need extra assistance when evacuating.

◆ Make sure your escape plan (the "you-are-here" plan) is prominently labeled and includes identifying locations on staircases. These plans should be posted where all residents can see.

◆ Once an emergency has started, remain calm.

◆ Contact emergency personnel immediately.

◆ Don't get involved beyond your capabilities. You're not a police officer or a fireman, so be careful what you attempt to do.

◆ Follow the emergency plans that have already been set up and practiced.

Light the Way

Once the power goes out in a building, it can become very frightening to those trying to escape. People can panic and injuries can occur. Buildings should have exit signs and motion-sensor lighting equipped with a battery backup that lasts at least 90 minutes past a power outage. This gives occupants a chance to see and safely exit the building. Or, consider photoluminescent lights.

Productivity Tips

Photoluminescent lights are like glow-in-the-dark stickers, but stronger. Some companies sell sleeves that slip over fluorescent tubes to light the way. Hyline Safety Lighting (www.hylinesafety.com) recommends that light sleeves be installed on 10 to 20 percent of all fixtures throughout your building so no one is left in the dark during a power failure.

An article in *The Cooperator* (www.cooperator.com), a co-op and condo monthly magazine, examines the cost of installing, maintaining, and powering one exit sign over the course of 10 years. The article explained that an electric exit sign using two incandescent bulbs would cost $1,614 for 10 years, a fluorescent sign would cost $933, and an LED sign would cost roughly $448. A photoluminescent exit sign would cost only $215, a number that reflects only the installation cost.

Consider a backup or emergency power system as well. Uninterrupted power supply is a service that's available from power companies. When the power fails, the building is run by battery power. This will allow time for computer programs to be saved, emergency evacuation to take place, and occupants to get out of elevators.

The Least You Need to Know

◆ Think of the worst-case scenarios and have plans for each, just in case one of those scenarios happens.

◆ Safety is a team effort with you, your staff, and the occupants all doing their part.

◆ It's important to know the basics of safety, but make sure you check your local building codes and laws to keep up with the most recent requirements.

◆ Have an evacuation plan in place and practice it regularly with your staff and your tenants.

Chapter 16

Security

In This Chapter

- ◆ Keeping everyone safe and sound
- ◆ Security for every budget
- ◆ Teaching the tenants well
- ◆ Knowing how to respond to different emergencies
- ◆ Working positively with the media

On any given day, hundreds (maybe thousands) of residents, guests, contractors, staff, and others can walk in and out of your buildings and on the property. Everyone is an open target to potential security risks, such as intruders, burglars, vagrants, suspicious packages, vandalism, illegal activity, and even terrorism. Having a security plan in place is vital to keeping everyone and everything safe and sound.

What security measures you should have depends on the size of the building and, of course, the budget. Not every building can afford, nor does every building want or need, state-of-the-art security technologies. But every property must have some simple methods of staying safe and an effective method of alerting tenants if something goes wrong.

This chapter examines security technologies such as cameras, locks, and intercoms. It also discusses the role of your doorman, concierge, and other security personnel as your first line of security defense. You and your staff will become familiar with identifying potentially dangerous people and packages. And, finally, it will also provide methods of staying in touch with your tenants during and after a crisis.

Security Check

The first method of creating a successful security plan is to just use your eyes. Look around. On a regular basis, do a visual assessment of the building with your staff—the more eyes looking around, the more security issues you may find.

What are you looking for? You're looking for broken locks, doors, and windows that allow easy access to the building. Identify windows that are covered from debris or shrubbery outside of doors or windows that provide a hiding place for intruders.

If you already have security measures in place—such as cameras or alarms—examine them to make sure they aren't broken or missing. Once you have created a list, you can tackle any repairs, replacements, or upgrades—from additional basic security to more advanced state-of-the-art technologies. If your building is already a major security risk, however, call in a professional. The pro will assess the building right away and offer recommendations for increasing its safety.

Think Complete

When you're analyzing your building's security needs and lapses, look at the building as a whole. Don't just think about one item, such as protecting the front door or securing the windows. Think about every part of the building and how a comprehensive security plan must be in place for your building to be secure.

Things to Avoid

Without an emergency or security plan in place, the property can be found liable if something happens and there are injuries involved. This was the case in the 1993 World Trade Center bombing, when a car bomb was detonated by terrorists in the underground parking garage below Tower One. Six people died and thousands were injured. At the time, the Trade Center was found two-thirds liable because management didn't have a good evacuation plan.

Keep 'Em Out

One of the simplest ways to deter problems is to fence them out. Some fences and gates come with electronic sensors and electronic shocks that recognize when someone is climbing over them.

And, don't forget that well-lit areas also discourage intruders. In Chapter 15, we discussed the importance of lighting so that tenants and residents don't get hurt. Being able to see those entering and leaving the building and in alleys and parking lots is an important part of the security plan. If you don't already have them, install sensor-activated lights (wireless versions are available) that switch on when motion is detected.

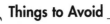

Things to Avoid

All security systems, especially those that are electrical, should comply with the National Fire Protection Association and the International Code Council.

Say Cheese!

One of the most common security measures used is closed-circuit video cameras. They can be installed in elevators, lobbies, and other common areas of any building. Today's cameras are high tech and digital, which means the picture quality is better (bye, bye videotapes!). You can enter the date, time, and camera number to call up any frame of the picture you want—no fast forwarding or rewinding necessary. Digital cameras can be motion sensitive, too. So, once an elevator starts moving, for example, it will start recording.

Keys

Traditional keys can be easily duplicated and handed out to anyone. A more secure, yet simple, security option doesn't need keys at all. It's a keyless entry system that can be monitored via a computer program. These systems provide a trail of the tenants in the building. Want to know who was in the hotel gym last? The computer tracks it. At the same time, the computer can check a guest's name against denied party lists, sex offender lists,

Things to Avoid

No matter what security system is in the building, remind tenants and staff that, no matter what, common sense is your best defense. No one is to open the door and hold it open for the person behind him. Often, this is how trouble gets into the building.

and terrorist lists. These technologies are more commonly used in schools, hospitals, and government-type buildings.

We're also getting closer to having more Matrix-type securities in the buildings. Biometrics—in which you place the palm of your hand or fingertips on a sensor to open a door—is going to become more commonplace, and an eye scanner is also in the works.

The Human Element

Video cameras are very successful crime deterrents, but your property should still have a personal security touch. This doesn't mean gargantuan Men in Black–style bouncers standing at your door. What it does mean is relying on those who man the doors—including the doorman or concierge—to help keep the building safe. Contracting a security guard or outside security firm is also a good idea.

Doorman and Concierge

The doorman and concierge, once just greeters, now play a pivotal role in building security by monitoring those who enter the building. If someone is questionable, they should know how to prevent them from entering the building. There should be strict guidelines in place for food and other deliveries and moving in and out. The staff should be made aware of any restrictions.

Make certain the staff knows how to report all possible criminal behavior (for example, a domestic violence argument or children entering a suspicious apartment). They should not, however, accuse a tenant of anything illegal! Simply have the staff point such things out to you so you can investigate with the proper authorities. This is important because if nobody does anything and someone gets hurt, it can become a serious liability issue.

Security Guard

The difference between your security guard and an outside security firm is that the in-house officer is an employee of your management company and may even live on the premises. An outside security firm is in charge of hiring the officers, and the guard usually doesn't live on the property. In some states, security guards must be trained and certified, and a background check must be run. An outside security firm provides the training, certification, and background checks on their own employees. But make sure that you receive proof that the guards have completed background checks.

Tenant Awareness

With staff security in place, the next step is to educate the tenants. It's important to hold meetings or contact your tenants through e-mail, association websites, or by newsletter to let them know what's expected of them during an emergency. For example, tenants should know to never give copies of their keys out or prop open access doors.

With everyone educated on safety, it reduces the chances that something will happen. If something serious does happen, all parties will know how to properly and quickly respond.

Suspicious Packages

If anyone sees a package that looks out of place and no one is claiming it, what should you, a staff member, or a tenant do? Who should they call? According to the United States Postal Service (www.usps.com), some typical characteristics that should trigger suspicion include letters or parcels that …

- Have any powdery substance on the outside.

- Are unexpected or from someone unfamiliar to you.

- Have excessive postage, a handwritten or poorly typed address, incorrect titles or titles with no name, or misspellings of common words.

- Are addressed to someone no longer with your organization or are otherwise outdated.

- Have no return address, or have one that can't be verified as legitimate.

- Are of unusual weight, given their size, or are lopsided or oddly shaped.

- Have an unusual amount of tape.

- Are marked with restrictive endorsements, such as "Personal" or "Confidential."

- Have strange odors or stains.

The Centers for Disease Control and Prevention suggest educating your staff and tenants on the following tips if they come across such a package:

♦ Do not shake or empty the contents of any suspicious package or envelope.

♦ Do not carry the package or envelope, show it to others, or allow others to examine it.

♦ Put the package or envelope down on a stable surface; do not sniff, touch, taste, or look closely at it or at any contents which may have spilled.

♦ Alert others in the area about the suspicious package or envelope. Leave the area, close any doors, and take actions to prevent others from entering the area. If possible, shut off any ventilation system (this reduces the chances of chemicals from being released into the air).

♦ Wash hands with soap and water to prevent spreading potentially infectious material to face or skin. Seek additional instructions for exposed or potentially exposed persons.

♦ Staff members should notify a supervisor, a security officer, or a law enforcement official. Tenants should contact the super or management or, if that's not possible, contact the local law enforcement agency.

♦ If possible, create a list of persons who were in the room or area when this suspicious letter or package was recognized and a list of persons who also may have handled this package or letter. Give this list to both the local public health authorities and law enforcement officials.

Office Buildings and Shopping Malls

Office buildings and shopping malls have their own security concerns. For example, medical office buildings may need to have 24-hour access. But, at the same time, they may also need to have additional security.

Shopping malls also run the risk of violence, theft, and vandalism. A security system is vital within the mall. Although undercover security guards can do the job, it's also good to have uniformed security personnel visible to all customers—it's a big deterrent to potential problems.

Productivity Tips _____

Proper landscaping can also help your building stay secure. Make certain that shrubbery isn't placed where it can be a hiding spot for predators or where it obscures the first-floor windows.

Responding to an Emergency

An emergency situation can happen at any time, anywhere. How you respond to it, and how fast, can sometimes be the difference between life and death. This is where your emergency plan comes into action—follow what you've been practicing. Remain calm and move quickly. The first 10 to 15 minutes of an emergency are what counts. Let's examine a few different types of security-type emergencies and how you should respond.

For example, the National Retail Federation provides basic guidelines for individuals present during an active shooting incident:

♦ Assess the situation

♦ React

♦ Evacuate (in a hide out or shelter)

♦ Take action

♦ Call 911 when it is safe to do so

Productivity Tips _____

Make certain that your building has adequate insurance to protect against any security issues, including terrorism, fire, and theft.

For more information, the organization provides the "2008 NRF ICSC Emergency Response Protocols to Active Shooters" at their website, www.nrf.com.

Do you know about any illegal activity in the back of a store on your property? What are you going to do? If you don't do something, you could lose other tenants who may know about the situation and do not see you reacting to it. And remember that being a successful property manager means having a solid reputation. Not reporting illegal activity will not only ruin your reputation, it can subject you to lawsuits from unhappy tenants.

Expecting the Unexpected

Anything can happen on your property each and every day, even things you have never experienced before. For example, a helicopter flies into the building (it happened in New York City), a shooter goes on a rampage at the mall (it's happened in several spots around the country), or a car crashes into your shopping mall. Don't ever say, "It can't happen here." The truth is, anything can happen—from the weird to the ridiculous. Plan for anything.

Who's Going to Be in Charge?

This is vital. In an emergency, who is going to be in charge of evacuations? Who will contact 911? Who will evacuate the residents who need assistance? Once you know who is going to be in charge of what, practice a run-through of an evacuation or an emergency drill.

Family First

One problem you'll encounter when you have an emergency is that, while managers and staff want to do their jobs, they may be more concerned about contacting their own families. That's understandable. So, when you're developing a security plan or an emergency plan, your entire team should know the basics on what each person does in case a fellow staff member is hurt during the emergency.

Remain Calm

It sounds obvious, but when an emergency strikes, not everybody has a cool head. As manager, you need to be in control and act professional. Everybody—from board members to staff to tenants—will look to you for leadership and, if you aren't in control, everyone else may panic.

Handling the Media

Ah, the media. As soon as something happens, they are on the property searching for answers and interviews, even before you've gotten through the crisis. In this instantaneous, media-driven world, it's important to be able to deal with the media and have a communication strategy in place.

Lorraine Howell is the owner of Media Skills Training (www.mediaskillstraining.com), where she teaches business owners, CEOs, and management teams to speak with confidence and impact in an enjoyable and down to earth way. She provides these tips to property managers when handling a media interview.

Howell explains that it's really difficult to appreciate the First Amendment in the middle of a controversy, but the media has an important job to do, too. If you treat the media like "the enemy," your chances of successfully surviving a controversy are diminished.

You Can't Control the Media

Give up the notion of trying to control the media. You can only control your response to them and how you communicate your message. Don't push cameras away or ignore the questions. It's better to manage a situation by being prepared and responsive.

Stick to the Facts

When answering a reporter's questions, don't lie. Don't make stuff up or assume something is happening. For example, if there was a fire in the building, you should state where the fire was, what floor it was on, who was hurt (without giving out names due to privacy issues), and so on. A reporter may ask what the cause of the fire was. Do not assume. If you don't know, tell them, "it is under investigation." Was there a shooting on the property? You might want to let law enforcement talk about the shooter instead of you. To quote *Dragnet*, "Nothing but the facts, ma'am!"

Establish a Contact Point

Establish a contact point where reporters can get information and press updates. Assign someone to respond to press inquiries. It doesn't have to be you, but it needs to be someone you can depend on, who is well-spoken, and who clearly knows what's going on. If you have time, provide handouts giving reporters background information or answers to frequently asked questions. Having the media on your property is an opportunity to get the correct information about your property out. If you have established good working relationships with the media prior to the problem, you are way ahead of the game.

Do's and Don'ts

Howell offers some important Do's and Don'ts:

- ◆ Don't ever lie, mislead, or stonewall. It will come back and hurt you every time!

- ◆ Don't speculate. Stick to the known facts. Don't respond to hypothetical questions.

- ◆ Stay calm and breathe! Don't get angry or defensive, and don't take hostile questions personally.

- ◆ Be direct and responsive. "No comment" is not a response. It leaves the impression you are trying to hide something. It's best to address questions, give whatever information you can, and indicate a willingness to update the media as the story unfolds.

- ◆ Acknowledge the human side. Express empathy, sympathy, concern, and other appropriate feelings for any victims, families, employees, clients, or anyone else who may be directly impacted. The priorities should always be the safety and well-being of the people involved.

- ◆ Take the initiative. In a crisis or controversy, people are looking for leadership. State what action is being taken in response to the problem. Stay away from declarative comments about responsibility or causes until all the facts are known. Keep the media informed as much as possible. Remind your audience about your commitment to getting answers, and bridge back to your main message when appropriate.

- ◆ Stay on track. Don't let questions lead you astray. Left-field questions don't always require answers, and they can be used to bridge back to your message. Here are some suggested responses:

  - ◆ "I'm not familiar with that issue, but what is important here is ..."

  - ◆ "I've heard that issue raised before, and we prefer to look at it this way ..."

  - ◆ "I can't address those specifics until our investigation is completed, but in general, it usually works this way ..."

It's also okay to say "I don't know" and commit to getting the information and getting back to the reporter as soon as possible.

◆ Get rid of the jargon. Translate complicated ideas, issues, or technologies into plain language. Use examples, metaphors, and analogies to reinforce the image you are trying to convey.

◆ Put your important points first. Don't bury the "lead"! Get to the meat of the matter as soon as possible. You can always back up and explain or give background information.

It's important to understand that, while the media wants answers, they are *not* the priority, especially while an emergency is still happening. Once you're ready to speak to the media, however, it's better to be prepared.

In today's world, every little bit of security helps when it comes to staying safe. Unfortunately, too many types of security on the premises can actually make the tenants more uncomfortable. Good security comes down to finding the right balance that makes everyone feel safe.

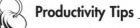

Productivity Tips

Once local police or firemen arrive on the property, let them take over the situation. For example, there is a shooter in the building, and you have an evacuation plan for part of the tenants of the building. But the local police show up on the scene and have a different evacuation plan based on the location of the shooter. Follow their lead.

The Least You Need to Know

◆ Having a safe, secure building should be one of your most important goals as a property manager.

◆ Don't have an "it can't happen to us" attitude; anything can happen, so be prepared.

◆ Staff should be thoroughly trained on what to do for all different types of emergencies.

◆ Security plans should be evaluated yearly to make sure you are addressing current issues with current technologies.

Part 4

Handling It All

Being a successful property manager also means looking toward the future. It means constantly working on improving your skills, networking to meet peers, and even switching jobs to move up the corporate ladder where you'll handle a bigger portfolio or oversee other property managers. This part will tell you how to network, attend trade shows, achieve additional certifications, and switch jobs to advance your career.

If you're the entrepreneurial type, this part will also tell you how to fly solo and start your own business. You'll learn the basics of writing a business plan and financing your business, the licenses you need, and the potential benefits of partnering with another manager.

So, congratulations! At the end of this book, you will have all the tools needed to become a successful property manager!

Chapter **17**

Managing Time and Stress

In This Chapter

- ◆ Applying time-management skills
- ◆ Keeping track of it all
- ◆ Managing your stress
- ◆ Keeping your cool
- ◆ Utilizing technology

What attributes should a successful property manager have? That's easy—eight arms to handle multiple phone calls and e-mails, two heads to see what's going on at all times, a pair of roller skates to run from place to place, the ability to put out fires, and courage! Why? You need courage to face a to-do list that will almost always be more than a mile long. In addition, there are businesses and lives at stake, tenants to make happy, and investments worth millions of dollars to care for.

Your never-ending to-do list might include—but certainly isn't limited to—arranging building repairs, negotiating leases, writing financial statements, visiting sites, choosing contractors, working with board members and associations, and expecting the unexpected. Handling emergencies—such as a leaky pipe or broken door, a staff member who quits in the middle of the day, or a weather-related crisis (such as a tornado)—is a typical part of your day.

This chapter helps you take stock of all your time guzzlers and stressors, and helps you find solutions to keep it all under control. By implementing various strategies to reduce your stress level and better manage your time, you will become a much better property manager.

Managing Your Time

When it comes to time, remember two things: no matter how you look at it, there are only 24 hours in a day, although most people want to add more hours to the day and more days to the months. And there really isn't a one-solution-fits-all to efficiently managing your time. Successful property managers use a combination of time-management tactics that work for them, such as the following:

- Online software programs
- Voice mail
- Personal digital assistants (such as BlackBerry or Palm Pilot)

The right solution for you is a personal choice. You can ask other property managers for time and stress-management ideas, but what works for them may not work for you. You might also have to go through several rounds of trial-and-error before you find the right techniques. For example, one manager uses Google calendar—an online calendar service—while another prefers an old fashioned pen and appointment book.

> ### Notes from the Field
>
> A 2007 DayTimers survey found that the majority of Americans have difficulties with stress, cutting down the number of hours worked per week, and finding and enjoying leisure time. In fact, 61 percent noted that they were unable to reduce stress in their life during the past year. Fifty-seven percent were unable to enjoy as much leisure time as they would like, while 89 percent were unable to work fewer hours in 2007.

Time Flies ...

How are you spending your day? Are e-mails overwhelming you? When you actually keep track of how much time you're spending on e-mails, you discover that it's 7½ hours per week! Or perhaps you're spending too much time traveling back and forth to properties when, instead, you could consolidate visits and save time. Or perhaps you're always crunched to get your end-of-the-month paperwork done because you haven't balanced your time well. Keep track of how much time you're spending doing your daily tasks, and you'll get a better idea of where you need to improve your time-management skills.

Here is a sample entry from John Jameson, a fictitious portfolio residential property manager:

8:30 A.M. to 8:45 A.M.—Checked e-mails

8:45 A.M. to 10 A.M.—Held meeting with staff

10 A.M. to 11 A.M.—Answered e-mails and phone calls

11 A.M. to 11:30 A.M.—Handled plumbing crisis in Building 1

11:30 A.M. to 12 P.M.—Answered e-mails

12 P.M. to 1 P.M.—Lunch

1 P.M. to 2 P.M.—Wrote draft of financial paper, but was interrupted by phone calls and a search for other paperwork

2 P.M. to 3 P.M.—Visited Building 2 and performed a walk-through with those tenants who are moving out

3 P.M. to 3:15 P.M.—Returned to office, checked e-mails, and prepared for tonight's meeting

3:15 P.M. to 4 P.M.—Visited building again to collect rent, and made deposit

4 P.M. to 4:15 P.M.—Missed meeting at 3:15 (wrote it down on paper, but forgot to put it in schedule)

There are several flaws to this schedule:

◆ No structure: There are random times during which he spent way too much time answering e-mails and phone calls.

◆ No consolidation: He isn't consolidating tasks—he made two nonurgent trips to the same building in one day instead of one. How could this be improved?

John could designate certain times during the day for e-mail and answer only those that are urgent. Everyone expects an immediate answer to their e-mails, but the truth is that all nonurgent correspondence can wait and be answered in one sitting at, say, the end of the day. Then he would have the 10 A.M. to 11 A.M. time slot to prepare for the meeting. Further, he could combine his walk-throughs and the rent collections into one visit. The one positive note about this diary entry is that the property manager has some flexibility to react to an emergency situation.

Flexibility Is Key

One property manager admitted that her biggest time-management problem used to be when she had everything all perfectly mapped out for her day and then—bam!—a water pipe burst or a staff member quit. Then that nice, neatly planned out schedule was thrown into disarray and her stress level went through the roof.

By learning to be more flexible in her planning, she was less stressed when an emergency hit. Of course when a tenant calls or e-mails that they need help right away, you need to listen to or give the e-mail a cursory read to decipher a true emergency from one that can wait or be delegated to another staff member. If the situation needs to be handled immediately, you have the flexibility of moving other nonurgent matters around so the situation can be dealt with.

Write It Down

Jan Jasper, a productivity expert and workflow coach in the New York City area, and author of *Take Back Your Time: How to Regain Control of Work, Information, and Technology* (St. Martin's Press, 1999), urges managers to write down or put in their personal digital assistants (PDAs) everything they need to do each day. "It helps to see the big picture and prioritize and it also saves you time by avoiding making two trips for what could be done in one trip."

She also suggests jotting down a few notes about where you left off, so you are aware of what your next step is when you come in the next day. Of course, you'll have new items to add to your list, but this prevents any chance of forgetfulness. Likewise, if you're interrupted—and you're going to be—she suggests making notes of where you left off so you don't need to reinvent the wheel when you return to the task at hand.

Assessing and Prioritizing

Once you are done writing everything down, it's time to prioritize your to-do list to see what needs more of your attention. Janet Bledsoe, an Operational Supervisor for the Miller Properties (11 properties) in Austin, Texas, has a list of what needs to be done at the beginning, the middle, and the end of each month, which helps to prioritize the rest of her schedule.

At the first of the month:

♦ Collecting rent and making deposits

♦ Leasing

♦ Renewals

♦ Walking move outs and processing the paperwork

♦ High volume of work orders and corresponding with residents

♦ Late rent notices after the grace period in the lease contract

The middle of the month:

♦ Eviction notices (should go out no later than the 10th for her state)

♦ Cleaning up the move out paperwork

♦ Any reports that are required

♦ Renewal letters that are in the lease contract's time frame

♦ Meetings with vendors

♦ Filing evictions by the 15th (her company's requirements)

The end of the month:

♦ Increased leasing traffic

♦ Scheduling move out walk-through

♦ Processing the bills

♦ Closing out any reports

♦ Making a project list for the next month and wrap up old list items

Productivity Tips

Jan Jasper, productivity expert, urges managers not to use their entire desk surface as a giant in-box. Instead, separate papers according to the action required. Create individual action folders for papers, such as contracts to review, work in progress, bills to pay, units to rent, and so on. These folders are only for active items—when tasks are completed, file the corresponding papers.

Tag Team Management

As we talked about earlier in the book, a property manager should have a team of professionals to turn to if various situations arise. If you don't already have one, it's time to create one. This prevents you from getting caught up in a legal or financial battle when it's either the lawyer's or accountant's responsibility to handle it, unless you are called upon to get involved. In addition, you can also call on staff to complete smaller tasks while you take care of more important matters. For example, staff can be appointed to answer and return phone calls and e-mails.

Technology Tips

There are cell phones and PDAs that are available to help you do your job as property manager and do it well, but if you're not really techno-savvy here are some basic tips to get you started.

Voice Mail

Contrary to popular thinking, having a call go to voice mail is not a bad thing. You can then sort through the messages and prioritize. For example, Joe Smith in 1A leaves a message questioning the bylaws policy of guest overnights. Sallie Jones in 4B leaves a voice mail stating that she feels a warm spot in the wall when her toaster is being used. Because Ms. Jones's problem can cause a potential fire, she becomes the priority. Later tonight, you can e-mail Joe back and let him know about the guest overnight bylaws.

Jasper says to make sure your greeting encourages callers to leave clear messages. For example, your outgoing message can say, "To help me respond to you, please state which building you're calling about, and your phone number at the beginning and end of your message. I will return all nonurgent phone calls within 24 hours." Make certain you do so.

Enhancing E-Mail Efficiency

When you are e-mailing someone back, remember that the e-mail is a legal document that can and will be used against you. Make sure you write professionally. If you are confirming something in writing with a tenant, contractor, or owner, make sure they do the same in return. Jasper suggests using e-mails to help you stay organized by changing the e-mail header to something clearer once you read it. You should have individual e-mail folders for each building. For example, "If the e-mail topic is how the lobby isn't clean, change the subject line to 'Lobby 300 State St.' when you reply," says Jasper. "This will save you time later and helps keep good records." Then, file the e-mail in a folder earmarked "300."

Jeffrey T. Lame, chief operating officer at READCO Management in New York, says that he has trained his staff to become more adept at handling the barrage of e-mails and phone calls that come into the office using the "3-D time management program: Do it, Delegate it, or Dump it."

PC Property Manager

There are many software programs to help you become a successful property manager. For example, managers utilize basic software programs such as Microsoft Outlook, which schedules events easily and sends you a reminder so you don't forget. Microsoft Outlook can be synchronized with your PDA, so if someone makes a change to a meeting or a phone number in the office, it will automatically update your PDA.

Chip Hoever, of Somerset Management Group in Somerset, New Jersey, uses his BlackBerry to schedule meetings with the owner of a new building that is still under construction. The PDA automatically reminds him of the event as it gets closer, so he can prepare accordingly. "I don't know how we did it before," he says.

Mike Levy, president of Levy Consulting in Fort Collins, Colorado, uses several software programs to help him better manage his time. He uses Microsoft Outlook Calendar and Tasks to manage his workload; uses colored flags to prioritize the e-mails that he needs to follow up on; and uses free online conferencing services to conduct conference calls with multiple people (saving time and transportation), screen calls, and more.

Productivity Tips

If you want to learn more time-management skills or to improve on the skills you've already learned, consider taking a time-management course. Organizations such as the American Management Association (www.american-management-association.org) offer seminars that teach goal-setting, prioritizing, multitasking, and more.

Stress Management

According to the National Institute for Occupational Safety and Health, job stress is how your body reacts—both physically and emotionally—when a job becomes too much to handle. Job stress can lead to a host of problems, including fatigue, injury, headaches, poor health, absenteeism, and more. The American Institute of Stress reports one study that shows a whopping 80 percent of workers feel stress on the job—nearly half say they need help in learning how to manage stress and 42 percent say their coworkers need such help.

Every job has its stressful moments—some more than others—and property management is no exception. But it's how you deal with the stress that makes you a successful property manager.

What's Your Stress?

What's stressing you out? Start by noting, in the same journal or diary that you are using for time management, what daily incidents cause you stress. Write an "s" or mark the incident with a star so you can return to it later and find a way to reduce the stress in case it happens again.

One property manager in Boston, Massachusetts, said that the most stressful parts of her job are unit/owner lawsuits and newly developed buildings, where the unit owners are not up to speed on condo ownership. Mike Levy noticed that his stress level would rise when properties were vacant. He realized, however, that no matter how tense he was over the vacancies, that tension wasn't going to resolve the problem.

> **Productivity Tips**
>
> Want to measure your stress load? Visit www.stress.org/topic-workplace.htm and take their "How Much Job Stress Do You Have?" test.

So, he instituted a new policy: if a property isn't rented in a certain number of weeks, he would lower the price by 5 percent. This policy reduced his stress—he knew exactly what he had to do and when. He began instituting policies for other situations. For late-paying tenants (another stressor), he sets one firm deadline and provides a three-day notice if they do not follow through with payment.

Clear Your Plate

You can pile up good food on a plate, but eventually it overflows and spills onto the floor. Does that describe your day? Is it too much? Is it overflowing? Or do you have a well-balanced day? Are there techniques like Levy's that you use or can create to reduce your stress level? If so, you might be able to balance your day a little bit better.

Take It One at a Time

If you have trouble concentrating on one task at a time, set an alarm clock for, say, 10 minutes, and work only on that task—lease agreements, for example—until the bell sounds.

> **Notes from the Field**
>
> "If you're interested in 'balancing' work and pleasure, stop trying to balance them. Instead make your work more pleasurable."
>
> —Donald Trump

Take Mental Health Breaks

We all need mental health breaks. When you feel like you need one, step back and remove yourself from the situation. Unless you are involved in an emergency that you cannot break free from, take a few minutes to walk away and regroup. Go for a walk, exercise, get a healthy snack, or do something that makes you feel a little more relaxed.

One property manager discusses her work problems with her co-worker, who often helps put the situation in perspective.

One property manager who specializes in resort management tag teams with her partner when things get stressful. This removes her from the situation and the guests and allows her to come back a little more relaxed.

Work Harder

While it might sound contradictory to the previous advice, plowing through your to-do list when you're stressed out and seeing results can help reduce your stress level.

Randy Pausch, a Carnegie Mellon University professor and author of *The Last Lecture* (Hyperion, 2008), once said of working hard, "Don't complain, just work harder." (He shows a picture of Jackie Robinson). "It was in his contract not to complain, even when the fans spit on him. You can spend it complaining or playing the game hard. The latter is likely to be more effective."

Prioritize the list first and work on the most important issues of the day.

Take Care of You

When we are stressed we tend to eat poorly, grabbing fast food and sweets on the run. We don't sleep well and we forgo exercising so we can finish our work. Big mistakes. One of the most important things you can do, even during your busiest time, is take care of you. Don't skip meals or eat on the run. Try to take five minutes to sit down, close off the world from your eating time, and enjoy your meal.

The short-term effects of exercise actually increase the body's stress level—increased heart rate, increased need for fuel, stress on muscles and joints, and increased blood pressure. But, the opposite is true in the long term. People who exercise regularly typically have lower resting heart rates, better blood pressure, and a higher degree of fitness that helps their body cope with stressful events. "I don't have time for exercise" is no excuse. Instead, make certain to make time!

Pushing Paperwork

With each transaction (renting units, signing leases, hiring contractors, etc.) you will have a very long paper trail. There are also lease agreements, purchase and sale agreements, rules, contracts, bylaws, maintenance repair work orders, tax documents, financial reports … the list goes on. You will also have to maintain mounds of market data, neighborhood information, tenant laws, zoning regulations, minutes from meetings, and property values. Let's not forget payroll, evaluations, and communications from staff members, too.

If this book was written several decades ago—before the advent of property management software, PDAs, and laptops, and the adoption of a more environmentally friendly attitude—a residential property manager's job would look like this:

- Type up monthly newsletter or management report; go to the copy center.

- Copy and deliver fliers to 485 units.

- Log maintenance requests by hand.

- Return maintenance calls or questions from residents.

- File updated resident documentation in appropriate folders.

- Run from one property to another, gathering necessary information during an emergency, and make sure emergency contingency plans are being properly carried out.

Today, it's a different world. Forget flyers—simply use your phone to send one message to every resident's answering machine, cell phone, pager, or PDA. Residents can log into a website to be kept updated on community events, file maintenance requests, update family situations, change emergency phone numbers, download any necessary forms, or change account profiles on the spot. In the event of an emergency, you can search information on any resident from your current location, access files, and post news and updates.

Utilizing the Internet

In the past, just the mere mention of creating a website was enough to make an association's treasurer cringe, anticipating a severe blow to the budget's bottom line—and rightfully so. Hiring a website design firm to create a website for even a medium-sized association or development could cost upward of $10,000. That's not even taking into account other costs, including system administration, hosting, monthly maintenance, and updates.

Fortunately, that's no longer the case. Now, affordable software programs and websites, such as Association Voice (www.associationvoice.com) and BuildingLink (www. buildinglink.com), are preformatted and allow associations the luxury of signing up, logging in, and getting started. Compared to paper-based newsletters and flyers, it's a very affordable alternative.

These websites are just two examples of preformatted websites that have archiving, newsletters, discussion rooms, and other functions already available for customers. Instead of creating a website from scratch, associations "rent" preformatted programs for a monthly fee. For example, a small association could spend as little as $50 per month, adding extras and more sophisticated features as their budget allows.

Even the most rudimentary web packages can include such useful features as the following:

♦ E-mail notification.

♦ Spreadsheets.

♦ Secured resident profile information.

♦ Online newsletters.

♦ Record keeping.

Productivity Tips

To offset the fees of a website, associations usually add the resident's portion of the monthly website fee into their monthly management fees.

- Special sections for board of directors information.

- Doorman can notify residents of packages.

- Discussion forums where managers, boards, committees, and members can talk to each other.

- Customer support. The only hardware requirement for the association is an Internet browser system.

- Security features, storing digital photographs and signatures to verify their identity upon entering the property.

- Online rent and association payment.

Just remember that human interaction is a large part of your job as property manager, so don't let any computer programs replace face-to-face communication. Your tenants still want to know that you are there for them when they need you. And, most importantly, don't forget to say thank you to staff and contractors for a job well done. Everybody likes a little gratitude, and it really keeps the work atmosphere calmer.

Staying Calm, Cool, and Collected

A property manager's job can be stressful even in well-managed buildings. There's tension between residents, nonpaying tenants, vacancies, and emergencies. In the meantime, paperwork is piling up, e-mails aren't getting answered, and phone calls aren't being returned. Residents are wondering what's going on.

There is good news, though. You don't need to resort to being one of Spider-man's arch nemesis, Doc Oc (a scientist/villain with multiple robotic arms), to be a successful property manager. All you need to do is follow these time- and stress-management superpowers, er … tips, to handle the tasks at hand, no matter what happens next.

You can also stay calm with laughter, which they do say is the best medicine. Of course you don't want to laugh at tenants or contractors, but you can laugh at situations, take a break and read a funny joke, or listen to a comedy CD as you're traveling from property to property.

Real-World Example

Ask any property manager about their day and they will tell you that every day can be busy, but every day can also be different, unusual, and sometimes downright funny. The stories they could tell! That's the good thing about a career as a property manager. You will never have the same day twice. Kimberly Smith, a corporate housing property manager in Denver, Colorado, tells about the tenant who got locked in his own kitchen!

"Our company has an after-hours emergency pager that a tenant can call to alert the on-call manager when there is an after-hours emergency. Around 2 A.M., I received calls from a tenant who was trapped in his kitchen and couldn't get out. It was very disturbing to think a tenant had locked themselves in the kitchen in the middle of the night and had to spend the night on the kitchen floor. I became more worried, however, when I checked and verified the unit. There was no door leading to the kitchen! The next day, after the tenant came down from their drug high, it was decided that the tenant would vacate the property."

The Least You Need to Know

◆ Planning your day is an effective tool, but don't plan every second. Leave room for emergencies.

◆ Like most things, even time-management solutions are personal. Find what works for you.

◆ Property managers should have a support team of professionals and staff members they can turn to for help.

◆ There are tools, including online software programs, that you can use to help better manage your time.

Chapter 18

Advancing Your Career

In This Chapter

- Climbing the corporate ladder
- Tapping into resources
- Networking your way to the top
- Switching jobs and moving up

If you're an entry level property manager and you are ready to move up the ladder, or maybe you have been in your current position for quite some time and are ready for the next rung, this chapter is for you. Maybe you are ready to branch out and supervise other managers or manage multiple properties. Maybe you want to try a new type of property management. Maybe you're a small-town manager who wants to handle bigger properties in bigger cities or who wants to switch companies. Whatever your career aspirations, it's important to have strategies in place so you can achieve those goals.

Consider this chapter your map to get you where you want to go. Although some people travel without directions or a destination in mind—and it's certainly possible—charting your course allows you to ensure a path directly to your goals. Of course, like any trip, there might be obstacles in your path—bumps in the road—but knowing what you want and how you're going to get to the next step in your career puts you farther down the road than those who end up at a fork in the road.

Trade Organizations and Associations

To take your career to the next level, look into the trade associations that you belong to. If you are a property manager, chances are you're also a member of one of the national property management trade associations such as the Building Owners and Managers Association (BOMA), the Institute of Real Estate Management (IREM), and the National Association of Residential Property Managers (NARPM). If you have your real estate license, you may be a member of the National Association of Realtors (NAR) or your local builders association.

BOMA holds regular meetings for its members, which are attended by property managers, service providers, and vendors. The IREM offers online, home study, and classroom courses. The National Property Management Association (NPMA, www.npma. org) offers educational courses throughout the country.

Check your state and local trade associations, too. In New York, for example, the New York Association of Realty Managers (NYARM, www.nyarm.org) offers courses, workshops, and an entire school devoted to property management. These courses focus on national and New York–only material. Trade organizations provide many networking and leadership opportunities for you through committees and boards, educational courses, and discounts on goods and services, whether offered by the organization or through affiliates.

If you are already a member, make sure you're maximizing the organization's benefits. If you're not, you could be missing out on some viable opportunities to enhance your career. For example, you could attend monthly meetings and sign up for members-only courses to network with other managers and developers.

Chambers of Commerce

A Chamber of Commerce advocates for local businesses and even provides conferences, educational classes and workshops, and social opportunities for its members (great for managers of smaller properties who may be more isolated). Joining your local Chamber of Commerce provides many opportunities to increase your business skills, meet other associates in the area through ribbon cuttings and networking events, and promote and market yourself and your business. The only requirement to join is an annual fee, and many chambers offer discounted programs and health insurance, too.

Network with a Purpose

It's been said that it's not what you know, it's who you know. Of course, in property management, what you know is vital to your day-to-day responsibilities. But who you know—and who you may get to know—can help you advance in your career. Networking, which is about building relationships and alliances, is an effective tool that helps you get ahead in your career.

Networking 101

How does networking work? Say, for example, you attend a business meeting. During the social hour, you mix and mingle with the other members and chat with a manager from a nearby commercial retail center. You exchange business cards and call each other to exchange recommendations for vendors. He lets you know he's looking for a new super; you recommend someone. You chat with him about moving up the ladder; he suggests that you talk to his boss who is hiring a property manager for a new facility—bigger title and bigger salary. You've successfully networked.

If you can't attend meetings, you can still network. As a property manager, you meet people in the industry all the time. Stay in touch and, if they ever need help, do your part and exchange business cards. At some point, you may be able to ask them for help. People outside your industry might make good connections, too. For example, you're dining in a nice Italian restaurant and the maître d' comes over to see how his guests are doing. In conversation, you tell him what you do for a living. He gives you his card and you give him yours. It pays off six months later, when he calls to tell you his cousin just bought a building for his new business and needs to hire a property manager.

> **Productivity Tips**
>
> Always keep updated business cards on you, even if you're going out for personal reasons. You never know!

Business Network International

Business Network International (BNI, www.bni.com) is one example of a networking organization where, at the monthly meetings, the primary purpose is to exchange business cards with other members. When those members meet someone who could use your services, they recommend you—simple as that. BNI provides tools to network more effectively, including referral slips, meetings, newsletters, trade shows, workshops, and more.

How can networking organizations, such as BNI, help you move ahead in your career? It can help the same way it helped when you went to the restaurant and met someone looking for a property manager. For example, you may meet someone who owns a storage warehouse. He is moving and wants to hire someone to maintain the warehouse. Or you may meet a dentist who just bought a building for his practice and needs a manager. Opportunities exist, and you have to network to find them.

Continuing Education and Conferences

In Chapter 2, we went over the importance of a college or trade school education to kick-start your property management career. Once you graduate, you can take continuing education courses—offered through four-year and community colleges and associations and as online courses—to supplement your education and training. Through continuing education courses, you can fulfill trade organization or licensing requirements, learn a new skill or a new language, or even earn a new certificate. Such pursuits are great ways to advance your career.

Productivity Tips

Looking for conferences in your area? Check with organizations to which you belong and your local Chamber of Commerce. You can also search www.allconferences.com to see what else is available.

There are additional degree and certificate programs, and these courses have a fee. Your employer may pay all or part of the fees for you to attend, especially if you are taking a course related to your job. For example, you may take a course on bookkeeping or Microsoft Office Excel (a computer spreadsheet program) that helps you improve the financial side of your business.

Managers can also choose to attend trade association conferences to both learn something new and network. Don't attend a conference without having an idea of what you want out of it. For example, some people attend conferences to get away from the day-to-day routine of work and to socialize with peers. Others use conferences as a way to meet vendors, learn new skills, and network.

Promotions

There are smart strategies you could be doing to move a promotion along.

Pick the Right Company

Does your company give you room to grow or have you reached your fullest potential? While it's good to know what the opportunity for growth is before taking on a position with the company, it's never too late. Some firms will actually create a position for someone they want to stay. If you feel stuck, however, consider moving to a bigger firm where there is room for growth.

Keep Track of Your Successes

Keep track of your successes if you want to get your boss's attention. For example, make note that you improved your property's bottom line by 10 percent and reduced the vacancy rate. Keep a journal of when and how you accomplished this feat. Does your company send out media releases announcing employee accomplishments? If so, make sure you're on that list when you have something to announce. When it's time for your yearly evaluation, make sure you bring your list of accomplishments.

Apply for a Job

When a position opens up in the company, apply for it! Make an appointment, bring your resumé and your list of accomplishments to the table, and tell them what a good job you are doing. Let the right people know that you want the job, but don't gripe if someone else gets it.

Take on Additional Responsibilities

Consider taking on additional responsibilities to prove that you can handle more. Do a good job, and your higher-ups might notice that you take initiative and that you are willing to support your company when needed. Just be sure to accomplish what you say you can accomplish. It's good to take on more, but if you really don't understand the task at hand and end up not being able to deliver, it won't bode well for you and your aspirations.

What Not to Do

In Harry E. Chambers's *Getting Promoted, Real Strategies for Advancing Your Career* (Basic Books, 1999), the author mentions several ways you can sabotage or derail your career, such as …

- ◆ Being tardy or taking many absences.

- ◆ Bringing personal problems to work.

- ◆ Having inappropriate work relationships.

- ◆ Having a negative attitude.

- ◆ Spreading rumors and gossip.

- ◆ Losing your cool.

- ◆ Insubordination—inappropriately answering back to authority.

- ◆ Defensiveness.

- ◆ Failing to keep your skills current.

- ◆ Blaming others.

- ◆ Exhibiting a reluctance to make decisions.

Here's the bottom line: do your job and do it the right way. Be the utmost professional, do your tasks, and let your boss know you're interested in additional responsibilities and a promotion. Without expressing your interest, they may pass you over, believing you are content in your job and uninterested in moving up.

Developing a Niche

To help you stand out from others working toward the same goals, you might want to develop a niche in your career. For example, you can become a licensed property manager who specializes in storage warehouses, or co-ops, or senior living centers. Although you might think it would narrow your opportunities, it might actually open more doors for you. Companies seek out people who specialize in certain areas.

How do you develop a niche? Think of particular skills or knowledge that you possess. Have you sat on the board of directors for your condo association or co-op building? You can focus on those skills.

Things to Avoid _____

Don't specialize in a particular area—say commercial realty—just to specialize. You want to be happy and be sure you like it, even if there are ample opportunities. If you prefer residential property management, stick to that.

Stand Out!

Here's an interesting scenario: you're happy in your job and don't want to leave, but you want opportunities to promote your name in the industry. It's possible! Plenty of interesting opportunities to get your name in the media and in front of your peers, customers, and potential clients await you.

Write Articles

Most professional trade journals—magazines just for your property management industry—are always looking for experts to write articles for their readers. Have you gone through an interesting and unique experience and want to share it with other managers? It might make an interesting article for others to read. Some publications want these articles submitted for free (you and your company get the exposure and publicity) and some pay. It's a great way to make extra income.

You can meet editors or publishers speaking or presenting exhibits at property management conferences, so strike up a conversation. Or, you could visit the magazine's website and find their e-mail address. E-mail them and tell them your background and what you are interested in writing about; make sure it's helpful to their readers and not a mini-advertisement for your company. Make sure you read several back issues of the publication first, so you're not pitching an idea that's already been written about.

Productivity Tips _____

If you're interested in writing, keep a folder of article ideas. You can then refer to something interesting that happened that you might have otherwise forgotten. When you write an article, get a copy of it or link it from their website to your website, blog, or social networking page. Make sure you add it to your resumé as well. One article assignment will help you get another article assignment.

Create a Blog

If you don't want to write for a magazine or newspaper, but you want some creative freedom, start a *blog*. There are many property management blogs on the Internet. Some managers write about what's happening in a particular area of real estate, such as commercial or storage. Other managers provide tips and suggestions for property managers based on their experiences. Still others provide opinions on the current market trends while others use it to promote their company and successes.

You can start a blog for free. Websites such as Blogger.com and Wordpress.com are two popular sites for bloggers. The sites walk you through the process of setting up a blog—from naming it to choosing a template design. If you have computer website experience, you can add graphics and other information beyond the templates.

def•i•ni•tion

A **blog** is a website that is similar to an online journal or diary. Someone who writes a blog is called a blogger. Blogs can provide information, opinions, links to articles, information on speeches or other media events, pictures, and more.

Once you have the blog up and running, let everyone know—clients, peers, and the media—and be sure to update it at least two to three times a week.

Remember, however, that this is a professional blog, so use your real name and keep it separate from any personal blogs. Do not include anything in either a personal or professional blog that could later hamper your career. Once you are blogging, add a link to your website and in your e-mail signature. Professional writers and the media often look to blogs for experts to include in stories and on television.

Write a Book

Have a lot to say on a particular subject? Think it would make an entire book? You might want to become an author. There are many books on property management, but if you have a unique angle that hasn't been done before, you may be able to catch a publisher's interest. Books often start with a book proposal. You can find out how to write a book proposal by looking on the Internet or visiting such writer's websites as www.writersdigest.com. You may also want to team up with a professional writer who has experience writing about real estate or property management topics and who has contacts in the publishing industry.

Writing a book can lead to interviews with trade journals and requests to speak at conferences and seminars. You can also organize and run your own workshops on your book topic.

Be Interviewed

Reporters are always looking for experts to interview and quote in articles. If you want to be interviewed, start by contacting the reporters of the articles you read. Let the reporters know what your expertise is and how you can help them in their next article. Remember, however, that the writer will identify you and your company in the article, but it's not an advertisement and they are under no obligation to quote you or your business name at all.

If you want to keep on top of what writers are working on, visit Peter Shankman's free Help a Reporter website (www.helpareporter.com). Every day, reporters contact Shankman with requests for sources for their articles. He compiles these requests and e-mails them to those who have joined his free subscriber list. From here, you can see if writers are working on articles in your area of expertise. Simply respond to the writer's request and let them know your background. The writer will contact you if they feel that your background fits their request.

Become a Speaker

When you attend conferences and workshops, there are speakers telling you how to be an effective property manager or telling you about new legislation or a new technique. That could be you. If you are a good speaker and can create basic presentations, associations are always on the lookout for good workshop and keynote speakers. You could be paid to speak at seminars for trade associations, colleges, conferences, or even as a special guest speaker for other property management companies.

If you're not the best speaker, take courses to improve your skills and then try the speaking circuit. Consider joining an organization—such as Toastmasters International (www.toastmasters.org)—that teaches you (at your own pace) how to write and improve your communication and leadership skills, while fostering confidence and personal growth.

Once you feel comfortable, tap into your networking system and let them know what topics you are qualified to talk about.

Write out your speech, practice it until you can say it from note cards, and you'll be ready to go. Just like writing an article, once you complete your first speech, you can use that experience to catapult yourself to other speaking engagements.

Volunteer

If you're a member of a property management trade organization, consider volunteering. These associations need help on committees and at trade shows. It's a great way to get your name out there, obtain opportunities for speaking engagements and networking. You can often earn reduced conferences fees and be asked to travel on behalf—and sometimes at the expense—of the association. There are also volunteer opportunities with your local Chamber of Commerce and other business organizations, too.

Finding a New Job

You've worked very hard over the years, achieved many successes, and worked through several failures. But right now, you're just plain burned out. Your current building might be stressful and filled with drama, or maybe the management company has had you stuck in the same position for years while others advance. You've had enough. Do you need a change of scenery? Can't advance in your current position? Are you not-so-thrilled with your current position? Need to find a new job? CareerBuilder.com suggests the following reasons to look for, or accept, a new job:

   ◆ You'll reduce your stress level. Is your job very stressful? Stress is a big cause of absenteeism and other work-related problems. So, if you're not finding any joy in your job, it might be a good idea to move on.

   ◆ You'll advance your career. Moving onto another job may mean more money and responsibilities. Even a lateral move into the same position for a different company could make you feel better if it's less stressful and there's more room for advancement.

   ◆ You'll get better benefits.

   ◆ You'll have more time. Perhaps your new job will be closer to home and you'll cut down on commute time.

Use Your Networking Skills

If you're searching for a new position, use your networking skills and reach out to those you've met before and let them know. Remember all those business cards you saved? Now is the time to contact them and let them know you're available if anyone is hiring.

Business professionals are now using social networking websites such as LinkedIn (www.linkedin.com) and Facebook (www.facebook.com) to network with other professionals. You can contact others through these sites and let them know when you are searching for a new position, but be careful. You don't want to jeopardize your current position. Also, do not talk negatively about your firm on the Internet. It can come back to haunt you later.

Employer Websites

Interested in working for a particular property management company? Then visit their website. For example, the fictional Smith Property Management, located 10 miles away from you, might have a job listing for a property manager under their "Employment Opportunities" or "Careers" section on their website. You can apply directly by submitting your resumé online and keep tabs on the job opportunities.

You can also find job opportunities through career websites such as Monster.com or CareerBuilder.com, and the career sections of Craigslist. You can narrow down your selections by keyword(s), location, salary, and so on. Use more than one website to expand your options. Just remember that, if you are e-mailing a resumé, write a professional cover letter and not a friendly e-mail that you would send to family or friends, filled with smiley faces and abbreviated wording.

Things to Avoid

Not everyone is comfortable sending a resumé through the Internet. So, if you're concerned, make sure you protect your personal information. You can do this by creating an e-mail address that is different from your personal e-mail address. Never include your Social Security number or address. Instead, provide a basic telephone number so the employer can contact you if they are interested.

Trade Associations

Your trade associations can post jobs as well. Some job banks are a members-only perk, but others allow public viewing. These associations also have sections for uploading resumés that employers can scan when searching for an applicant.

Recruiters

Finding a job the old-fashioned way still works—make an appointment with a headhunter and submit your resumé, and they will scan their list of potential opportunities. Remember, however, that the recruiter's job is to find their client—the employer—the best possible candidate for the job. Their responsibility is not to find you a job, so make sure you use more than one type of job search.

A recruiter will set up an interview to see if you are qualified for one or more of their jobs. If you are, they will send you to the employer for an interview. Act professionally, send a thank you letter after the interview, and follow up with your recruiter.

Layoffs

It happens—employees are laid off from their jobs, whether because of restructuring within the organization or because of troubled economic times. Nobody likes the idea of being laid off, and it stings emotionally and physically, but you can handle it and come out even better on the other side.

It's normal to experience a wide range of emotions if you are laid off, including anger, sadness, confusion, fear, and shock. This is normal—but, if it becomes anything more serious, please see a professional counselor. Employment counselors usually advise those who have been laid off to take a few days for themselves and then begin contacting connections. Again, keep your opinions on the company to yourself when you are talking to potential employers. Here is what you should do next:

◆ Update your resumé (actually, it would be a smart idea to keep your resumé updated as you go along in your current job, adding in accomplishments, responsibilities, and so on).

◆ Visit job boards and read newspaper classifieds.

◆ Stay on top of what's happening in your industry.

Real-World Examples

It's always inspiring to read about what others have done in the industry. How did they get where they are now? What's important to them? How did they climb the ladder of success? Can you do what they did?

Tom Moss

Tom Moss holds a degree in business administration with a concentration in marketing. He obtained his real estate sales license while living in central Florida. After graduating from college, Moss worked at a four-star resort in central Florida. The resort is owned by a major entertainment company, and Moss worked at the front desk and concierge desk. He says the resort, and the entire company, placed a very strong emphasis on delivering exceptional customer service. "That training provided a good foundation for me," he says.

After working in the hotel business, he managed an apartment complex for about a year, and has since been at Quest Center in St. Charles, Illinois.

Ty Youle

In the 1980s, Ty Youle of Youle Realty, LLC, moved to Fort Collins, Colorado, and networked with a local real estate agent. He had a career as a teacher, with a Master's degree in physical education. In 1983, he earned his real estate license. Just out of a relationship and not knowing what he wanted to do with his life, Youle asked the agent for advice. She asked him what he liked to do. His response? "Manage properties."

With the agent's encouragement, he started his own business. Today, Youle Realty has an accountant and manages about 195 properties in Fort Collins, Loveland, Nunn, Wellington, Windsor, and nearby Wyoming. He says he manages, "with honesty and integrity, and has great systems and rapport with my owners and tenants."

"The tenants deserve to be listened to and be taken care of," he says. "They pay rent and deserve to have things fixed. I make no mark up, only a percentage of a property rented, and I do not have my own maintenance crew, et cetera, so owners know I am honest."

"I believe property management can be a good experience for owners and tenants. I diffuse any conflict, make a win-win for owners and tenants, treat everyone with respect, and am very happy and confident in what I specialize in."

The Least You Need to Know

◆ Opportunities are all around you—just keep your eyes open!

◆ If you are truly unhappy in your job, stay on top of what's available until you find what's right for you.

◆ There are many creative ways of advancing your career without even leaving your current job.

◆ Property managers can be a great source of expertise for the media on housing and real estate issues.

Chapter 19

Starting Your Own Business

In This Chapter

◆ Striking out on your own

◆ Planning your business

◆ Taking your office everywhere

◆ Learning from other managers

After reading all of these chapters, you should be confident and prepared to make it in the world as a successful property manager. But maybe instead of working for someone else, you would rather own your own business. If real estate is your passion and you have that entrepreneurial spirit to own your own business, this chapter will help you make that dream come true.

According to the U.S. Census Bureau and the Bureau of Labor Statistics, 3 out of every 1,000 adults in the United States—0.3 percent of the population—started a new business in 2007. The bad news? Not everyone succeeds—actually, 50 percent of those businesses will fail in the first five years. What's going to make your business different? Honestly, you. How hard you work and how you set your business apart from the others is going to be the difference between success and failure.

This chapter will show you, step-by-step, how to take the plunge and start your own successful property management business.

Are You Ready?

Get ready, get set, go! Or stop. Wait a second. Are you *really* ready to own your own business? Owning a business takes a lot of hard work—most people don't even realize how much time they must dedicate to getting their new project off the ground. Are you ready for the extra push it will take?

The Small Business Administration suggests that you ask yourself these questions before embarking on entrepreneurship:

◆ Do you have the physical and emotional stamina to run a business? Business ownership can be exciting, but it's also a lot of work. Can you face six or seven 12-hour workdays every week?

◆ How well do you plan and organize? Research indicates that poor planning is responsible for most business failures. Good organization of financials, inventory, schedules, and production can help you avoid many pitfalls.

◆ Is your drive strong enough? Running a business can wear you down emotionally. Some business owners quickly burn out from having to carry all the responsibility for the success of their business on their own shoulders. Strong motivation will help you survive slowdowns and burnout.

◆ How will the business affect your family? The first few years of starting a business can be hard on family life. It's important for family members to know what to expect and for you to be able to trust that they will support you during this time. There may be financial difficulties until the business becomes profitable, which could take months or years. You may have to adjust to a lower standard of living or put family assets at risk in the short term.

If you've said "yes" to these questions, then you are ready to give entrepreneurship a try. Now, the question is: do you go solo or bring in a partner?

Sole Proprietor

Do you like the idea of being solely in charge of the business? If so, then you might want to be a sole proprietor. If you are a sole proprietor, you own an unincorporated business by yourself. There are pros and cons of being a sole proprietor. There are tax advantages, such as the ability to deduct your business losses.

However, the disadvantage of being a sole proprietor is that it leaves you completely liable for any debts you may incur or lawsuits that may be filed, even against your employees. So, for example, if a superintendent completes a maintenance job that damages a unit, that unit owner can sue for damages and come after your personal assets.

Partnership

When you own a business, you can make all of the decisions by yourself, or you can partner with someone. A partner can take some of the stress off of you when starting a new business. For example, you can each take over certain responsibilities and cover for each other on days off. You can also partner with someone because the partner has access to financial resources or may be skilled in an area that you aren't—for example, accounting or marketing.

You need to ask yourself if you could work full time with this person or if they would be better in an employee or consultant position.

> **Notes from the Field**
>
> Maria wanted to start her own property management firm, but was nervous about going it alone. She partnered with Nancy, who had a similar background. The problem is that she didn't know Nancy as well as she thought she did and the two of them often butt heads on business decisions. As a result, they decided to dissolve the partnership and go their separate ways. Maria says she learned the hard way that you need to really know your partner before going into business together.

The Wall Street Journal suggests asking yourself these questions about your partner to gauge how well you might work together:

- Do you and your partner share personal and professional values, ideas, and goals?

- Do you trust your partner's motivations and character?

- In what areas of everyday life and business do you agree?

- What will happen if a spouse wants to join the business, a partner acts unethically, or a partner wants to move?

Another point to consider is that relationships and friendships change when partnering with someone close.

Notes from the Field

An attorney can make sure you have all your paperwork ducks in a row and have them signed, sealed, and delivered. Partnerships and agreements should be written out and signed by both parties. If anyone is financing the business, all the terms of the business should be outlined in a contract. The contracts should also outline what happens to the business and its assets when one or both parties want to leave.

Franchises

If you don't want to start your business from scratch, purchasing a franchise might be a better option. A franchise is an already established business that leases its name and provides support for anyone who wants to start a business using their business model and name. You are still the boss, but you have someone to turn to if you need assistance.

Franchise companies can provide help in advertising, marketing, training, live support, and financial support as well.

Corporations and LLCs

Now, if owning a business has you a bit nervous about putting your assets on the line, you could form a corporation. A corporation allows you to separate your business from your personal assets. You can incorporate by yourself or with a partner. A small business would incorporate as an S business—which doesn't pay corporate taxes— while a larger business would incorporate as a C business.

Productivity Tips

The IRS (www.irs.gov) Small Business/Self-Employed online classroom offers a series of self-directed workshops on a variety of topics for small business owners. The workshop topics include tax regulations, setting up your home office, setting up a retirement plan, and more.

Another option would be to start your company as a Limited Liability Corporation (LLC). An LLC protects your personal assets in the event of a lawsuit or debt. You can do this solo or with a partner(s). With an LLC, you can collect profits through your membership. However, this form of partnership is a little pricey. You should consult with both an attorney and an accountant to determine which is the best option for you.

Know Your Competition

Before you start your own business, you should know something about your competition. Who are they? How long have they been in business? What services do they offer? If you were opening up a hamburger stand, you would visit the neighboring fast-food joint to know what they are serving and how their business is growing. Property management isn't any different—check out the competition.

Take time to research the other property management companies in the area. Talk to the tenants. Considering commercial management? Visit the office buildings and talk to the tenants. Are they happy? What do they like and dislike about the management company? What would they want that they don't have now? How will your company stand out from this one?

Productivity Tips

There is a great resource for starting your business called Landlord Source (www.landlordsource.com), which has policies and procedures for property management companies. The owner, Jean Storms, has owned her own property management company for over 25 years.

Establish a Client Base

Of course, a property management company needs properties to manage, but where do you find them? If you have already established your real estate career, spread the word and let your contacts know what you're doing, so they'll consider you if an opportunity arises. If you're just starting out, you are going to have to prove yourself. Be ready to answer tough questions, especially "Why should we trust you with our property?"

Answer this question honestly and professionally. Focus on your strengths. Do you have a marketing background that will help you bring in tenants? Are you experienced in building maintenance? Have you been condo association president? Let them know. It would be a good idea to have professional references, as well.

Target Market

Who is going to buy your services? If you've created a property management niche for yourself—say, you specialize in senior communities—are there any such facilities in your area? Senior communities? Multifamily housing? Determine who your audience is before you start your business. You don't want to invest in a business that won't sell, right?

For example, let's say your business wasn't property management, but rather selling snow tires. Your business is located in an area that doesn't often see snow and there are three other existing tire shops in the area that service cars, change oil, and offer snow tires. The odds of selling well in a market like that are slim. You need to find out who your customers are and what they need. Then, you can target your business accordingly.

Creating a Business Plan

Every business should have a plan. A solid business plan can help you manage your business better and is essential if you need financing from a lender or partner. Gwen Moran, coauthor of *The Complete Idiot's Guide to Business Plans* (Alpha, 2005), says that the plan should answer five key questions, which she outlines and describes next.

What Is Your Business?

Your plan should reflect a solid understanding of current market conditions and how your product or service is better. Industry analysis is essential, whether you're operating within a particular geographic region or a specific industry. Do your homework by reading trade journals and tapping research from key industry associations and your local Small Business Development Center or chapter of the Service Corps of Retired Executives (SCORE).

Who Is Working in Your Business?

Having the right people working on and in your business is essential. Include bios and key talents for each partner and all employees, professional advisors, and consultants you intend to employ in your business. It's important to have proper staffing projections so that you understand the investments you will need to make in appropriate personnel.

Notes from the Field
According to *Kiplinger's* magazine, property management for corporations, institutional real estate investment fund management, and consulting combined to generate at least 26 percent earnings growth in 2007.

Why Is Your Business Better?

Your business should have a unique selling proposition (USP). In other words, they need a reason why customers will choose your business rather than someone else's business. Are you the upscale purveyor who provides the best service in the area? Or, are you a discount provider who can beat almost anyone on price? Knowing your place in the market is essential to helping you evaluate everything from your competition to your profit margins. Lenders and investors will want to see that you understand where your business fits into the competitive landscape.

Where Will You Find Customers?

A business without customers is like a fish without water. You need a sufficient supply of customers to survive. In your business plan, define your key customers as clearly as possible. Who are your primary and secondary markets? How many of them are there? How will you reach them to market and sell to them? If you can't answer these questions, you don't have a viable business.

How Much Money Will Your Business Need?

From investing in properties to making upgrades and repairs to simply buying office equipment, running a property management business can take on many forms and have many expenses. You need to have a good handle on how much money is essential for starting, running, and growing your business. Work with your financial advisor or accountant to prepare proper financial benchmarks.

Moran says that "by reviewing your plan regularly—at least quarterly—you can determine whether your business is achieving its financial goals or whether adjustments need to be made. In addition, your plan should map out how the business will grow, including projections for future revenue, personnel, and other growth factors.

The process of writing your business plan requires that you think through every aspect of your business and how it will operate. By working out challenges on paper before you commit real blood, sweat, tears, and dollars, you can better ensure that you will be prepared for your business launch and trajectory to success."

Things to Avoid

You'll need an Employer Identification Number (EIN), also known as a Federal Tax Identification Number, which is used to identify a business entity. If you're starting as a sole proprietor, you can use your Social Security number; if not, apply for an EIN number through the IRS.

Show Me the Money

Some businesses can be started on a shoestring budget. For example, managing a small property that someone else owns is less expensive than buying your own building with the idea of managing it. You'll also need income to pay staff and benefits. Where is this money coming from?

Here are a few financing options:

- ◆ **Fund it yourself.** You can use your own personal savings—called self-funding—to start your business. You would be paying yourself back.

- ◆ **Borrow it.** Starting out with debt isn't the ideal situation, but most businesses start out this way. Borrowing money from a bank, family member, creditor, or other entity, are options for getting your business off the ground.

- ◆ **Use equity capital.** Equity capital is money raised by a business in exchange for a share of ownership in the company. In other words, they pay you and get a stake in the business, through stocks.

- ◆ **Contact the Small Business Administration (SBA).** The SBA provides a number of financial assistance programs for small businesses. Visit their website to evaluate your eligibility for these programs. Depending on the program, you'll need credit approval.

Remember, the first few years of getting a business off the ground can be trying—both emotionally and financially. If you're seeing a profit, don't jump to spending the money. Instead, work on a bare-bones mentality—buy only what's necessary to run your business and wait until you are a little more stable before spending on anything but essentials.

Business Licenses

It's vital to have the required business licenses for your area. Your state or local governments may have a division of local licenses or a department of economic development that can tell you exactly what you need. Remember, you may also need a real estate broker's license to show and sell apartments. Refer back to Chapter 2 to learn how to get your real estate broker's license.

Office

One of the first things you might need for your new company is office space. It's important to have an office that is close to, or in some cases on, the property you are managing. If you are managing multiple properties, one office on or near one of the properties is sufficient—you don't need multiple offices. Your office is where you will hire employees, sign leases, and keep maintenance logs and other paperwork.

Keep in mind that this is an expense, but you need an office that offers sufficient space and that is safe and secure.

Virtual Office

Most property managers are on-the-go and only report to the office to complete paperwork and answer phone calls and e-mails. Thanks to today's technology, however, you no longer have to be stuck in a brick-and-mortar office or cubicle to get the job done.

Think about it—wireless laptops and handheld devices allow you to check your voice mail and access the Internet to get your e-mail from wherever you are. With one click, you're texting your superintendent with maintenance requests, scheduling appointments to show vacancies, reviewing applications, or referring potential customers to your website.

Staff

You'll need staff to get your business started, unless you plan on doing the work yourself. You can hire new employees through networking, especially if you have previously worked in the industry or if you advertise in the newspapers (small fee) or on Internet sites such as Craigslist (free or fee-based depending on your area). You can also contact local employment agencies, trade and builder organizations, colleges, and so on. When hiring your own staff, make sure to follow the hiring guidelines in Chapter 11.

Business Insurance

Business insurance is like home or car insurance—it protects you. In this case, business insurance protects you if your business is sued or should something happen to your property. Some examples of business insurance you may need are as follows:

- ◆ Property insurance, which insures you if you have any loss or damage to the office or property (in this case, we're just talking about your actual office).

- ◆ Casualty insurance, which covers loss in case of an accident.

- ◆ Liability insurance, which insures you if you're sued for negligence. This is a biggie!

- ◆ Workers' compensation, which protects your employees should they get hurt on the job. Check with your local and state government for guidelines.

- ◆ Health insurance, which insures health-care services for you and your staff.

- ◆ Life and disability insurance, which protects the business in case of the untimely death of you or a partner.

You may need additional policies, such as commercial auto insurance and business interruption insurance. It's a good idea to get named as additional insured on the property you are managing for no additional cost. You should have this requirement in your management agreement.

Advertising and Marketing

You're ready for business! Time to advertise. This can be accomplished by placing ads in local newspapers, telephone books, billboards, and even on the radio. You can also place a banner ad on the local chamber website as well as on the website of your local board of Realtors. Make sure you have a website ready to go, so you can point people to your online calling card. Mention the website in all communications or advertisements.

Real-World Examples

Everyone enters the property management field in a different way. There are those who started as real estate agents and moved into property management. There are those who started a career in a different field—say, business—and decided that managing a building was what they wanted to do. There are those who manage farmhouses and those who run multimillion-dollar properties. Each manager got where they are in either traditional or unconventional ways, but they all ended up in the same place— as successful property managers.

Self-Employed Manager: Jaime Raskulinecz

Raskulinecz had been in the health-care industry for over 20 years. But, when her business partner started a property management company and didn't really have sales and marketing experience, she stepped in and formed a partnership.

Today, she is a certified purchasing manager (CPM) and a licensed real estate broker in New Jersey. She has been the chief executive officer of Rainbow Property Management in Verona, New Jersey, since 1994. The company has two support staffers.

◆ *Why did you start your own company?* "I had been downsized a couple of times by health-care companies—closing offices, and so on—and I always did a great job of bringing in business. I decided I wanted to do it for myself."

◆ *What are the hardships about starting a property management business?* "Money is probably the biggest hurdle. We overcame that by using savings as our capitalization and being very frugal until we started making some money."

◆ *What do you consider the benefits of being a self-employed property manager?* "They're too numerous to mention all of them. But I thrive on working for myself, being able to make decisions that make sense to me, and having the flexibility that goes along with it. And, it seems, I don't mind the responsibility that comes with that."

◆ *Do you still take educational courses?* "I do take courses if they interest me, to keep fresh and on top of what's happening now. But I'm also a voracious reader."

◆ *What's your most important piece of advice?* "Having enough money is a given, but tenacity is the biggest trait I think you need."

Cabin Property Manager: Dianne J. Mallernee

Dianne J. Mallernee is the owner and property manager for Di's Mountain Get-A-Way in Blue Ridge, Georgia, a cabin rental company. Mallernee previews properties to determine if the cabin is what the renters are looking for.

◆ *What are your responsibilities?* "I provide a list of what needs to be done to the rentals—new furniture, more pictures, and so on. I can also do the work. I have decorated several cabins, had landscaping done, and more. I do all reservations and the monthly payouts, and I work with the accountant to get all the financial information in."

◆ *What staff do you have?* "I have a housekeeper, a maintenance person, and a lawn person, so we take care of all the owners needs. I have someone who is in charge of the website. We do it all and, in the end, hopefully we have made a little money for the owners to offset their expenses and for the company as well."

Former Journalist: Tiffany Owens

Tiffany Owens was a journalist/writer/editor by trade, but also an avid gardener and culinary enthusiast. Her husband, David, was a former firefighter, city water auditor, cable splicer, and leak detection specialist. With their hands-on experience, they started on the property management business path in 2006, billing themselves as the Modern Day Nomads professional caretaking team.

Today, they are the caretakers for a 150+ acre, former-working farm in midcoast Maine. It includes nine buildings—a farmhouse, several big barns, a former piggery, a shepherds' hut, and a three-level home.

◆ *What were the hardships you dealt with while starting your own company?* "Not having references at first; however, we used our former professional references to start out with."

◆ *What are the benefits?* "Creating your own schedule, a salaried position that allows for some down time for creative endeavors, traveling the country, and getting paid for it."

◆ *What's the most important piece of advice you would give to someone who is starting their own property management company?* "Be sure that you and your employers are a good fit. Also, a good website is the best investment to getting hired."

Licensed Real Estate Broker: Wendy Heyman

Wendy Heyman started as a property manager in a more traditional way. She was a licensed real estate broker and a condominium owner. Five years ago, she opened her own property management firm, SGH Property Management, in Boston, Massachusetts. Today, she manages condo buildings ranging in size from 4 to 35 units. She also manages individual investment properties.

- *What are the benefits of owning your own company?* "Being my own boss, scheduling my time, and establishing my own goals and meeting them."

- *What are the hardships?* "Balancing life, raising my two children on my own, and knowing when it's time to take a break from the business … that's a longer conversation!"

- *What advice do you have for others?* "Get your systems in place before you start. You'll save yourself a lot of time, versus if you're just plugging in data and figuring it out as you go."

Founder/Principal of Wachtler Knopf Equities, LLC: Philip Wachtler

Philip Wachtler's real estate background dates back to the late 1980s when he worked for a Small Business Investment Company (SBIC). Their target investments were lending to small businesses secured by their real estate. When the businesses defaulted, the firm took back the properties and it was Wachtler's responsibility to manage the asset until it was sold.

He managed a strip of retail stores; a mixed-use building; a warehouse; and a 200+ acre property that included an airport, horse stables, and open land.

- *Why did you move into property management?* "Once the properties were liquidated, I realized that I really enjoyed property management. I was employed by The Tilles Investment Company on Long Island in April, 2000, as director. By September, I was the vice president of leasing and managed the three million square feet of office/warehouse properties that the Tilles family owned.

  A few years later, the opportunity to own 450,000 square feet of prime office space became available on Long Island, and Wachtler Knopf Equities was formed. I run the business on a day-to-day basis, and my partner Daniel Knopf is a silent, nonactive partner."

◆ *What's been the main hardship of starting and running your own business?* "It's a doubled-edged sword. You make a tough decision and you live or die by it. There is no other person to deflect the blame on for a bad decision and the good thing is you get the glory for the ones that go right.

For example, in one building, I felt that the hallways were too plain and we needed to 'theme' it. I looked around and thought it might be nice to make the building have an old aviation theme throughout the 150,000 square feet. I went online and bought every black and white aviation photo available and hung them up. The photos added so much character to the building and they looked like they should have always been there. I made a decision, it worked, and people like it. It could have easily been a huge waste."

◆ *What are the benefits?* "Clearly, it's the satisfaction of doing a good job both for the tenants and my investors. I run all 12 properties, which now total over 800,000 square feet, like a bed and breakfast. There are millions of square feet of office space available, run by larger companies with much bigger budgets. I need to set myself apart from the pack by being different.

I have put flowers in the ladies' rooms on Valentines Day, bought Girl Scout Cookies for all my tenants, rented an ice cream truck, and gave out ice cream to all my tenants. I have personally cooked all the food at a barbeque last fall, and I run periodic blood drives. One tenant came up to me and said, 'You make coming to work fun and thanked me with a big smile.' That, to me, translates to doing a good job if my tenants are happy, my investors are happy, and then I'm happy."

◆ *What advice can you give others?* "Listen. Be a sponge and absorb what your tenants want and need and what you can do, and then do it. Nothing makes a person feel that they have been heard more than you delivering what they asked for.

Put yourself in their shoes: Do you want to be cold? Would you want your mother to use a filthy bathroom? Do you want to walk through a dirty lobby? Do you want the driveways plowed where you live/work? Run the buildings as if they are your own house and take as much pride in your job as you would in yourself, because in the end it's all up to you and it's on you and your reputation."

The Least You Need to Know

- Don't let the hard work of starting your own property management company stop you if that's your dream.

- Don't open the doors until you've examined all avenues and completed all paperwork.

- Remember that once the doors are open, the marketing and advertising doesn't stop—always look for new opportunities.

- You don't need to reinvent the wheel—get involved with associations, and you will find others that are willing to assist you.

- Believe in yourself—you are a successful property manager!

Glossary

Accredited Residential Manager (ARM)   An individual who has met the requirements of a certification program from the Institute of Real Estate Management (IREM). An ARM manages residential and apartment properties, rental mobile homes, rental condominiums and single-family houses, and condominiums.

aerator   A device that combines water with air to increase water spray velocity, which reduces splash, saves water, and conserves energy.

agenda   An agreed-upon list of things to be done or discussed in a particular order during a meeting or negotiation.

anchor store   One of the larger stores in a mall, usually a department store. An anchor store is typically found at the end of each mall, thereby "anchoring" the mall. *Also known as* the key tenant or draw tenant.

arbitrator   A private, neutral person chosen to arbitrate a disagreement, as opposed to a court of law. Resolving a disagreement with an arbitrator is substantially less expensive than resolving it in a court of law.

assessment   An extra monthly payment from each unit owner that covers an estimated repair cost.

asset manager   This individual focuses on the property's finances for an investor.

blog   A website similar to an online journal or diary that includes information, opinion, links to articles, information on speeches or other media events, pictures, and so on.

blogger   Someone who writes a blog.

board of directors   A group of persons chosen to govern the affairs of a building or association. The board of directors is made up of volunteers who live in the building.

bylaws   In a cooperative, these are the rules to abide by, which dictate the building's do's and don'ts.

capital budget   The budget that plans for long-term repairs and replacements or for equipment or systems.

carbon footprint   The effect that activities have on the climate.

cash flow   The amount of monies received from rental income each month less the amount paid out on expenses.

CC&R's   The abbreviations of convenants, conditions, and restrictions—the rules that come with a condo, PUD, or townhome; usually required to be included with your rental lease.

Certified Property Manager (CPM)   A designation whereby an individual has met the requirements of IREM's course for property managers.

collective bargaining   The process whereby workers organize together to meet, converse, and compromise with their employers regarding the work environment.

commercial property   This consists of retail shopping centers, office buildings, hotels, warehouses and other industrial facilities, and shopping centers.

commercial property managers   Individuals who oversee income-producing commercial properties: retail or office spaces, shopping centers, industrial spaces, and storage facilities.

community manager   A manager of a condominium or homeowners' association.

congregate living   This type of dwelling offers seniors independent living in their own apartments, either as a rental or as a purchase; these homes offer additional care services.

cooperative   Consists of a group of apartments—often a high-rise apartment building—in which units are owned by the corporation and residents are stockholders of the units. *Also known as* a co-op.

discrimination   Unfair treatment of a person or a group on the basis of prejudice.

facilities management   Management of large commercial properties such as offices or colleges.

Facilities Management Administrator (FMA)   Certification provided through the Building Owners and Managers Institute (BOMI). One must complete seven mandatory courses, one elective course, and one ethics course.

flex space   Light industrial warehouses being converted to office space.

garden housing   Apartment with access to common lawn space or gardens. Such buildings are no more than two or three stories, and are found in suburbs.

grace period   The time period after rent is due during which a tenant is allowed pay without penalty. If the grace period is met without payment, the tenant will be charged a late fee.

homeowners' associations (HOAs)   Legal entities created at condominium and housing associations.

landlord   The lessor or owner who rents out the property to another.

liability   The state of being legally obliged and responsible.

Master Property Manager (MPM)   Certification through the National Association of Residential Property Managers (NARPM).

mediator   Someone who acts as a neutral party, listening to both sides in a dispute and making a decision.

mid-rise   Buildings that are 5 to 10 stories high.

mixed-use   A popular form of building development, in which the street level of the building is devoted to commercial use and the upper floors are dedicated to residences. Mixed-use can also mean commercial properties that combine medical and retail.

naturally occurring retirement community (NORC)   Apartment buildings, housing complexes, or neighborhoods for senior citizens that started out as communities for tenants of all ages. Such communities turned into housing for senior citizens over time, as the tenants aged.

net operating income   The amount of money a property is making through rents and other revenue-generating sources.

occupancy rate   Percentage of all rental units in a property that are occupied or rented at a given time.

operating budget   An annual budget that includes such expenses as salaries, taxes, utilities, maintenance fees, insurance, and so on.

planned unit development (PUD)   A type of building development as well as a regulatory process. A PUD is a designed grouping of varied and compatible land uses—such as housing, recreation, commercial centers, and industrial parks—all within one contained development or subdivision.

podcaster   Someone who hosts or creates podcasts.

property manager   Responsible for the day-to-day operations of buildings.

proprietary lease   A lease used for cooperatives that gives a shareowner the right to live in his or her particular unit.

Real Property Administrator (RPA)   Certification through the BOMI, which is an organization of property management firms, owners, and trade associations. An RPA requires the completion of six mandatory courses, one elective course, and an ethics course.

remediation   The removal of a contaminant to protect human health and the environment.

reserve studies   Performed by a qualified engineer who calculates how much money is needed to cover replacements and repairs throughout a building or property.

Residential Management Professional (RMP)   An individual who has met the requirements of the National Association of Residential Property Managers (NARPM), a national association designed for real estate professionals. This person must be a currently licensed real estate agent for a period of not less than two years, must manage a minimum of 25 residential units, and must complete 18 hours of NARPM-approved RMP coursework and an ethics course.

security deposit   Monies held by the manager when the tenant signs a lease, in case the tenant doesn't pay the rent or causes any kind of damage to the property.

skyscraper   A tall, continuously habitable building. There is no official rule that states how high a skyscraper has to be, but most are those that are considered higher than other buildings in the area and that stick out over the skyline.

special assessment   A one-time fee to raise money to cover an unexpected fee. Usually, an assessment is only done in an emergency situation, when other methods of raising money have been exhausted.

subsidized housing   Housing that is supported by the government. It is meant for those who have low to moderate income.

superintendent   A person who takes care of the building repairs. *Also known as* a super.

sustainability   The ability to stay for a long time period. It's now more frequently used with talk of saving the environment and the life span of a building product.

Systems Maintenance Technician (SMT) and **Systems Maintenance Administrator (SMA)**   A certification provided through the BOMI. An individual must complete eight mandatory courses, one elective course, and an ethics course. Both SMT and SMA courses detail specific operating systems. The SMA program includes additional courses covering environmental issues, administration, and building design and maintenance.

tenant   Person who pays rent to occupy the property.

uninterrupted power supply (UPS)   Supplies emergency power to a building when power goes out, for approximately 5 to 15 minutes, until power is restored. Generators may protect your systems for up to another 30 minutes.

vacancy rate   Percentage of all rental units in a building that are unoccupied compared to the total number of units in the building.

Appendix B

Resources

This appendix contains a listing of resources regarding professional associations, books, publications, and others to help you gather information and stay up to date on numerous aspects of property management.

Professional Associations

American Institute of Architects (AIA)
1735 New York Avenue, NW
Washington, DC, 20006
www.aia.org
1-800-AIA-3837

This professional association for licensed architects serves as the voice of the architectural profession and provides resources, information, and guidance to architects around the world.

American National Standards Institute (ANSI)
1819 L Street, 6th Floor
Washington, DC, 20036
www.ansi.org
202-293-8020

Founded in 1918, the institute oversees guidelines, creation, and use of norms that directly impact businesses. ANSI also is engaged in accrediting programs that assess conformation to standards, including globally recognized cross-sector programs.

American Society for Industrial Security International (ASIS)
1625 Prince Street
Alexandria, VA, 22314-2818
www.asisonline.org
703-519-6200

ASIS International is the largest organization for security professionals. Founded in 1955, it is dedicated to increasing effectiveness and productivity through the development of educational programs and materials addressing broad security interests.

American Society for Testing and Materials International (ASTM)
100 Barr Harbor Drive
PO Box C700
West Conshohocken, PA, 19428-2959
www.astm.org
610-832-9500

Originally known as the American Society for Testing and Materials, it is the largest voluntary standards development organization in the world.

Americans with Disabilities Act (ADA)
U.S. Department of Justice
950 Pennsylvania Avenue, NW
Civil Rights Section, NYA
Washington, DC, 20530
www.ada.gov
1-800-514-0301

This federal civil rights act prohibits discrimination against people with disabilities in everyday activities, and became effective in January 1992 for businesses of all sizes.

Asbestos Hazard Emergency Response Act (AHERA)
U.S. Department of Labor
Occupational Safety and Health Administration
200 Constitution Avenue, NW
Washington, DC, 20210
www.osha.gov
1-800-321-6742

In this act, find information on asbestos hazards and the public's protection.

Building Owners and Managers Association (BOMA) International
1101 15th Street, NW, Suite 800
Washington, DC, 20005
www.boma.org
202-408-2662

BOMA International was founded in 1907 as the National Association of Building Owners and Managers. Its present name was established in 1968 as it broadened into Canada and other affiliates around the world.

Building Owners and Managers Institute (BOMI)
1 Park Place, Suite 475
Annapolis, MD, 21401
www.bomi-edu.org
410-974-1410 or 1-800-235-BOMI

BOMI is an independent organization established in 1970 to provide educational resources for property owners and property management professionals.

Building Owners and Managers Institute International
1 Park Place, Suite 475
Annapolis, MD, 21401
www.bomi.org
410-974-1410 or 1-800-235-BOMI

BOMI International's mission is to provide educational products and services to property and facility management sectors.

Certified Commercial Investment Members (CCIM) Institute
430 North Michigan Avenue, Suite 800
Chicago, IL, 60611-4092
www.ccim.com
312-321-4460

The institute confers the CCIM designation and is affiliated with the National Association of Realtors. Networking, education, and technology impact and influence the way members do business.

Community Associations Institute (CAI)
225 Reinekers Lane, Suite 300
Alexandria, VA, 22314
www.caionline.org
703-548-8600 or 1-888-224-4321

CAI provides education and resources to volunteer homeowners responsible for community associations. The organization also provides experts with information on community management and law, and acts as an advocate for legislative and regulatory policies.

Dun & Bradstreet
103 JFK Parkway
Short Hills, NJ, 07078
www.dnb.com
1-800-333-0505

In 1841, businessman Lewis Tappan established a network of correspondents that would function as a reliable, consistent, and objective source for credit information. The sole purpose was to provide business information to customers. Today, the company covers more than 125 million businesses worldwide and constantly improves the quality of its global bases.

ENERGY STAR, U.S. Environmental Protection Agency (EPA)
1200 Pennsylvania Avenue, NW
Washington, DC, 20460
www.energystar.gov
1-888-782-7937

ENERGY STAR is a joint program of the U.S. EPA and the U.S. Department of Energy, helping consumers save money and protect the environment through energy-efficient products and practices.

Federal Housing Administration (FHA)
U.S. Department of Housing and Urban Development
451 7th Street, SW
Washington, DC, 20410
www.hud.gov
202-708-1112

FHA provides mortgage insurance on loans made by FHA-approved lenders throughout the United States and its territories. FHA insures mortgages on single- and multi-family dwellings, including manufactured homes and hospitals.

Federal National Mortgage Association (FNMA), better known as Fannie Mae
3900 Wisconsin Avenue, NW
Washington, DC, 20016-2892
www.fanniemae.com
202-752-7000 or Resource Center 1-800-732-6643

Fannie Mae operates in the United States as a secondary mortgage market. They work with lenders, brokers, and other primary mortgage market parties to ensure they have funds to lend to home buyers at affordable rates.

Green Roof for Healthy Cities (GRHC)
406 King Street East
Toronto, ON, M5A1L4, Canada
www.greenroofs.org
416-971-4494

Founded in 1999, the association consists of public and private organizations. It is a rapidly growing not-for-profit industry association. Its mission is to increase the awareness of the economic, social, and environmental benefits of green roof infrastructure and the development of green building products and services.

Inside Self Storage, Customer Service
PO Box 3439
Northbrook, IL, 60065-3439
www.insideselfstorage.com
847-564-9969 or 1-800-581-1811

Inside Self Storage offers information on the self-storage market. They provide resources through their expos, webinars, subscriptions, educational institute, and more.

Institute of Real Estate Management (IREM)
430 North Michigan Avenue
Chicago, IL, 60611
www.irem.org
1-800-837-0706

For 75 years, IREM has provided resources, education, and information for real estate management professionals serving both multifamily and commercial real estate sectors. It is an affiliate of the National Association of Realtors.

International Council of Shopping Centers (ICSC)
1221 Avenue of the Americas, 41st Floor
New York, NY, 10020-1099
www.icsc.org
646-728-3800

Founded in 1957, it is the global trade association of the shopping centers industry. ICSC links with more than 25 national and regional shopping center councils throughout the world. Its aim is to advance the development of the shopping center industry and to establish individual shopping centers in the community.

Leadership in Energy and Environmental Design (LEED)
1800 Massachusetts Avenue, NW, Suite 300
Washington, DC, 20036
www.usgbc.org
1-800-795-1747

LEED's Green Building Rating System encourages and accelerates global adoption of sustainable green building and development practices. Its third-party certification program is a nationally accepted benchmark for the design, construction, and operation of green buildings.

National Apartment Association (NAA)
4300 Wilson Boulevard, Suite 400
Arlington, VA, 22203
www.naahq.org
703-518-6141

Its mission is to serve the interest of multifamily housing owners, managers, developers, and suppliers. The association is a leading advocate for quality rental housing and provides education and training opportunities. The NAA Educational Institute offers six designation programs and promotes the apartment industry as a career choice.

National Association of Home Builders (NAHB)
Multifamily Housing Council
1201 15th Street, NW
Washington, DC, 20005
www.nahb.org
202-266-8200 ext. 0 or 1-800-368-5242

Established in January 1981, the National Association of Home Builders Multifamily Housing Council was formed to serve the multifamily industry. The Council represents the specific interests of condominium and rental apartment builders, developers, owners, and managers.

National Association of Industrial and Office Properties
2201 Cooperative Way, 3rd Floor
Herndon, VA, 20171-3034
www.naiop.org
703-904-7100

This association is the leading trade association for professionals in industrial, office, and mixed-use commercial real estate. Founded in 1967, it provides networking opportunities, educational programs, research, and legislative representation.

National Association of Realtors (NAR)
430 North Michigan Avenue
Chicago, IL, 60611
www.realtor.org
1-800-874-6500

Founded in 1908, the main purpose of the organization is to help members become more profitable and successful.

National Association of Residential Property Managers (NARPM)
638 Independence Parkway, Suite 100
Chesapeake, VA, 23320
www.narpm.org
1-800-782-3452

NARPM is a nonprofit trade association of real estate professionals managing singe-family and small residential properties. Its newsletter, created in 1988, has grown to an award-winning, full-color news magazine. The association also offers educational and professional recognition courses.

National Board of Certification for Community Association Managers
225 Reinekers Lane, Suite 310
Alexandria, VA, 22314
www.nbccam.org
703-836-6902 or 866-779-CMCA

This national board administers the national certification program for community association managers. It is an independent nonprofit corporation affiliated with Community Association Institute since 1995 and is committed to helping association homeowners protect their investment.

National Business Incubator Association (NBIA)
20 East Circle Drive, #37198
Athens, OH, 45701-3571
www.nbia.org
740-593-4331

NBIA is the leading organization in advancing business incubation and entrepreneur-ship. The organization provides professionals with information, education, advocacy, and networking resources. NBIA is a private nonprofit member organization.

National Retail Federation (NRF)
325 7th Street, NW, Suite 1100
Washington, DC, 20004
www.nrf.com
202-783-7971 or 1-800-673-4692

NRF is the largest retail trade organization whose members come from all retail for-mats and channels of distribution. The NRF Foundation offers development and educational programs and a magazine addressed to the senior retail professional.

The New York State Energy Research and Development Authority (NYSERDA)
17 Columbia Circle
Albany, NY, 12203-6399
getenergysmart.org/multifamilyhomes/existingbuilding/buildingowner.aspx
1-866-NYSERDA or 518-862-1090

A public benefit corporation created in 1975, its mission is to use innovation and technology to solve some of the most difficult energy and environment problems in New York State, thereby improving the state's economy.

Occupational Safety and Health Act (OSHA)
200 Constitution Avenue, NW
Washington, DC, 20210
www.osha.gov
1-800-321-6742

Established in 1970 by the Department of Labor, OSHA assures safe and healthy working conditions for workers.

Professional Landcare Network (PLANET)
950 Herndon Parkway, Suite 450
Herndon, VA, 20170
www.landcarenetwork.org
703-736-9666 or 1-800-395-2622

PLANET, a professional landscape network, is an international association serving lawn care professionals, landscape management contractors, design/build/installation professionals, and interior plantscapers. PLANET provides a business foundation enabling members to evaluate and better manage their companies. The Associated Landscape Contractors of America (ALCA) and The Professional Lawn Care Association of America (PLCAA) joined in 2005 to become a larger network of green industry professionals. PLANET is an international association that emerged as a result and provides members with a business foundation that helps them better manage their companies. The organization develops and maintains programs covering business management, government affairs, public relations, and more.

Retail Week
Greater London House
Hampstead Road
London, NW17EJ
www.retail-week.com/Property/index.html
+44(0)2077285000

Retail Week is the United Kingdom's leading provider of retail industry news, retail employment listings, and marketing reports.

U.S. Department of Homeland Security
Washington, DC, 20528
www.dhs.gov
202-282-8000

Homeland Security leverages resources within federal, state, and local governments, coordinating multiple agencies into a single integrated agency that focuses on protecting the American people and their homeland. Over 87,000 different governmental jurisdictions at the federal, state, and local levels have homeland security responsibilities.

U.S. Department of Housing and Urban Development (HUD)
451 7th Street, SW
Washington, DC, 20410
www.hud.gov
202-708-1112

HUD's mission is to increase home ownership, support development in the community, and increase access to affordable housing free of discrimination.

U.S. Green Building Council (USGBC)
1800 Massachusetts Avenue, NW, Suite 300
Washington, DC, 20036
www.usgbc.org
1-800-795-1747

This is a nonprofit organization committed to expanding sustainable building practices.

Books

The Complete Idiot's Guide to Green Building and Remodeling, by John Barrows and Lisa Iannucci (Alpha Books, 2009).

Leases & Rental Agreements, by Marcia Stewart (Nolo, 2007)

The Rental Property Manager's Toolbox: A Complete Guide Including Pre-Written Forms, Agreements, Letters, and Legal Notices: With Companion CD-ROM, by Jamaine Burrell (Atlantic Publishing Company, 2006).

Publications

The Cooperator
Yale Robbins, Inc.
102 Madison Avenue, 5th Floor
New York, NY, 10016
www.cooperator.com
212-683-5700

This is a real estate publisher covering New York City and nine other states throughout the Northeast, Mid-Atlantic, and Midwest regions. It provides invaluable resources to the industry's commercial and residential sectors.

Food Management
Penton Media, Inc.
Attention Editorial
1300 East 9th Street
Cleveland, OH, 44114
www.food-management.com
216-696-7000

This magazine provides ideas for food-service directors, managers, and chefs that affect the noncommercial food service industry. *Food Management* also informs readers about equipment and new products and supplies layout and design articles.

Multifamily Executive
1 Thomas Circle, NW, Suite 600
Washington, DC, 20005
www.multifamilyexecutive.com
202-452-0800

This magazine addresses real solutions to operational, financial, design, and property management issues.

National Real Estate Investor
Penton Media Publication
249 West 17th Street
New York, NY, 10011
www.nreionline.com
866-505-7173

This magazine has readership that represents a cross-section of disciplines. It is considered an authority on commercial real estate trends. The magazine also provides information on varied topics pertaining to office, industrial, retail, hotel, and multi-family markets.

Newsletter

Multi-Housing News
Nielsen Business Media
6800 Jericho Turnpike, Suite 102E
Syosset, NY, 11791
www.multihousingnews.com
516-682-6041

This newsletter provides leaders of the multihousing industry with the most current and complete news, information, and analysis to help industry leaders more efficiently and profitably run businesses.

Software

Property Solutions International, Inc.
522 South 100 West
Provo, UT, 84601
www.propertysolutions.com
877-826-9700 or 801-375-5522

This software group provides software to the multifamily housing industry. It streamlines and simplifies management tasks and integrates the apartment community with management.

Websites

Association Voice, Inc.
1 Cherry Center
501 South Cherry Street, Suite 100
Denver, CO, 80246
www.associationvoice.com
1-800-959-3442

Beginning in 2000, Association Voice has led the industry in community website services for homeowner associations and management companies.

Facilities Management Link
FMLink Group, LLC
PO Box 59557
Potomac, MD, 20859-9557
www.fmlink.com
301-365-1600

FMLink is a publication blending information from its own sources and outside sources, including leading magazines and associations in the field.

Sample Documents

The documents contained in this appendix will help you manage your properties more efficiently and effectively by using actual examples for you to review.

Association Voice

If you're managing a homeowners' association, you know how much work is involved. Online portals, like Association Voice (www.associationvoice. com), allow a property manager to conduct all business through one website. In the past, if you wanted a specialized computer program for your association or building, you had to either have it custom made for you, or the computer expert would need to come to your office, install it on any work-related computers, and sit with you for a tutorial on how to use the system. If something went wrong, you had to spend hours on the phone with customer service or make an appointment and wait.

Times have changed. Today, programs like these allow you to just log into a website and use the template that has already been created for you. Programs, such as this one, provide you with a one-stop shopping website. You can communicate with residents and keep records for yourself, and residents can find everything they need on the site as well.

Photo Credit: Drew Regitz.

To understand how a program like this works, Association Voice takes you on a virtual tour of the fictional Canyon Ranch Country Club estates. When you first log in, you see that the home page caters to your association. There are areas residents can click on for news and announcements, resident services, a resource center, classifieds, and more. Residents can log in and check their records and payments, find forms that they may need, and send e-mails to you. The classifieds section is a great place for an online garage sale—residents can sell items and businesses can post help-wanted ads.

There are so many benefits to programs such as these for property managers. You can conduct all of your correspondence with residents and keep track of repairs and requests. You can post social events and information on important items. For example, you can post that you're having construction done in the parking lot and that you want the residents to be aware of the extra trucks and equipment when they walk to their cars. It's also a great way to promote your association to the community and potential new tenants. It's an affordable marketing and communication tool. If anything happens, online tech support is available. There are many programs to choose from, so it's important to take a demo tour to make sure it has everything for your particular needs.

Simplify

PhotoCredit: SimplfiyEm.com. Property Management Software by TReXGlobal.com.

Some software programs focus on specific aspects of property management. This program, SimplifyEm (www.simplifyem.com), is a free online tool for tracking rental income and expenses.

It has all the forms a manager needs to keep track of investment property income and expenses. When tax time comes, the program includes the required tax forms so the manager can fill them out and send them in. This software program focuses solely on the financial aspect of a property, which is a time consuming and demanding aspect of property management. By having your forms and information in one place, you can use the same software to print out important tax documents.

Keep in mind, however, that unless you have a strong financial or tax background, you should consult with your accountant to make sure that all forms are correctly filled out. In addition, your accountant can point out tax breaks that you might not have been unaware of or that you might have missed.

Rental Application

Photo Credit: Great American Business Products, www. gabpproperty.com.

CREDIT RENTAL APPLICATION

(Each co-resident must submit a separate application.)

Approved _____ Not Approved _____
No. Assigned _____
Address _____
Amt. Deposit Received _____
Date Deposit Received _____
Date of Occupancy _____
Date of Lease _____
Rating _____
Priority _____

Date _____
Property Name _____
Address Requested _____

Name _____ Date of Birth _____
    (First)   (Middle)   (Last)
Social Security No. _____ Driver's License No. _____ State _____
Spouse/Roommate Name _____ Date of Birth _____
Social Security No. _____ Driver's License No. _____ State _____

Present Address	City		State	Zip	Phone	Years
Owner/Manager	Address				Phone	
Previous Address	City		State	Zip	Phone	Years
Owner or Manager	Address				Phone	
Current Employer	Address				Phone	Years
Position	Salary	Supervisor's Name			Phone	
Previous Employer	Address				Phone	Years
Position	Salary	Supervisor's Name			Phone	
Spouse's Employer	Address				Phone	Years
Position	Salary	Supervisor's Name			Phone	

In case of emergency notify:
Name _____ Address _____ Phone _____

Residence Desired _____ Date of occupancy _____ Minimum occupancy expected _____
    (Number of Bedrooms)
Have you ever broken a lease or been evicted from any type of housing? _____
If yes, please explain: (You may use the back of this form for additional space if necessary.) _____

Names of other occupants: (All persons occupying premises must be listed.)

Name	Relationship	Age
_____	_____	_____
_____	_____	_____
_____	_____	_____

How many autos (including company cars) would you keep at this address? _____
Make _____ Color _____ Year _____ License No. _____
Make _____ Color _____ Year _____ License No. _____
Do you have any pets? _____ If so, indicate kind, weight, breed, age _____
How did you find out about us? _____

REFERENCES
Bank _____ Address _____ Acct. No. _____

Major Credit Card (Number)	Expires	Major Credit Card (Number)	Expires
Open Accounts _____	Phone _____	Amount Owed _____	
Open Accounts _____	Phone _____	Amount Owed _____	
Personal _____	Address _____	Phone _____	
Personal _____	Address _____	Phone _____	

You have my permission to run a credit check ☐ Yes ☐ No. A credit check will appear on your credit report as an inquiry. This application and the contents thereof are represented, by me, to be accurate and complete.
Signature _____
Spouse's Signature _____

There are so many forms you have to sign and file as property manager. This is an example of one such form—a credit application form—from Great American Business Products. It's a form that a potential tenant fills out and returns to you. Based on this information, as well as a possible in-person interview, you will decide whether this person should be a tenant in your building.

As you can see, the form features five sections: employment, rental history, lease information, credit, and references. It also separates deposit and occupancy information. The front version of the form is in English, and the back is in Spanish.

On a rental application form, you are allowed to ask for the following: name and Social Security number; address and phone number; current landlord's name; employer's name, address, and telephone number; job title, annual income, and employment information going back five years; relative references and identity of nearest relative; release for credit report; and signatures of applicants. The good news is that, by using a template form like this, the questions are already outlined for you, taking the second guessing out of what can and cannot be asked.

Lease Renewal Application

A lease renewal agreement is pretty much what it sounds like; it's an agreement when a tenant's lease is about to expire that allows the tenant to continue living there. A lease is renewed for a specified time period. If a lease renewal is not signed, the tenant switches over to a month-to-month arrangement.

A form, like the following one from Great American Business Products (www. gabpproperty.com), indicates several things. First, the property name is mentioned as well as the name of the tenant and landlord or management company. The agreement also confirms price. This is important because a lease can be renewed at a greater rate than the last lease. So, if you are looking to increase the rent—say $100—this is the time to do it and get it in writing.

Most important, this agreement should specify any other changes that have occurred since the original lease agreement.

Photo Credit: Great American Business Products, www. gabpproperty.com.

Your lease will expire on:

_____

We are looking forward to your continuing to lease with us. Please sign all copies of this lease renewal and return to us.

To

Thank You,
The Management

RENEWAL OF LEASE

THIS RENEWAL AGREEMENT dated _____ YEAR

will become a part of the original lease dated _____ YEAR

between _____, Lessor,

and _____, Lessee,

for the unit located at _____
NUMBER   BLDG.

_____
STREET ADDRESS   CITY & STATE

known as _____
NAME OF BLDG. OR PROJECT

The lease is hereby extended for an additional term of _____ months

beginning _____ and ending _____
YEAR   YEAR

and the RENTAL RATE during this period shall be _____

_____ Dollars ($ _____) per month.

All other conditions of the Lease shall remain in effect, and no condition of the lease shall be deemed waived by this Renewal Agreement.

_____
Lessor or Agent

_____
Lessee

_____
Lessee

Warning Notice

Sometimes your job requires you to give out warnings to tenants for inappropriate behavior. These behaviors may include, but certainly aren't limited to, the following: destroying property, violating the rental agreement, unauthorized pets, and noise complaints. When warning a tenant about a problem, you can contact them in several ways. If it's a first warning, you could call them to discuss the problem and give them a few days to rectify the situation.

Index

F

J-K-L

...ete *Idiot's Guides*®

...all of your real estate needs.

Profitable tips for bargain-hunting buyers

Buying Foreclosures
SECOND EDITION

Bobbi Dempsey and
Todd Beitler

978-1-59257-721-7

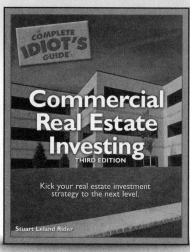

Commercial Real Estate Investing
THIRD EDITION

Kick your real estate investment strategy to the next level.

Stuart Leland Rider

978-1-59257-468-1

Real Estate Investing Basics

Savvy strategies and timely tactics to ensure your property is a money-maker

HOUSE FOR RENT

David J. Decker and
George G. Sheldon

978-1-59257-516-9

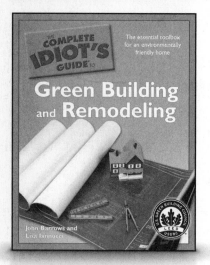

The essential toolbox for an environmentally friendly home

Green Building and Remodeling

John Barrows and
Lisa Iannucci

978-1-59257-828-3

THE POCKET **IDIOT'S** GUIDE to

Home Inspections

◆ An idiot-proof introduction to the home inspection process for buyers *and* sellers

◆ Quick and easy guidance on the most common problems and how to spot them

◆ Expert advice on what's involved in making repairs

Bobbi Dempsey and
Mike Kuhn

978-1-59257-216-8

Fast fixes for every part of your home

Simple Home Repair

Judy Ostrow

978-1-59257-665-4

A

ALPHA

idiotsguides.com